Essentialism in the Thought of Karl Marx

Essentialism in the Thought of Karl Marx

Scott Meikle

OPEN COURT PUBLISHING COMPANY
LA SALLE, ILLINOIS 61301

OPEN COURT and the above logo are registered in
the U.S. Patent and Trademark Office

Published by arrangement with Gerald Duckworth & Co. Ltd., London.

OC 873   10 9 8 7 6 5 4 3 2 1

ISBN 0-912050-75-6

Printed and bound in the United Kingdom

Contents

The first principles of the universe are atoms and empty space; everything else is merely thought to exist.

Democritus, cited by Marx in his
Doctoral Dissertation, MECW I, 79

He is a *sceptic* as regards the *necessary essence* of things, so as to be a *courtier* as regards their *accidental appearance*.

Marx on Gustav Hugo, *MECW* I, 204

'The one thing which is important for Marx is to find the law of the phenomena ... Of still greater importance to him is the law ... of their development, i.e. of their transition from one form into another ... Marx treats the social movement as a process of natural history governed by laws ...' Here the reviewer pictures what he takes to be my own actual method, in a striking and, as far as concerns my own application of it, generous way. But what else is he depicting but the dialectical method?

Marx, *Capital* I
Afterword to Second German Edition

Preface

Though this book deals with the method and philosophy of Marx, it is not intended only for students of Marx's method or philosophers. It is intended for the general student of Marx with whatever background, whether sociology, economics, history or political theory, and for the general Marxist reader.

The object of the book is twofold. The first is to show that Marx's conception of science, his basic categories and forms of explanation, are essentialist, and therefore radically different in their nature from what they are taken to be in much contemporary Marxist thought. The second is to illustrate, and to some extent clarify, the sort of essentialism held by Marx, to show that it is invulnerable to the familiar forms of attack made upon essentialism, and that, far from being a weakness in Marx's thought, essentialism is its greatest strength and the powerhouse of his explanatory theories.

If these objectives are met, even partially, we shall have begun to uncover the lost nature of Marx's political economy. Among the writings of modern Marxists there is less than an abundance of anything closely resembling Marx's political economy. There is a lot of economics and sociology of change written in Marx's terminology, but they are not at all the same thing. At the heart of Marx's political economy lie categories of which little use is made today: *law*, *form* and *necessity*. Marx himself wrote that he sought 'the laws of motion of modern society', and he endorsed the judgment of an early reviewer of volume one of *Capital* that he sought 'the *law* of the phenomena ... of their development, i.e. of their transition from one *form* into another ... the *necessity* of successive determinate orders of social conditions' (Afterword to the Second German Edn., *Cap*. I, italics added). It is from the categories of essentialist metaphysics that Marx's characteristic conceptions of law, form and necessity arise, and they are as different as chalk from cheese from the currently familiar conceptions, in use by many Marxists, which arise from empiricist or atomist metaphysics. Consequently, without their recovery, and the recovery of essentialism in general, there is no possibility of Marxian political economy being written once again.

Essentialism has been intellectually despised so widely and for so long that the fear of being accused of it has sunk deep roots. This might help to explain why Marxists, and in particular Marxist philosophers, have been tardy and less than perspicacious in identifying and evaluating the significance for Marxism of certain recent and widely discussed developments (by Kripke and others) in the heartland of conventional anglophone philosophy, viz. the emergence of essentialism in semantic theory, philosophy of logic and metaphysics. Much time and effort has been expended in initiating anglophone Marxists into successive francophone Marxoid vogues. Now, ironically, French Marxists have increasingly turned towards English-speaking Marxists for some straw to clutch at as they have felt the ground on which French Marxist thought stood giving way beneath their feet. While employed in these unrewarding labours, English-speaking Marxists (philosophers especially) have largely failed even to notice the fundamental shifts that have made their beginnings in conventional philosophy, and have therefore quite failed to develop them and to exploit their potential for recovering Marx's thought from the pit of confusion into which the history of this century has sunk it.

A full explication of Marx's essentialism and its connections with Aristotle and Hegel would require a great deal more detailed philosophical work, which this book does not attempt. That will be the matter of a subsequent work. The point of this book is to point towards the right methodological spirit in which to read Marx, and thereby to reveal the need for the more detailed work.

The aims of this book, which are described in greater detail in Chapter 1 Sections (i) and (ii), involve bridging three areas: the history of ideas, philosophy, and history and historiography. Crossing such lines of demarcation is hazardous and usually engenders complaints that one has fallen between stools. But an exaggerated fear of making mistakes is a besetting vice, especially of academics, and it often induces them to stay firmly glued to the particular stool upon which they were perched in their training. Whether such conservatism and territoriality succeeds in the avoidance of error is questionable; that it is an obstacle to understanding is certain.

If the tone of this book is at times polemical, this is not unconnected with the difficulty of penetrating the accreted layers of atomist (q.v. below and Glossary) prejudice to be encountered in the social sciences and humanities. Such prejudice is by no means limited to non-Marxists; indeed, it is the norm in what is quite widely regarded today as the best in Marxist work. I try to avoid using

polemic in place of argument, but its presence alone is usually enough
to prompt that criticism.

The obstacles to recovering Marx's theories in our period are very
considerable. To the degree that I have been at all successful in
demonstrating that Marx was an essentialist and in helping towards
the clarification of the nature of that essentialism, this can be only at
the cost or gain of throwing up problems in comparable degree about
Marx's categories and the theories built upon them. I have tried in
some cases to contribute to the formulation of some of these
problems, and in other cases to contribute to their solution. Whether
one regards the exposure of these problems as a gain or a cost
depends, I believe, on whether one is pro-Marx or anti-Marx.
Marxists will see them as problems needing thought and
investigation. Non-Marxists or anti-Marxists will see them, not as
occasions for deeper thought, but as occasions for no further thought
and as providing yet further reasons for treating Marx as a duck long
known to be dead, or a duck whose grip on life is so tenuous that if it
is to survive it must have copious intellectual blood transfusions from
atomism. Scientific human thought lives and develops through
discovering problems and seeking solutions to them. Any system of
thought that is problem-free cannot be scientific; indeed it cannot be
genuine thought.

John Divers, Geoffrey de Ste. Croix, Milton Fisk, David Ruben,
Patrick Shaw, Mino Carchedi, Patrick O'Donnell and Peter
McMylor were generous in reading and evaluating part or whole of
the work in its preparation. Stephen Kupfer, Hillel Ticktin and
Geoffrey Kay were abundant sources of ideas, criticism and
encouragement. Stephen Clark will be able to judge my debt to his
own original work *Aristotle's Man.*

Works cited frequently are referred to by abbreviations, and a list
of them is given opposite. Quotations from *Capital* are not taken
uniformly from a single edition, but from both the Moscow and
Pelican editions. The advantages of sense gained seemed to
outweigh the awkwardness. For convenience all references to Marx's
early works are given, where possible, to Colletti's Pelican edition
KMEW = *Karl Marx: Early Writings* (see Abbreviations).

University of Glasgow   S.M.
June 1984

Abbreviations

*Cap.*I   K. Marx, *Capital.* Vol.I. Two editions in English translation have been used, and which of them was used in a particular citation is indicated in the accompanying footnote: (1) the Moore and Aveling translation, London (1970); (2) the translation by Ben Fowkes, London (1976).

*Cap.*II   K. Marx, *Capital*, Vol.II, Moscow (1967); London (1970).

*Cap.*III   K. Marx, *Capital*, Vol.III, Moscow (1971); London (1972).

CHDS   K. Marx, 'Critique of Hegel's doctrine of the state'; see *KMEW*.

CSAGW   G.E.M. de Ste. Croix, *The Class Struggle in the Ancient Greek World*, London/Ithaca, NY (1981).

De An.   Aristotle, *De Anima.*

De Gen. An. Aristotle, *De Generatione Animalium.*

EE   Aristotle, *Eudemian Ethics.*

EPM   K. Marx, *Economic and Philosophical Manuscripts*; see *KMEW*.

GI   K. Marx, *The German Ideology*; citations from *MECW* 5.

Gr.   K. Marx, *Grundrisse*, trs. Martin Nicolaus, London (1973 and repr.).

HMR   M. Mandelbaum, *History, Man and Reason; A Study in
          Nineteenth Century Thought*, Baltimore (1971).

IMP   *Issues in Marxist Philosophy*, eds. J. Mepham and D.H.
          Ruben, Vol.I, *Dialectics and Method*; Vol.II, *Materialism*;
          Vol.III, *Epistemology, Science and Idealogy*; Brighton (1979).

KMEW   *Karl Marx: Early Writings*, ed. L. Colletti, London (1974
          and repr.).

KMTH   G.A. Cohen, *Karl Marx's Theory of History, A Defence*,
          London (1978, repr., with corrections 1979)

MECW   K. Marx and F. Engels, *Collected Works*, an English edn.
          in 50 vols (Moscow/London/New York, 1975ff), Vols
          I-XVIII, and Vols XXVIII and XXXIX of
          correspondence appeared in 1975-83.

Met.   Aristotle, *Metaphysics*.

MEW   K. Marx and F. Engels, *Werke* I-XXXIX (Dietz Verlag,
          East Berlin, 1961-8).

NE   Aristotle, *Nicomachean Ethics*.

Post.An. Aristotle, *Posterior Analytics.*|

TMMC   R. Rosdolsky, *The Making of Marx's 'Capital'*, London
          (1977).

TFC   R.H. Hilton, *The Transition from Feudalism to Capitalism,*
          London (1976), with introduction by Hilton.

TSV   K. Marx, *Theories of Surplus Value* (Vol.IV of *Capital*). Part
          I, Moscow (1963 and repr.); Part II, Moscow (1968);
          Part III, Moscow (1971).

1

Introduction

(i) The object

The three principal elements of Marx's work are: first, his dialectical method; second, his theory of history which is the application of dialectics to human society; and third, his analysis of the value-form in history, which culminates in his systematisation of the laws of capitalist economy. Much has been written about the last two which, while being useful and having various strengths, is partly enfeebled and distorted by confusion over the first: dialectics. My object in this book is to help to begin to rectify this confusion.

Much of what is written today from within the Marxist tradition is as deeply flawed in method and conception as most of what is written about Marxism from outside it. This is true in political economy, in sociology, and in political, historical and philosophical analysis. There is little today that can be viewed as constituting the regeneration of Marxism that was expected and hoped for in the 1960s, in spite of the enormous increase in published material which is in one way or another Marxist. On the contrary, there is no shortage of evidence of profound and pervasive methodological disorientation, and it shows itself most starkly in the spectrum of attitudes taken to dialectics.

At one end of the spectrum there are Marxists who simply find dialectics an embarrassment. Some deal with this embarrassment by making dialectics an object of gentle derision, and by seeking to show that Marx's thought loses nothing by jettisoning it. Others avoid the embarrassment by seeking to show that there is nothing that can be said or explained in dialectical terms which cannot be said or explained equally well in 'ordinary down-to-earth' terms. In attempting to dig out, or recover, what dialectics really is in Marx's thought, the falsehood of these positions will become evident.

At the other end of the spectrum, there are those Marxists who are convinced, as was Marx himself, that dialectics is the very heart and soul of Marx's way of going about things, and of how he thinks things *are*. The trouble is that authors at this end of the spectrum often fall short of a full understanding of what dialectics is, and of a precise enough understanding of how it differs from its opposed methods and conceptions. As a result their explanations of it are inadequate to convince anyone who is not already convinced that there is anything substantial in dialectics, much less that it is intellectually firmer and of greater explanatory power than opposing methods.

Some, like Henri Lefebvre, offer grandiloquent and triumphal accounts which, though brief and unilluminating, manage to be inconsistent also. Lefebvre transcends this weakness by a turn of phrase which allows it to masquerade as a strength: dialectics is many apparently incompatible things at once which can only be integrated into 'an open totality perpetually in the process of being transcended'.[1] Nonsense of this kind merely contrives to feed the suspicion that dialectics is the last resort of the scoundrel. That suspicion has a genuine historical basis which cannot be ignored. Leopold Trepper, the leader of the Red Orchestra, gives an eloquent illustration of its reality in his autobiography.[2]

The most eminent of the authors who favour dialectics is Rosdolsky. He had dialectics in his bones and could not think in any other way. But he was quite unable to say what it was. In his great work *The Making of Marx's Capital* he tries time and again to express and communicate what it is, and with a passion that evinces his perception of it as the bedrock of Marxism. Yet he fails to convey what he is plainly burning to convey, and resorts either to unhelpful comments about the kinship of Marx's terminology with that of Hegel, or to scarcely more helpful appeals to the authority of

[1] H. Lefebvre, *Dialectical Materialism*, London (1968), 111. See also 86-109 where he sets out his contradictory exhaltation.

[2] During his sojourn in Stalin's prisons Trepper learned the story of two brothers serving in a military hospital in Belorussia who had to decide 'what attitude to adopt in the face of the German advance. In the end one of the two, who was the head doctor, could not bring himself to abandon his patients, and decided to stay and take care of them under enemy occupation. In this way he saved many lives. The other brother, who wanted to avoid falling into the hands of the Nazis at any price, fled ... and joined the partisans. After the war, both brothers were arrested. The head doctor was accused of collaborating with the enemy, the other with having fled and abandoned his patients. Long live the dialectic!' Leopold Trepper, *The Great Game*, London (1979), 371.

Lukács.[3] In other words, he does not succeed in getting to the bottom of things. In this respect he is representative of the supporters of dialectics. But it is not good enough to be more or less on the right lines. It is necessary to be able explicitly to identify what those lines are, so that they may be both used the more effectively and shown to be right. Part of the object of this book is to bring into the light of day, and to formulate explicitly, what that dialectics is which authors such as Rosdolsky use to such effect but explain to so little effect when called upon to say what it is.

Dialectics is not inherently difficult; indeed, as will become clear, it is straightforward and coherent, particularly when contrasted with the convoluted sort of things that are accepted nowadays (or were until quite recently) as orthodox non-Marxist accounts of reality, scientific 'method' and explanation. It has, none the less, become a mire; or rather, it has been made into one.

The historical developments which led to the loss of dialectics led to the loss of much else besides. They led also to the almost total loss of what some have a less than fully justified conviction of still retaining, namely, Marx's understanding of the nature of the historical process and of human social development. Indeed much more of Marx's understanding has been lost than even the most critical Marxist and student of the history of the world working-class movement often suspects.

Marx's understanding of the historical process embodies categories of essence, law and necessity, and these are categories about which Marxists have become coy to the point of silence. Essence, law and necessity lie at the heart of Marx's theoretical and practical enterprise, as indeed they must for any serious theory. Marx explicitly endorsed the view that what he sought were 'the special laws that regulate the origin, existence, development and death of a given social organism and its replacement by another, higher one'.[4] If there is no secure foundation for these categories, Marx is sunk. (Why else should they have been such favoured objects of attack during the greater part of this century?) Yet little effective effort has been made to provide, or recover, any such foundation. The reasons for this are the same as those for the eclipse of dialectics, with which the categories of essence, law and necessity are intimately connected, as we shall see. So the task of recovering

---

[3] R. Rosdolsky, *TMMC.* See 42 n.177; 45 n.135; 49 n.149; 51 n.164; 78 n.24; 142 n.3; etc.
[4] *Cap.*I, Pelican, 102.

dialectics is at the same time the task of recovering Marx's essentialism, his conception of law and necessity in the historical process, and thus his conception of the real nature of the historical process. This, in turn, connects with Marx's view of history as a process which will (barring accidents) lead to the full realisation of human society and therewith fully realise the social nature of mankind: a process which will produce for the first time true humanity.

What is needed, and missing, is the underpinning philosophy upon which Marx's now unfamiliar conceptions of science and explanation are founded. Non-Marxist social scientists and historians have had a good deal of such work to fall back on when they needed it. Marxists have not. In some ways this is odd, because the conception of science with which Marx worked, and the categorial foundations on which it rested, have as long and respectable a pedigree in human thought as those from which non- or anti-Marxists have worked. Dialectics, essentialism and organicism did not begin with Hegel or Marx. They have an impeccable lineage stretching back to Aristotle, their first systematic expositor, of whom both Hegel and Marx were considerable students.

To begin the recovery of that underpinning philosophy, therefore, must involve uncovering the entire tradition of thought deriving from Aristotle which has been obliterated by the Democritean atomism of the twentieth century. I shall discuss Hegel and Aristotle, as exponents of that tradition, in Chapters 2 and 7. The discussion will not pretend to the dimensions of a thorough exercise in the history of ideas. That certainly needs to be done, but it will not be attempted here. I shall select aspects of those authors which are immediately pertinent to the main object: the recovery of Marx.

Twentieth-century methodological orthodoxy, which is commonly and loosely referred to as 'empiricism', is based on a metaphysics of *atomism*. That of Marx, Hegel and Aristotle is based on a metaphysics of *essentialism*. (The meaning of these terms will be made clearer in Sections iii and iv of this chapter.)[5] The object of this book is to show that the work of Marx is thoroughly essentialist in every respect, and that this is the source of its explanatory strength. In order to do this, the core of the essentialist tradition has to be rescued from the atomistic reinterpretation and misappropriation of Aristotle and Marx.

[5] A more detailed treatment is given in Chapter 7.

(ii) The plan

The main argument of the book, from Chapters 2 to 6, shows the fundamental place that essentialism and organicist categories (basically Aristotelian) have in Marx's thought, and argues that they are the source of his explanatory power. I shall contend that nothing in Marx can be properly and fully understood without an understanding of their role, whether in his theory of history, his theory of money, his conception of the value-form and its line of development, his differences with classical political economy, his theory of the formation of categories, his theory of the supersession of market economy by freely associated producers, or whatever else.

This is set against the history and development of the greater part of what has constituted 'Marxist' thought and interpretation since the 1930s and earlier, which has often been atomistic and anti-essentialist in character, or an impossible attempt to reconcile the two. One effect of this is to lay bare the importance to Marx of the Hegelian philosophy of history; something which many have wished to minimise or deny.

Another is to show the importance of teleology in Marx's thought, though the explication of the form of teleology he (and Aristotle) used is left to Chapter 7. Since teleology has been made such a bogey by positivists, it would have been better if its elucidation could have been incorporated earlier, say in the first couple of chapters. But it could not; so the reader's attention is directed to the final chapter.

If the theses of these chapters had to be stated in bald outline they would be as follows. (1) The history of human society is the history of the value-form: first, its process of coming-to-be; second, its life and development to the level of a world system; third, its passing-away and supersession. (2) At the same time, the history of human class society is the history of forms of extraction of surplus labour; first, as based on dependence or unfree labour; second, as based on the supply of human social labour under the value-form (wage-labour); third, as based on production of freely associated producers. (3) The entire process is that of the realisation of the final form (completion) of the nature or essence of human society and, *pari passu*, the realisation of the social nature of humanity.

The substance of the book concerns anyone with an interest in Marx and Marxism, and I have tried to write it in a way that avoids putting obstacles in the path of those whose training may not have included much or anything that is, in the present form of intellectual division of labour, labelled 'philosophy'. But the book is really about the philosophical categories and method embodied in Marx's thought about history and the value-form; that is an inescapable fact that could not be wished away, and it presented certain problems. I have tried to deal with them by adopting a number of strategies. Such contrasts between the two fundamental traditions of atomistics and dialectics as are required for reading the main body of the book are introduced in a descriptive way in the remaining sections of this chapter. Finally, a glossary has been added to help with some technical terms that could not be avoided.

Those inclined to go a bit further with the fundamental basis will find an outline account in the final Chapter 7. That chapter does not aim to *establish* at a basic level the superiority of essentialism or dialectics over atomism, even though it is written a little *parti-pris*. The superiority of dialectics over atomistics as a method for comprehending human social development is, I believe, sufficiently manifest in the main argument from Chapters 2 to 6. The more general question, however, of the superiority of dialectics in general is another matter on which most minds are made up anyway, and which could not be tackled in this or any other single book, nor probably by any single author.

(iii) Accident and necessity in history

There is a theory of history which has been unfashionable for several decades, among Marxists and non-Marxists alike: the organicist or essentialist conception of history. It is inseparable from the 'dialectical method' by which Marx set such great store, and without which 'dialectics' can only remain the contaminated and vacuous tag it has become, worth no more than the quiet derision directed at it by G.A. Cohen in his account of Marx's theory of history.[6] How could Marx, with his clear and merciless judgment that spared nothing, have valued so highly something that was a vacuous tag? There must be more to it. The missing elements are to be found, I believe, in organicist historiography, and beneath that in the categories of essentialist metaphysics upon which that historiography rests.

This can be approached more easily through a connected question which has been an embarrassment to Marxist historians, social scientists and philosophers for a very long time, and which few other than E.H. Carr have ever dared tackle head on.

Carr devotes an elegant half-chapter of *What is History?* to the role

[6] G.A. Cohen, *KMTH.*

of the accidental in the historical process. In the course of it he dryly observes that it is in periods of uncertainty and decay that historians are wont 'to indulge in extensive reflections on chance'[7] and to discover great wisdom in the theory of history as a chapter of accidents. The insight is illuminating, but Carr allows it only a restricted application to particular authors and countries: the later Meinecke, H.A.L. Fisher, Bernard Berenson, Isaiah Berlin and Karl Popper. In the present century, however, we are dealing not with historians of individual declining countries, but with historians of a declining class. The true scope of Carr's insight is the greater part of historical, social and philosophical thought of this century.

In the second half of Carr's chapter, dealing with whatever may be the antithesis of accident in history, he runs out of things to say, and becomes noticeably leaden-footed and professorial. He cannot identify the antithesis, other than as those things that are 'caused'. That is no good at all, because everything including accidents have causes. He tries to clear a path by making out that there is a 'hierarchy of causes', which allows the historian to reach what he calls his 'rational interpretation'. This is no good either, because we are still in the dark about what the antithesis of accident is (and we are not told by what principles causes are to be hierarchised). Without the antithesis Carr is still stuck with the single category of the accidental, and so at the end of the day he largely remains within the same luxuriant thicket as the accidentalists in whose direction he had aimed so much richly deserved scorn.

The antithesis of accident, of course, is *necessity*. Carr could not bring himself to say it, because it has become an unmentionable which everyone falls over themselves to disclaim (usually without having much idea what it is). But problems are not solved by running away from them. There is a real problem, and unless one is willing to embrace the inconsequentiality of the accidental view, the problem must be faced. To disclaim both accidentalism and necessity at the same time is not possible. There are only three categorial possibilities: there is only the accidental; there is only the necessary; there are both accidents and necessities. The first two cannot be defended, so we are left with the third. But the embarrassing problem remains: what acceptable account can be given of necessity in history?

Facing up to the problem is made even less attractive by the fact that, having faced up to it, you are immediately plunged into an even more malodorous unmentionable: essence. If we are to admit both

[7] E.H. Carr, *What is History?*, Penguin (1981), 99-100.

accidents and necessities, then we have to admit real essences or natures. For it is possible to identify those changes that are necessary, and to discriminate them from those that are accidental, only in relation to a real nature or essence, whose accidents and necessities they are. It is only against a thing's essence that we are able to chart its accidents. And it is from a thing's essence or nature that the necessities in its line of genesis, development and decay arise.

Many today are potty-trained to jump at the very mention of essences. Althusser, a pretty thorough accidentalist himself, is as rude about them as Popper.[8] Needless to say, this has been reproduced in all the sub-Althusserian vogues that have each had their moments in various parts of Europe and elsewhere since the 1960s. A historian like de Ste. Croix, on the other hand, bases himself firmly on the view that the society he is studying has an essence;[9] that like other class societies it is *in its essence* a social organism for the extraction of surplus labour from one class by another; and that the accidents and necessities in its history are to be identified and disentangled with constant reference to that essence. In this, he is doing no more than basing himself on Marx who was an unalloyed essentialist, formed and steeped in the study of Aristotle (as well as Hegel), and who expressed the essentialism of his understanding of human history with perfect lucidity in *Capital* III: 'The specific economic form in which unpaid surplus labour is pumped out of the direct producers ... reveals the innermost secret, the hidden basis of the entire social structure.'[10]

The theoretical core of the opposition between essentialism and atomism (or accidentalism) is absolute.[11] It begins with ancient Greek thought in the struggle between the atomists and Aristotle, carefully reviewed by Marx in his *Doctoral Dissertation* (so he knew all

---

[8] Althusser rejects all the dialectical and essentialist categories and a few others besides: 'essence, identity, unity, negation, fission, supersession, totality, simplicity, etc.', *For Marx*, London (1969) 197. He goes on to repudiate what he calls 'the ideological myth of a philosophy of origins and its organic concepts ... There is no longer any original essence, only an ever-pre-givenness, however far knowledge delves into its past ... If this is the case, it is clear that the "womb" of the Hegelian dialectic has been proscribed and that its organic categories, in so far as they are specific and positively determined, cannot survive it with theoretical status' (ibid., 198-9). His accidentalism is particularly clear in his use of his term 'overdetermination' which amounts to little more, or no more, than coincidence.

[9] G.E.M de Ste. Croix, *CSAGW*.

[10] *Cap.*III, Pelican, 927; cited and discussed by de Ste. Croix, *CSAGW*, 51.

[11] An excellent philosophical account is given by Milton Fisk, 'Dialectic and ontology', in *IMP*, Vol.I.

about it). On the one hand there were Democritus and Epicurus, who thought of reality as atomistic small-bits that combine and repel in the void, and who had a hard job accounting for the persisting natures of things, species and genera on that basis. On the other hand there was Aristotle, who realised that no account of such things could be possible without admitting a category of form (or essence), because what a thing is, and what things if its kind are, cannot possibly be explained in terms of their constituent matter (atoms), since that changes while the entity retains its nature and identity over time.

Atomism and essentialism have been fighting it out ever since; forms of essentialism being dominant throughout the middle ages; atomism becoming dominant in the 'modern' period with Descartes, Hobbes, Hume and the eighteenth-century mechanists; essentialism reappearing again with Hegel, nineteenth-century idealism and its progeny including Marx. Some time later, atomism regained the ascendent, outside Marxism and to a considerable extent within it. (The really fundamental distinction for Marxists is that between essentialism and atomism. The *diamat* of 'official' Marxism had as its basic distinction that between Idealism and Materialism; a reductive materialist account was then given of materialism which, because it gave no adequate place to whole entities with natures, readily led into atomism; hence enormous confusion.)

The difference is between those, on the one hand, who think that there are organic wholes with real natures and necessities (the essentialists and organicists), and those on the other who think there are no (knowable?) essences (the atomists, 'empiricists', anti-essentialists) together with those who think maybe there are essences, or maybe there probably are, but who do not particularly want to talk about them and would rather get on with composing symphonies of accidental relations between appearances (the empirio-Marxists).

The difference appears most striking in accounts of change. The essentialist distinguishes two kinds of change, those that are merely accidental and those that are necessary (or, as Marxists often describe them, those that are 'expressions' of something deeper). An organic entity, whether it is a cat or a society, undergoes changes of both kinds. If a kitten gets run over before reaching maturity, then it meets with an accident; that is one kind of change. But a kitten that develops into a mature cat does not thereby meet with an accident. That is another kind of change; not an accidental one, but one that is necessary. The potential for such a change is in the nature of a thing of that kind and anything lacking the potential for that change *is* not a thing of that kind and must be of another kind.

Marx regards societies as whole entities or organisms, and the categories he typically employs for identifying them and the changes they undergo are the (Aristotelian) categories of essence and form; form and matter (or content); necessary and accidental change; potential and realisations of potential; adequate form, finished form, etc. This is nowhere clearer than in his treatment of the value-form, which is the heart of *Capital*. His treatment begins with an essence in embryo, 'The Elementary or Accidental Form of Value', and proceeds through a series of necessary metamorphoses of the form until it finally universalises itself over the whole of society with the attainment of its final form, capital, where the supply of social labour itself has the value-form thrust upon it. The metamorphoses are *necessary*, not in being inevitable (they cannot be since accident can frustrate the development), but as being the realisations of potentials inherent in the very value-form itself.

The atomist typically sees only one sort of change: 'events'. The category of 'event' is a characteristic category of atomist metaphysics, and its special virtue is that it serves the need of the atomist to have a blanket category into which to fuse, or confuse, accidental change and non-accidental change. It has to fuse them. In denying the existence of real essences, it denies the existence of those items in which necessary changes occur as realisation of inherent potentials. Consequently it has to deny necessary change, and is thereby committed to going through with one or another of the tortuous strategies in the philosophy of science whose object is to seek to deal with all forms of change as accidents (strategies, it has to be said, that have not been conspicuously successful).

The category of law accordingly becomes that of a mere regularity or epistemological constant-conjunction of 'events' or 'event-types', rather than a statement of the real ontological lines of development of an essence. When Marx agreed that he sought 'the law of the phenomena' and that he 'treats the social movement as a process of natural history governed by laws',[12] the 'laws' he had in mind were plainly of this second kind: 'laws regulating the origin, existence, development and death of a given social organism and its replacement by another, higher one.'[13] Some have tried to interpret Marx in an atomist manner. For example, if the layers of G.A. Cohen's account are gone through in detail, his account of

[12] *Cap.*I, Pelican, 100-1.
[13] Ibid., 102.

'functional explanations' seems to leave us with 'universal conditionals' of the atomist stable familiar to philosophers in the form (x) $(Fx \rightarrow Gx)$.[14]

Marx's conception of law is teleological and all the better for it; any adequate account of law has to be so (see Chapter 7 below). The form of teleology that he uses, in common with Aristotle, is not an occultism in which the future acts causally upon the present, nor one in which teleological change is the fulfilment of the design of a hidden purposer. It is a theoretical correlate of recognising the fact that whole entities of their nature have potentials and lines of development, and that in their development, in fully coming-to-be, those entities are simply realising the potentials constituted in their natures.

(iv) Atomism and dialectics in the twentieth century

During most of the twentieth century the social and historical pressures at work have seen to it that the bureaucrat of knowledge has been in the ascendant, and that essentialism has accordingly been put at a discount. The bureaucrat of knowledge has a vested interest in things being complicated rather than simple; just as a pretentious but unaccomplished *savant* will have a vested interest in the truth being unsayable.

There has been a political basis for this. 'Multiple causality', an accidental interweaving of 'many factors', and a suspension of talk about real essences, suited Social Democracy as much as it suited Stalinism. If the society is essentially something, or is something essentially, then however much you may mess around with it in all sorts of ways, you do not alter what it *is* unless you change that something. For believers in 'socialism in one country', whether the

---

[14] Cohen holds that the form of explanation used by Marx is 'functional'. Functional explanation is 'a special type of causal explanation' (*KMTH*, 250), based on 'consequence explanations' (263). These in turn are based on 'consequence laws' which are universal conditional statements whose antecedent is a hypothetical causal statement (259). Marx's laws, however, are not universal conditionals, but, as Marx says, are *specific* to a 'given social organism' (cf. n. 4 above). Nor do they merely aim, as Cohen argues, to explain 'correspondencies' between 'base and superstructure', relating forces of production to relations of production, consciousness and institutions (e.g. 281). A preposterous atomist account of Marx's conception of law is offered by L. Addis, 'Freedom and the Marxist philosophy of history', *Philosophy of Science*, vol.33, nos. 1-2, 1966.

German social democrat of Weimar or the Stalinist inside or outside the Soviet Union, it was convenient not to be too clear about essential natures. It was even more convenient not to have them around at all, since it is then easier to blur the line between changes that change only accidents or appearances of the system and changes that change its nature. The more 'multi-factoral' the supposed reality, the wider the range of political goal packages you can entertain and sell.

The natural habitat of that repulsive creature, the bureaucrat of knowledge, is the thicket of accident. As an expert, he has charted its hidden pathways, or such of them as pass through his patch, and he has drawn up a map which others may consult on payment of a fee. He knows well the true complexity of things in the thicket, and while understanding the urges of the childlike to search for a unity, he is privy to the mature truth that there is none. His investment as an intellectual after all is at stake.

The idea that there is any such unity to be found in the affairs of mankind has been cast by Messrs. Worldlywisemen of the twentieth century as an illusion of the 'optimistic' nineteenth century, born of a naive belief in 'progress' and an infatuation with Darwin. Orthodox intellectuals have made it their business for decades to deride organicism and essentialism. This has been particularly conspicuous in political theory, the theory of history and in philosophy, where the principal proponents of essentialism, such as Aristotle, Hegel and Marx, have routinely been castigated for trading on a 'biological analogy', according to which the categories appropriate to biology are supposedly transferred in an illicit manner to areas where they have no rightful place, such as the study of human society and history. This is, of course, the merest tripe (see Chapter 2 (ii) and (iii) below). The categories of essentialist philosophy and method (dialectics, organicism, or whatever you want to call it) apply to, and precipitate explanation in, all areas alike which deal with historical processes of coming-to-be and passing-away in whole entities or systems, whether in natural history, the history of the physical universe or the history of human society.

With Marx, human self-understanding reached a point of attainment yet to be surpassed. Those whose interest was *not* to understand, or have others understand, sought to draw back from that high point, and they struck at its base: the categories of essentialist or dialectical method. Modern social science is the institutionalisation of that attack. Its effectiveness can be judged by the degree to which atomistic method has replaced essentialism within Marxism itself. Without essentialism, there is no possibility of reaching an understanding of change, for there can be no basis for distinguishing accidental from necessary change in a system; nor can it be possible to identify the *nature* of the system. History can then come to be seen only as the interplay of 'factors'. This accidentalism was rejected by E.H. Carr, but because of the historical hatchet-job done on dialectics, essentialism and organicism, he was unable to cope with its antithesis, necessity. In the absence of essences, the category of law becomes that of regularities between 'factors', rather than Marx's essentialist laws relating to the natures of whole entities. So law follows necessity and essence down the tubes.

Hilferding had already been driven to these conclusions years before Carr made his effort to resist them. Hilferding wrote, in his last work, that we must reject the 'conception of history as governed by laws', saying that 'we cannot speak of necessity in Marx's sense, but only of *chance* in the sense of Max Weber'.[15] Hilferding was driven into accidentalism; Carr could not extricate himself from it, despite his best efforts. At bottom, the reason was that he could not handle what had become the dry commonplace that the presence of essentialism in historiography was a silly mistake of the nineteenth century when, as Carr himself wrote, 'social scientists, taking their cue from biology, began to think of society as an organism'.[16] Carr was right to observe that the 'real importance of the Darwinian revolution was that Darwin ... brought history into science. Science was no longer concerned with something static and timeless, but with a process of change and development'.[17] The irony is that he was unable to make the reciprocal observation that if you drop the categories of essentialism and organicism, you take the science out of history.

In this century, dialectics (essentialism, organicism) has been expunged even from biology itself, and has been replaced by a crude non-explanatory atomism. To this end, Darwin has been portrayed as a harmless and loveable empiricist bumbler, never happier than when toying with masses of accidental facts, and quite innocent of anything so unamusing as a theory about how things really are. Only in recent years have theoretical biologists like Stephen Jay Gould begun to set the record straight, and to show that Darwin was

---

[15] Cited by L. Colleti, *From Rousseau to Lenin*, London (1972), 34.

[16] Carr, op.cit.,56. Even McBride tugs a forelock to the supposed 'biological analogy' when he 'casts grave doubt on his (Marx's) occasional, and Engels's frequent, assimilation of the socio-economic "laws" unearthed by his analysis to the "laws" of biology ...', *The Philosophy of Marx*, London (1977), 90.

[17] Carr, op.cit., 56-7.

anything but an atomist with a gentleman's contempt for theory.[18] Others, like C.H. Waddington and J.S. Haldane, had advanced cognate positions, but they had had to do so in an atmosphere of an atomism a good deal more rampant than it is now.

No matter how bad a press essences were given in the 1940s, 50s and 60s, there is no way of avoiding them now. Fortune is changing for them in theoretical biology, the philosophy of logic and in studies of prehistory such as those of Colin Renfrew. At the same time the currency of atomism has systematically depreciated as it has so persistently failed to redeem any of its inflated promises. There is, unfortunately, scant evidence that any of this has done much to embolden many Marxists out of their prostration to the declining dogmas of analytical atomism and back to organic dialectics.[19] There is evidence to the contrary; offers to defend Marxism have been made by updating it to the last intellectual atomist vogue but one. If you are in the business of updating, that is the strategy most likely to maximise the amount of egg that sticks to your face.

After Khruschev's secret speech, 'official' communist writers of history were released from compulsory adherence to what I believe Eric Hobsbawm once referred to as the theology of the three, five or seven stages. And 'unofficial' Marxists were relieved of the negative task of having to oppose that theology. Serious Marxists of most waters have ever since been striving to regenerate Marxism and historiography into something better than they had become, and the efforts were intensified after 1968. Some notable work was produced; yet there are few who feel that the present state of things is healthy or encouraging; indeed, there are some who feel that the regeneration has run bewilderingly into the sands.

But how can things be otherwise, when issues have not been joined at the decisive level? Unless they are so joined, all that can happen is that one wanders, like E.H. Carr, in a no man's land out of which there are two exits, accidentalism and essentialism, neither of which he feels able to take.

Once it is recognised that there are two exits only, the task is to

---

[18] See, for example, among others of his works, Stephen Jay Gould, *The Panda's Thumb*, 11, 19-26, int.al.

[19] It has to be said, however, that there is an increasing recognition that Marx's theories rest on a methodological base that is ontological rather than epistomological, and that those theories are teleological in character. Some of these tendencies are found in the following: Allen Wood, *Karl Marx*, London (1981); Carol Gould, *Marx's Social Ontology*, Cambridge (Mass.) and London (1978); William Leon McBride, op.cit.,n.16 above; Milton Fisk, *Nature and Necessity*, Bloomington and London (1973), and 'Dialectic and ontology' in *IMP*, Vol.I, *Dialectics and Method*.

decide which is the better. That choice, it will be argued here, is between Marx on the one hand and, on the other, all that is represented by Gustav Hugo (a luminary of 'the historical school of law', with many unconscious disciples today) of whom Marx wrote: 'He is a *sceptic* as regards the *necessary essence* of things, so as to be a *courtier* as regards their *accidental appearance.*'[20]

It is worth emphasising that Marx made a special study of the opposition between atomism and essentialism very early in his development and his mind was made up from then on. His *Doctoral Dissertation* is a consideration of the atomistic philosophy of nature (specifically of the ways in which, contrary to prevailing opinion, Epicurus developed that philosophy beyond Democritus). Much of the argument, however, amounts to an argued attack on the multi-factoral conception of reality as being made up of independent, 'mutually uninterested', and unrelated (or only accidentally related) autonomous components. The main conclusion that emerges is that the metaphysical basis of atomism is weak in explanatory potential, and problem-ridden where it is not incoherent. Since the metaphysical basis of ancient atomism does not differ greatly from that of modern atomism[21] (wherever it has influence, from physics to social science), it is regrettable that the *Doctoral Dissertation* should be so little attended to by those seeking to retrieve the understanding of Marx.

[20] *MECW* I, 204.
[21] See Patrick Suppes, 'Atistotle's concept of matter and its relation to modern concepts of matter', *Synthese* 28 (1974).

2

Historiography and Dialectical Philosophy

(i) The hidden agenda

Of all the cosy nostrums that make life comfortable for the academic routinist of the history of thought, one of the more cherished and venerable is that Marx thought of human society *as if* it were an organism; that he traded on a 'biological analogy'. In books and lecture courses, the evergreen 'biological analogy' is brought out like the family Christmas tree, decorated with all the familiar and homely embellishments that constitute the stock-in-trade of the routinist's pretence to knowledge: 'Karl Heinrich Marx, born in Trier in the year so-and-so ... was, of course, a man of his time, a Victorian; like so many Victorians, he was immensely impressed by Darwin, and thus, taking his cue from biology ...' and so on and so forth. Often enough, the 'biological analogy' is also brought on to facilitate the understanding of Aristotle, among others.

Marxists not uncommonly accommodate to this received wisdom in various ways. Marx's view that a new form of society is born in the womb of the old one, for example, has been referred to as 'the obstetric analogy' by G.A. Cohen. E.P. Thompson is wary of the 'vegetative, organic analogy'.[1]

It is not uncommon for the theoretical disputes of a given time to take the form, in part, of disputes about how to interpret philosophers of the past. In our time, Aristotle and others have been made objects of attack, misrepresentation and misappropriation, precisely because of the very close connection Marx had with their tradition, the 'Aristotelian' tradition. They have become surrogate targets for Marx himself.

Over the past five decades or so, much of the intellectual discussion in many areas, particularly but not exclusively those

---

[1] *The Poverty of Theory*, London (1978), 121.

connected with social and political theory, has operated on two levels. There has been the formal agenda: democracy, the cognitive status of theories, pluralism, the 'relativity' of truth, the theory of justice, the principle of complementarity and so on. Much of what was real in those debates, however, was based on a hidden agenda: the wrongness of Marx and the naturalness of some form of market economy. This was clearer in the 1930s and 40s, when the hidden agenda was much nearer the surface, but it has been true throughout. The primary agenda became increasingly hidden through the 50s and 60s, but one needs only an average endowment of paranoia to trace its influence during that period, whereas it requires greater than average stupidity or dissimulation to fail to observe it. Since then the gap between the formal and hidden agendas has narrowed and is now fast aproaching vanishing point, in Europe at any rate.

In this chapter I wish to examine the relation between essentialist philosophy and the sort of theory of history which can be built upon it. We must look first at the alleged 'biological analogy', so feared by E.H. Carr and others. Occasionally I have used, or will use, the term 'organicism' alongside that of 'essentialism' to name the fundamental categorial framework upon which Aristotle, Hegel and Marx built. In Sections ii and iii it will become clear that essentialist thinkers, sometimes described as 'organicists', are using no analogy in their social and historical work. We shall see that the term 'organic' is a metaphor that is occasionally useful in describing what they do, and is not a description of any supposed analogy they use in what they do.

We shall look at the general affinities between the essentialist authors Aristotle, Hegel and Marx, and at the differences between them as essentialists. In particular, we shall consider in Section iv how Hegel arrived at his theory of history by means of an explicit development of Aristotle's theory of essence and change. In Section v we shall see just how Marx's theory of history was a development of Hegel's which both incorporated those aspects in which Hegel had developed beyond Aristotle, and at the same time made a return to the material essences of Aristotle in place of Hegel's ideal ones. It was in this way that Marx and Engels developed the 'materialist theory of history', which for them meant precisely a material form of Hegel's theory of history. Marx was led thereby into a *critical* appropriation of classical political economy. What he found in classical political economy were the categories required for a materialist version of Hegel's theory of history. But he found them there in an atomistic, uncritical and ungenetical form (or an 'analytic' form as he later calls it in *Theories of Surplus Value*), and he begins to reconstruct them on an essentialist basis in the *Economic and Philosophical MSS.*

(ii) Aristotle and the 'biological analogy'

(a) Aristotle's views on what is and is not scientific in historical writing are, naturally, thoroughly informed by his general philosophy of science, and thus by the essentialist categories of his general philosophy. In reaction to the Atthidographers, among others, Aristotle notoriously took the view that 'poetry is a more philosophical and serious thing than history, as it speaks rather of the general, history rather of the particular'.[2] In the histories he found nothing general, but only accounts of particular events that took place in a certain locality over a given period of time. Their basis, therefore, was chance, or accident, and in Aristotle's estimation that was no basis for science. For science deals with 'what happens always or for the most part', and what happens in that way does so not fortuitously, but 'by nature';[3] that is, in virtue of some real nature whose presence is revealed precisely in the fact that certain sorts of thing tend to happen 'always or for the most part'. The efforts of the historical writers failed to reveal any such essential forms, natures or 'causes', and were accordingly judged to be unserious. In dealing with particularity rather than with generality in the particular, they could provide little of worth, for 'the general is honoured because it reveals the cause'[4], and 'we have scientific knowledge when we know the cause'.[5] To know the cause, we must look for the general and identify a line of necessity, and that is possible only in relation to some identified whole in whose development or movement according to its nature (*ergon* or *telos*) the necessity lies.

Aristotle's unfavourable comparison of historians with poets did not mean that he thought some sort of scientific history impossible. It meant that he thought those historians were not attempting it. He certainly thought it possible to some degree because he considered human communities or societies to be natural growths, and accordingly considered that they were to be understood in the same general categories that give us understanding of any whole entity. In such work in the social and historical field as has come down to us, such as the *Politics* and the *Athenian Constitution*, we can see Aristotle

---

[2] *Poetics* 1451b5f.
[3] *Physics* 2. 198b33ff.
[4] *Post. An.* 88a5.
[5] Ibid., 71b30f.

doing this, and to great effect.

(b) Indeed, his analysis of the development of exchange relations in the *Politics* 1.9, and in the *Nicomachean Ethics* 5.5, shows clearly the penetrative power of essentialist categories and method, for among other things it brought him closer to an understanding of money than any author until the nineteenth century.[6] He identifies the circuits C-C, C-M-C, M-C-M, and M-M (not, of course, by means of Marx's symbolism but in his own way), and achieves this by following out his methodological principle that: 'He who considers things in their first growth and origin, whether of a state or anything else, will obtain the clearest view of them.'[7]

In the first form of association, the household, all things were held in common, and so there was no purpose for exchange to serve.[8] That purpose arose with the increased scope of association of the village, whose members were more separated and different and had things to exchange. This they did in a direct manner, one useful thing for another (i.e., without money).

When Aristotle introduces the second form of exchange relations he presents it explicitly as a *development* out of the primitive one: 'The other more complex form of exchange grew, as might have been inferred, out of the simpler.'[9] This form is the exchange of goods mediated by money, C-M-C, which has the advantages, as Aristotle explicitly notes in the *Nicomachean Ethics*, of separating the acts of sale and purchase which were fused in the simple circuit C-C, and of serving us 'as a guarantee of exchange in the future'.[10] He explains the appearance of the new form of circulation of goods, and the appearance of money, as a response to, and an integral part of, a developing social reality which leads over time to the displacement of the less developed form of exchange relations by the more developed.

The penetrative power of recent atomistic thought is well illustrated by the distinguished Aristotelian scholar the late Sir David Ross who failed to see the point here. Lacking any real understanding of the Aristotelian notions of essence and form and of transitions from less developed forms of an essence to more developed ones, he can only express surprise at what appears to him as Aristotle's stupidity: 'This notion of money as facilitating barter, instead of (practically) driving it out of the field, is a curious one.'

---

[6] This is argued in detail in my 'Aristotle and the political economy of the *polis*', *Journal of Hellenic Studies*, 99 (1979).

[7] *Politics* 1. 1252a24.

[8] Ibid., 1257a19-30.

[9] Ibid., 1257a30.

[10] *NE* 1133b10ff.

But he explains the curiosity, to the satisfaction of all good citizens who approach Aristotle from the lofty vantage point of twentieth-century atomistics, with the wonderful statement that 'it must be remembered that in economics ... Aristotle was almost the earliest worker'.[11] One could not wish for a clearer illustration of the tendency of atomist-analytics to see static disconnection, where there is connection and process.

When Aristotle comes to the third form, M-C-M, he introduces this too as a *necessary* development out of its preceding form, and understands it to have a development of its own (what Hegel would call its own 'principle'). He writes:

> When, in this way, a currency had once been instituted, there next arose, from the necessary process of exchange (i.e. exchange between commodities, with money merely serving as a measure), the other form of the art of acquisition, which consists in retail trade (conducted for profit). At first, we may allow, it was perhaps practised in a simple way (that is to say, money was still regarded as a measure, and not treated as a source of profit); but in the process of time, and as the result of experience, it was practised with a more studied technique which sought to discover the sources from which, and the methods by which, the greatest profit could be made.[12]

Each form is considered to have its own object, point or *telos*. The point of C-C and C-M-C alike, is to acquire something that is needed; its aim is the acquisition of wealth considered as use-value and not as exchange value. The aim of the circuit M-C-M, however, is different, and it is therefore considered as a form of quite a different nature. 'It is concerned only with getting a fund of money, and that only by the method of conducting the exchange of goods.'[13] 'Money is the beginning and end of this kind of exchange'; 'there is no limit to the end it seeks; and the end it seeks is wealth of the sort we have mentioned ... the mere acquisition of money'; 'all who are engaged in it increase their fund of currency without limit or pause.' All this, and a good deal more, is quoted by Marx in *Capital*, of course.[14] Marx gives credit only where it is strictly merited. And he found good reason to 'go back to the great investigator who was the first to analyse the value-form, like so many other forms of thought, society and nature. I mean Aristotle.'

[11] W.D. Ross, *Aristotle*, rev. edn., London (1949), 213.

[12] *Politics* 1257b1-4. The interpolations are E. Barker's, given in his *The Politics of Aristotle*, Oxford 1952.

[13] Ibid., 1257b21f.

[14] *Cap.* I, Pelican, 151-2; 253 n.6.

(c) Aristotle's method of looking for the general in the particular, for the underlying essence and the forms through which it develops, and for the point or *telos* of each form, paid off handsomely. None the less, that method is an abomination to the bureaucratic analytical mind: it is 'organicist' and 'teleological'; need one say more? Unless to add that it is un-American. The latter epithet is not always so far beneath the surface in the work *Aristotle's History of Athenian Democracy* prepared in the late 1950s between the Universities of Chicago and Berkeley by Day and Chambers. Their treatment serves well to illustrate the genre of anti-organicist or anti-essentialist cases against Aristotle, and there is little to be gained by examining other instances of the genre. However feeble their book may seem, it does have the merit of offering *arguments* (of a kind) for the view that there is an 'analogy' involved in treating social phenomena in an organicist manner, as Aristotle does. E.H. Carr offers no arguments, as we saw in Chapter 1 (iv); he simply assumes that such treatment must be analogical. Even a considerable scholar of nineteenth-century thought like Maurice Mandelbaum can speak repeatedly of a 'biological analogy' and 'organic analogy' underlying the thought of essentialists and organicists, without offering any attempt to justify the view that there is an analogy involved; it seems never to have crossed his mind that there might *be* no such analogy.[15]

They proceed to their misjudgment by a curious route. Rather than concluding from the powerful illumination that Aristotle was able to generate that the application of his general philosophical categories to history and society has something to be said for it, their argument is that whatever may be said for his results, he reached them by the objectionable method of applying the categories of his general philosophy to history and society. (These categories are outlined and discussed in Chapter 7.)

This line of argument requires of Day and Chambers that they produce a reason why it was wrong for Aristotle to do that. To do this they would have to produce arguments to show either (1) that there was something wrong with the categories of Aristotelian philosophy, or (2) that there was something wrong with their specific application to human society, or both. Day and Chambers attempt both strategies. They succeed, however, in producing nothing but egregious arguments, as usually happens when people have their conclusions established in advance and cast around for arguments later.

(1) On the first strategy, they do not assay a single argument

---

[15] Maurice Mandelbaum, *HMR*. The 'biological analogy' appears on pp.44-5, 47-8, 52 and 57; the 'organic analogy' appears on pp. 57 and 61 int. al.

against Aristotle's categories and scientific method. Instead, they make a series of *statements* that obviate the need for argument by locating Aristotle's place in the received academic-political demonology of the 1950s. Thus Aristotle could not conceive that 'changes and events occur in the world without any *master plan* or *overriding purpose*'.[16] (The un-American overtones of 'master plan' and 'overriding purpose' were not stressed with italicisation in the original.) Along with that goes the familiar incomprehension, or misrepresentation, of teleology as involving agency or ineluctable purpose (cf. Chapter 7, where the absurd form of teleology which Day and Chambers have in mind is distinguished from that of Aristotle and Marx): 'In a teleological system things are not merely as they are: they were made that way in fulfilment of some purpose – God's or Nature's, or History's.'[17] The role of God in Aristotle is something over which a measure of debate is possible. But the inclusion of 'History', with a capital H, among the list of possible teleological 'agencies' has no shred of justification in terms of Aristotelian scholarship. It simply points the finger: had Aristotle lived long enough, and emigrated, he might have had to plead the Fifth Amendment, and answer certain questions put to him 'yes' or 'no'.

(2) The second strategy is to argue that Aristotle's general categories are unsuitable to the study of society and history, however apt they may be in other areas. They suggest that to apply the categories of essentialist philosophy to a human society is to treat it as a natural growth, and this they object to. They do not argue that the categories cannot apply, nor that society is not a natural growth, nor that it is something else, an artifact. What they do instead is to suggest that a human society could be a natural growth *only if it were a plant or an animal*.[18] From the undoubted fact that human society is neither plant nor animal, they conclude that therefore the categories cannot apply literally, so that 'Aristotle's language is metaphorical'.[19]

There then follow the usual platitudes: 'Aristotle's terms ... were not indigenous to political philosophy. They were borrowed from another science altogether, that of biology.' Platitude is confirmed by appeal to authority: 'Sir David Ross justly observes that "his political thought was to some extent modelled on his biological

---

[16] J. Day and M. Chambers, *Aristotle's History of Athenian Democracy*, UCPP 73, 1962.
[17] Ibid., 40.
[18] Loc. cit.
[19] Ibid., 40-1.

researches". '[20]

Day and Chambers take exception, of course, to Aristotle's straightforward identification of social classes as 'parts of the state'. As all persons loyal to the Constitution know, classes are just 'labels', and they 'are attached to classes known in theory but probably not observed in fact'.[21] Thus, some of Aristotle's terms for parts of the state are not 'descriptive and neutral' but 'evaluative'. It is explained that the 'biological analogy' is leading Aristotle astray: 'no one is in doubt whether the part called the mouth of an animal has been correctly identified', for such identifications are purely descriptive. The identification of classes, however, is evaluative. But as Clark has pointed out: 'This is an error in biology: to identify any part (at least any anomoemerous part) is to evaluate it: that is, to say what its value, its function is in the economy. One may well hesitate to say which part is the mouth. The "parts" of an organism are not materially distinguished.'[22]

And so, without any serious argument except for a single bad one based on ignorance, Aristotle's philosophical categories, and their applicability to human society, are consigned to the pit.

Of course, people like Aristotle do nothing in an open, frontiersmanlike way. Such people prefer to make their entry, cleverly and subtly, by the back door. Day and Chambers, however, are not taken in by the clever manoeuvres of organicists-under-the-bed. They detect at once that Aristotle does not come right out and *say* that states are plants or animals. 'Aristotle did not, indeed, *explicitly* class states among biological organisms ... His method for politics was not borrowed laterally from biology directly across to politics.' Here their investigations unmask the whole organicist can of worms; they are able to reveal that 'his procedure was both subtler and stronger. He could appeal to general philosophical theory with its laws of motion and change, its causes and teleology – all that he had sought to establish in the *Physics* as binding on natural entities (*phuseis*). The hypothesis was not, "Whether the state can be explained as a biological organism is explained"; it was rather, "Whether the state can be explained *phusikôs*, by natural science (as biological organisms are explained)".'[23] That is correct.

Our two bounty hunters failed to appreciate that this last, acute, and truthful piece of scholarly discrimination quite undermines their own thesis of an illicit 'biological analogy', upon which their

[20] Ibid., 42.
[21] Ibid., 62.
[22] S.R.L. Clark, *Aristotle's Man*, Oxford (1975), 140.
[23] Day and Chambers, op.cit., 42.

prosecution of Aristotle rests. For where explanation is sought in terms of a general set of philosophical categories and its accompanying philosophy of science, the question cannot arise of the categories appropriate to 'one science' being illicitly and metaphorically transferred to 'another science' to which they are not 'indigenous'. It is just this confusion that vitiates all the other versions of this kind of attack on Aristotle's 'political' thought.

(d) The real basis of all this messing around by Day and Chambers is that they have an alternative viewpoint to the organicist one. It only peeps out at one point where they attempt to explain what must really be, in their view, the only literal content possible for Aristotle's 'metaphorical' language: 'When Aristotle says "The state exists by nature", he means something very much like "Human beings *choose* not to live alone but characteristically form communities". To some degree, then, Aristotle's language is metaphorical.'[24]

This is the only content they can understand Aristotle's view (that society is a natural growth) to have, because they share the atomist-analytical view of society, viz., that it is an aggregation of individuals who 'choose' to live together rather than alone. This is the conception that underlies all the modern contractarian theorists of the bourgeois epoch from Hobbes onwards. It represents the application to the area of society and the human sciences of the method set out by Descartes in *The Rules for the Direction of the Mind*, a form of which is embodied in the so called 'resoluto-compositive' method of Hobbes' *Leviathan*. If you are studying something big and hard, break it down into simpler and easier elements. If necessary, carry on until you have the atoms of the thing, then establish the principles by which you can combine the atoms, and then reconstitute the original big thing you started with. In application to society, the atoms are deemed to be individuals who choose. States and societies are 'logical constructions' out of atomistic 'individuals', just as 'things' were supposed to be out of 'sense-data'. In each case the real essence is evaporated. The roles in early bourgeois thought of 'the state of nature' and 'the original contract' are based on this atomistic social ontology, for such an ontology requires a special account of the 'consent' that binds together the atoms of 'civil society'.

The categories of atomist and essentialist thought are quite irreconcilable, but without being aware of it Day and Chambers are trying to 'make sense of' Aristotle by translating his essentialism into

---

[24] Ibid., 41 (italics added).

the atomism which is all they understand. This is profoundly unaristotelian. It is also ignorant. The essential strand of contractarian thinking about the origin and nature of states was not a creation of the modern world. It was a commonplace even to the ancients. Plato made this clear in the discussion with Adeimantus in Book 2 of the *Republic*.[25] From that discussion it is clear that in Plato's time, and probably before, it was a commonplace view that the basis of the state was that co-operation among individuals was the way to the more efficient and abundant supply of physical goods, 'food ... dwelling ... clothing and the like'. It is perfectly obvious from all Aristotle's discussions that his objective in these debates was precisely to combat such mundane and utilitarian banality, and to advance his own more far-reaching, and ultimately more rationally defensible kind of view about the *telos* of human association (or the state), as having to do with the higher provision of 'the good life' which realises the potentialities inherent in the essence of man.[26]

(iii) *The organicism and historicism of the nineteenth century*

It is still a potent, if boring, commonplace that the thought of the nineteenth century was characterised by a 'belief in Progress', in human social development, and in 'organicist' laws of such development. Such ideas are collectively denominated 'historicism', usually by those opposed to them.

The commonplace is false: first, because such ideas continued to exert the most powerful conceivable influence well into the twentieth century. Indeed it would appear that the concerted attack upon them began when their practical political expression in the German working class was at its most intense, namely, in early Weimar Germany with Ernst Troeltsche's *Der Historisismus und seine Probleme* (1922). As Marxism ('historicism') itself began to decay in consequence of developments mainly in the Soviet Union, the attack continued with Karl Heussi's *Die Krisis der Historisismus* (1932) and Friedrich Meinecke's *Die Entstehung des Historisismus* (1936).[27] To be sure, Max Weber had begun his attack on 'organicism' considerably earlier. In 1903 Weber was expressing his hostility to the ' "organic"

---

[25] Plato, *Republic* 369b-371e.
[26] *Politics* 1252b29.
[27] These works are cited by Mandelbaum *HMR* 41. As it happens, it was only in 1935 that Karl Popper 'began to write about Marxism with the intention of publishing what I wrote'; *Unended Quest, An Intellectual Autobiography*, Glasgow (1980) 35.

theory of society with its unavoidable biological analogies'.[28] The merits of his work were not such that they immediately put an end to such thought. Rather, those merits became more apparent as the opponents of 'organicism' found themselves in urgent need of weapons with which to attack it.

The commonplace is false, secondly, because such ideas went back to the middle of the eighteenth century, if not earlier. They are fundamental to the authors of the Scottish Englightenment, Adam Smith, Adam Ferguson and John Millar. The 'four stage' theory of the development of human society, enunciated by Smith as 'hunting, pasturage, farming and commerce' in his *Lectures on Jurisprudence*,[29] and more fully developed in Book III of *Wealth of Nations*, could not have been formulated without a framework of categories based upon the supposed 'biological analogy' or 'organic analogy'. Ronald Meek observed that 'this "four stages" theory ... was destined ... to dominate socio-economic thought in Europe in the latter half of the eighteenth century'. (He added that it came to have 'crucial significance in the subsequent development of economics, sociology, anthropology, and historiography, right down to our own time'.)[30]

Meek sought to trace the origins of the four-stages theory in earlier authors from Aristotle onwards, and felt compelled to conclude that 'taking them as a whole, the anticipations are indeed so scarce and scattered, and in most cases so vague, that men like Smith and Turgot could hardly have discovered them (in so far as they in fact did so) if they had not known what they were looking for'.[31]

Their knowledge of what they were looking for clearly grew from the manifest features of the developing historical reality of their period which they were attempting to theorise. Smith, for example, was receiving information about peoples living in 'the rude state' in French and British colonies. He was also at the centre of jurisprudential reflections about forms of property and other matters, which arose from the attempts then being made to extend 'civilised society' into the Highlands of Scotland. These, however, were only the immediate phenomena.

The underlying reason why Smith and others were at that time receiving such information is the same reason that explains why they knew what they were looking for. It is that commodity-producing, or universal exchange based, society (Smith's stage of 'commerce') was

---

[28] Max Weber, *Roscher and Knies: The Logical Problems of Historical Economics*, NY and London (1975), 63.

[29] A. Smith, *Lectures on Jurisprudence*, ed. R.L. Meek et. al., Oxford 1978, B, 149.

[30] R.L. Meek, *Social Science and the Ignoble Savage*, Cambridge (1976), 2.

[31] Meek, op. cit., 35.

already well into its process of development in Europe, and was extending itself into other areas of the globe. It was in the process of universalising itself in Britain by bringing even the form of supply of human social labour within the value-form (i.e. wage-labour), and it was in the early stages of its process of development to the level of a world system of economy (cf.3 (v) below). Smith was able to attain his theory of history because he was so placed, historically, as to be able to use the form of society that had come-to-be (or was in the process of coming-to-be) in order to begin to come to an understanding of those forms that had existed in the past, versions of which still existed in the colonies and to some extent at home. Marx commented that the anatomy of man is the key to comprehending that of the ape. Smith's position was that he had the elements of the anatomy of the society of universalised exchange-value, and could use it as a key to comprehend the anatomies of earlier social forms.

The reactions of twentieth-century atomists to the 'holistic' or 'organicist' thought represented by Smith and Marx can be quite amazing. Mandelbaum, in the course of expounding the important role he sees of what he calls 'the concept of development' in nineteenth-century thought, expresses the surprise of the atomist at the very idea that there might be real entities with natures or essences, which undergo processes of non-accidental change (i.e. development): '... whenever we speak of a development we must always have in mind the idea of *something* which develops.'[32] In his understanding of what it is to do history, one could only entertain the idea of the existence of such a 'something' if one were employing an 'analogy' between a series of historical events and the developmental process of some item of organic nature such as a plant. Note the importance to his argument of the belief that only atomistic 'events', or series of them, can really count as admissible existents. 'Were a historian', he writes, 'to use this analogy with respect to a series of events which he had established, the development which he traced would not merely be the history of ... a certain period of time; it would be a history of a development process taking place within an enduring entity underlying the specific changes. The true subject of development would then be the entity itself, not merely a series of changes.'[33] Mandelbaum makes an honest effort to give the idea of such an entity a run for its money, but he cannot in the end accept it. On the other hand he finds it unnecessary to offer any shred of justification for *his belief* that mere 'events' are all that the explainer can be seeking to explain. The atomist preferred ontology of 'events'

---

[32] Mandelbaum, op. cit., 45.
[33] Ibid., 46.

was so dominant when Mandelbaum wrote that, it seems, the thought that the preference might need argued justification never crossed his mind. (See Chapter 1 (iii) and (iv) above; and Chapter 7 below.)

Mandelbaum's argument is based on the belief that only atomistic 'events' can really count as admissible existents (a belief that expresses the 'preferred ontology' of atomism). This belief is neither stated nor defended. It is simply assumed that atomistic events are all that there is to be explained, and consequently a further assumption is made about the possible form that this explanation can have. For if they *are* all that there is to explain, then there *is* nothing else to explain, nor can there be anything other than yet more events in terms of which to explain them. Whatever else may be wrong with this conception, it is objectionable because it rules out other possible forms that the explanation of events might take on grounds that are *a priori*. That in itself need not constitute a weakness were the *a priori* grounds sound. But we are not even told what they are. The assumptions made about what can really count as existing, about what there is to explain, and about what there is to explain in terms of, remain assumptions, without argument or justification. They are, in any case, implausible and unsustainable assumptions, and there are better reasons for avoiding them than for adopting them, as we shall argue in Chapter 7.

This atomism underlies Mandelbaum's inability to comprehend the idea that human society might actually *be* something. That inability is the cause of his failure adequately to explain the appearance of such thought as he considers to be characteristic of the nineteenth century: its holism, organicism, developmentalism, 'historicism', etc. An adequate explanation would have to give weight to Adam Smith and others, to the development of classical political economy, and to the developments of market economy which precipitated both.

The explanation offered by Mandelbaum is in the realm of ideas, and its key figure is Herder. Mandelbaum, in effect, explains the appearance of the idea that human society is a 'something' with lines of development, as a relation, or derivative, of Herder's religious ideas that there is truly only one single organism, and that all history is the growth of a single glorious tree: 'Reality is One, and the Divine is present in all the manifestations of this One' (the doctrine of divine immanence). Of course, he stresses profusely Herder's continual use of 'the analogy of growth, and other analogies from the sphere of living things. He spoke of seeds and plants, of buds and flowers, and used "blossoming" as a key metaphor in his conception of history.'[34]

[34] Ibid., 58.

(One wonders what Mandelbaum's own conception of human society could possibly be. He rejects as 'analogical' that it might be any kind of living thing or enduring entity; he rejects the idea that it can develop in a law-like way; and he cannot believe that it is a 'something' which is a subject of change. What is left? A non-living, unchanging thing, which is not even a thing?)

There is, of course, a reason why German philosophy took this road when it did, and it is pinpointed by Trotsky: 'The English and French bourgeoisie created a new society in their own image. The Germans came later, and they were compelled to live for a long time on the pale gruel of philosophy. The Germans invented the phrase "speculative world" which does not exist in English or French. While these nations were creating a new world the Germans were thinking one up.' Though he adds that 'the German bourgeoisie, although poor in political activity, created the classical philosophy, and that is no small achievement'.[35]

The exaggerated place given to Herder is the consequence of the failure to see the place that should have been given to the development of classical political economy and the theory of history that was part of it. (Mandelbaum has no real discussion of Smith, and Ricardo does not even appear in the index.) The real basis of the development of classical political economy, and with it all the categories of nineteenth-century thought that Mandelbaum is investigating, lay in the real developments that were taking place in human society towards a world system of commodity production and circulation. Since Mandelbaum believes such developments in the real world to be figments of an imagination befuddled by an 'organic analogy', he is not well placed to conduct 'A Study in Nineteenth Century Thought'; not, at any rate, one that is likely to result in illumination or explanation of any depth. Mandelbaum's generation was compelled to 'live on a pale gruel of philosophy'. That is why it all has come down, in his sort of view, to Herder, divine immanence and that sort of thing.

Thought has not gone forward from Smith and Marx. It has gone backwards. It cannot now even properly comprehend its own past. The idea of a process of social and historical development of the proportions contemplated by Smith and Marx is as difficult for the intellectuals of a declining class to handle in the realm of ideas, as the reality of that development in the here-and-now is for that declining class itself to handle in the realm of real affairs. It is, therefore, understandable that such intellectuals should have sought comfort in the 'theory' of the accidental interweaving of many factors.

[35] L. Trotsky, *The History of the Russian Revolution*, London (1977), 204-5.

The period in which Mandelbaum wrote was marked by the co-presence of virulent atomism (in the form of Logical Empiricism), and an even cruder pseudo-organicism (*histmat* and *diamat*) which was widely regarded on all sides as being orthodox Marxism. During that period of the Cold War and the long boom of post-war market economy, these items seldom had any serious encounter, and when encounters did take place (as, for example, in the work of political scientists and historians of ideas) they left ample room for discussion about the degree of seriousness attained. The Finns were notably active in this field, and von Wright wrote a rather official piece, the Eddington Memorial Lecture for 1968,[36] which took each side seriously and attempted to show a serious relationship between them.

Things have changed since. We have seen the emergence both of atomistic Marxists and of organicist anti-Marxists. Among the latter it is necessary to distinguish the scholars from the mountebanks. On the one hand there are scholars of the right who, in their genuine efforts to understand reality, have found recourse to a form of organicism unavoidable; Keith Middlemas, in his book *Politics in Industrial Society*, observes that the quantity of archival material available for studies like his own makes life easier for political scientists if they compartmentalise their work, and this he considers inadequate: 'Anything so complicated as a living organism ... can only be understood if its functioning is studied as a whole, rather than as isolated aspects.'[37] At the other end of the spectrum, there are now those on the right, such as Roger Scruton, to whom the bloody tatters of the national '*Geist*' have vouchsafed an ectoplasmic appearance.

(iv) Hegel: natural vs. dialectical processes of development

(a) The most notable but one of all Hegel's innovations was the abandonment of the mechanism then fashionable as the current form of atomism, and its replacement by the Aristotelian categories of essentialism and organicism. His most notable was the development of the refined dialectical form of those categories. Marx noted the former and recorded it in specific form (though in implied general form also) in the *Critique of Hegel's Doctrine of the State*: 'It is a great step forward to have seen that the political state is an organism and that, therefore, its various powers are no longer to be seen as

[36] G.H. von Wright, 'Time, change and contradiction', Cambridge, Nov. 1968.
[37] K. Middlemas, op.cit., London (1979), 11.

mechanical but as the product of living rational division of functions.'[38]

Hegel's philosophy of history, like the rest of his philosophy, is informed by Aristotelian categories from the outset, but he develops them and their specific application to history and society much further.[39] Indeed his conception of the historical process comes so close to that of Marx as to have left Marx with little more than tasks of adjustment on Hegel's work in order in order to arrive at his own theory. Althusser's judgment that there is an enormously difficult set of tasks involved in digging out the 'rational kernal' from Hegelian dialectic, and in finding out what is involved in 'inverting' Hegel so that he stands on his feet instead of his head, is a great piece of pompous professorial exaggeration. As we shall see, it is much less of an exaggeration to say that Hegel did not leave Marx with a great deal to do.

Hegel's first Aristotelian position, adopted at the beginning of the introduction to *The Philosophy of History*, is that which must be adopted by anyone attempting to advance knowledge rather than to keep it where it is or turn it back, viz. that *chance* is not the basis of phenomena; that there is law and order to be found in the phenomena. He chides Epicurus 'who ascribed all events to chance'.[40] Though Anaxagoras thought the world lawlike 'he did not apply the universal to the concrete;[41] only Socrates took the first step of comprehending the union of the concrete and the universal'.[42]

His second Aristotelian position is that he conceives the form of law in terms of the realisation of potentialities in a whole which has an essence in which those potentialities inhere. 'A principle, a law is

---

[38] *CHDS* in *KMEW*, 66.

[39] In order to pursue the main objective directly, we shall consider Hegel's *Philosophy of World History*, and the contrast he draws there between natural and dialectical processes of development, without much regard to the possibility or otherwise of reconciling that contrast with everything else he says elsewhere. It may be that Hegel's grander doctrine that Nature is Spirit in Otherness implies that Nature and natural change are historical. I shall leave this matter aside, since it is immaterial to the present objective. We are concerned with Marx, and he had already developed beyond Hegel's view of the relation between Nature and Spirit in his *Doctoral Dissertation*, where he espoused an Aristotelian (non-reductive) materialism in opposition to Hegel. Cf. *MECW* I, 64 int. al.

[40] G.W.F. Hegel, *Reason in History*, trs. Robert S. Hartman, NY (1953), 14. The translation by H.B. Nisbet, *Lectures on the Philosophy of World History; Introduction; Reason in History*, Cambridge 1975 (paperback 1980), is fuller but not always as lucid as Hartman's. J. Sibree's translation (London 1857 and repr.) is often useful in providing alternative renderings for the non-reader of German.

[41] Ibid., 13-14.

[42] Ibid., 15.

something *implicit*, which ... is not completely real (actual) ... not yet in reality ... a possibility.'[43]

His third Aristotelian or essentialist position is that the phenomena of history arise from a whole with an essence which undergoes transformation of form, and has an end or *telos*. The essence of history for Hegel is 'that freedom of spirit (which) is the very essence of man's nature',[44] and the *telos* of world history is 'the actualisation of this freedom' which Hegel identified as 'the final purpose of the world'.[45] As in Aristotle, necessity resides in the line of development in which a nature, if it does realise its potential, realises *that* potential. So Hegel's view of history is 'the union of freedom and necessity. We consider the inner development of the Spirit ... as necessary, while we refer to freedom the interests contained in men's conscious volitions.'[46]

(b) World history passes through stages (Aristotelian *metabolai*) in each of which a higher level of human consciousness of freedom is attained, and each stage has its own 'principle' or law.[47] 'The main efficient causation' that delivers these teleological stages, the means by which history moves, are 'the actions of men (which) spring from their needs, their passions, their interests ...'.[48] For the potentiality of the essence to become historically actual 'a second element must be added ... namely activity, actualisation', which for Hegel means the human will, passion and interest. 'Nothing great in the world has been accomplished without passion.' It is typical of Hegel, however, to stress that which is least historically specifiable in hard terms, rather than that which is so specifiable; thus he concentrates on 'passion' rather than on the more concretely specifiable 'interest'. Marx, of course, in his own theory reverses the stress. Hegel does this kind of thing systematically, and the reason for it, which, as we shall see, Marx lays bare, is that he is seeking to find some (not quite *any*) empirical embodiment for the schemata of *The Science of Logic* rather than to find the law of the empirical area of phenomena under investigation.

The teleology of history and its efficient causation necessarily interrelate in the production of history: 'First, the Idea, secondly, the complex of human passions; the one the warp, the other weft of the

[43] Ibid., 27.
[44] Ibid., 24.
[45] Loc. cit.
[46] Ibid., 31.
[47] Ibid., 70.
[48] Ibid., 26.

vast tapestry of world history.'[49] But they do not relate as equals in Hegel's scheme of things. It is the Idea that wears the trousers, and human will and interests are its instruments: 'These vast congeries of volitions, interests, and activities constitute the tools and the means of the World Spirit for attaining its purpose, bringing it to consciousness, and realising it.'[50] Hegel was well aware that this is difficult to swallow, and the idea was much criticised in his own time. He notes that 'One may indeed question whether those manifestations of vitality on the part of individuals and peoples in which they seek and satisfy their own purposes are, at the same time, the means and tools of a higher broader purpose of which they know nothing, which they realise unconsciously.'[51] But in spite of criticism he is insistent that: 'Reason governs the world and has consequently governed its history ... This Reason is immanent in historical existence and reaches its own perfection in and through this existence.'[52] Marx later reverses Hegel's prioritisation of teleology and efficient causation in an account of the historical process where the two can be seen to mesh, and which does not give grounds for suspicion that they really do not mesh at all but are made to appear to do so by rhetoric because the System requires it. Marx achieves this in the *Critique of Hegel's Doctrine of the State*, not arbitrarily or from some alternative preference, but by showing Hegel's prioritisation to be an inescapable consequence of his entire idealist project: 'Hegel's true interest is not the philosophy of right but logic.'[53]

(c) Hegel contrasts natural with historical change. He distinguishes, as Aristotle did not, between the manner in which organic categories apply in the history of human society and in organic nature. 'Change in nature, no matter how infinitely varied it is, shows only a constant cycle of repetition. In nature nothing new happens ... one and the same permanent character continuously reappears, and all change reverts to it.'[54] (We can discount Hegel's belief in the 'permanent character' of organic species as a factual error that makes no difference to his argument for a contrast between natural and historical social change.) 'Only the changes in the realm of Spirit create the novel. This characteristic suggests to man a feature entirely different from that of nature – the desire

[49] Ibid., 29.
[50] Ibid., 31.
[51] Loc. cit.
[52] Loc. cit.
[53] Marx, *CHDS*, 73.
[54] Hegel, op.cit., 68.

towards *perfectibility*. This principle, which brings change itself under laws, has been badly received ... by states which desire as their true right to be static or at least stable.'[55] This is an idea that Hegel was able to develop only feebly in his theory of history. It asks to be transformed into Marx's more persuasive idea that man himself can adapt society to himself and to the realisation of his own potentials, rather than adapting to it and to the requirements of some historical social (economic) system which thwarts him even though it is of his own making.

This contrast between natural change and historical change lies, according to Hegel, in differences in the natures of the two kinds of processes themselves. As a feature of organic natural entities, development is a straightforward process, relatively simple to comprehend at least in outline. Historical development is a more complex process, and its specific difference Hegel identifies (in *The Philosophy of History* at any rate) as its 'dialectical' character.

Development in 'organic natural objects ... proceeds from an inner ... principle, a simple essence, which first exists as a germ. From this simple existence it brings forth out of itself differentiations which connect it with other things. Thus it lives a life of continuous transformation.' But equally, it never produces anything novel, any new nature or essence, and all change reverts to the same thing; that is, it reproduces the same real nature, and all that is new in this process is the production of a new *numerically* different instance of the same identical essence.[56] As Hegel puts it, though 'it lives a life of continuous transformation ... we may look at it from the opposite point of view and see in it the *preservation* of the organic principle and its form'.[57] The organic natural object 'makes itself actually into that which it is in itself (potentially) ... The development of the organism proceeds in an immediate, direct (undialectical), unhindered manner. Nothing can interfere between the concept and its realisation, the inherent nature of the germ and the adaptation of its existence to this nature.' Accidents can happen in natural organic developments which frustrate their completion, but Hegel's point is that there is nothing in the nature of the development process itself, in the case of natural organic change, that interrupts the realisation of potentials.

---

[55] Loc. cit.

[56] One of the fundamental problems of essentialist philosophy is involved here, namely, whether the essence relates to the *individual* or to the *kind* to which the individual belongs. I shall shamelessly pass it by, though it will be touched upon at various points below.

[57] Hegel, op.cit. (italics added).

The contrast is with Spirit development or history, where the process of development is internally more complex. Here, the interplay between its component forces can frustrate development, advance or retard it in unforseen ways, without the benefit of extraneous accidents; this is an aspect of its nature as a *dialectical* process. The line of necessity in the development is not *immediate*, and frustratable only by external, material accident. It is *mediated*: 'The transition of its potentiality into actuality is mediated through consciousness and will.'[58] The crucial difference, therefore, between the natural and the historical process of development is the role of conscious human agency. Where natural development reproduces the same unchanged natures smoothly (barring accidents from outside the essence impinging on the process of internal development), historical development neither reproduces the same thing, nor is the process smooth.

(Allen Wood offers a useful discussion of the Hegelianism of 'Lukacs' idealistic notion that only conscious human practice confers a dialectical structure on thing'. He rightly observes that there is nothing in Marx to suggest that he held any such view, and that 'Marx parts company with Hegel precisely because Hegel makes the dialectical nature of thought the basis for the dialectical structure of reality, where Marx holds that just the reverse is the case'.[59] The soundness of Wood's judgment is, I believe, confirmed below in the next section of this chapter, and in Chapters 3 to 6.)

The process of historical development produces, not the same nature, but quite new forms of the nature; stages of attainment of consciousness of Spirit's freedom. And the historical process in which these transitions from potentiality to actuality are attained 'is not the harmless and unopposed simple growth of organic life … not mere formal self-development in general'.[60] Since it is mediated by consciousness, the process is a war within Spirit, or between less developed and more developed *forms* of the essence of Spirit, in which the lower, habitual one fights it out with the higher more advanced one, in a process of decay and generation. 'Thus Spirit is at war with itself. It must overcome itself as its own enemy and formidable obstacle. Development, which in nature is a quiet unfolding, is in Spirit a hard, infinite struggle against itself …'[61] Hegel considered this to be particularly clearly exemplified by those 'several large

[58] Ibid., 69.
[59] Allen Wood, *Karl Marx*, London (1981), 215.
[60] Hegel, op.cit., 70.
[61] Ibid., 69.

periods' of world history whose 'whole enormous gain of culture has been annihilated' without any apparent further development. The insufficiency of 'the merely formal view of development' is shown in its incapacity to explain why there should be such discontinuities or declines rather than continuing development. 'It must consider such events, and in particular such reversals, as external accidents' or chance;[62] and that is a category to which Hegel rightly thinks minimal resort should be had, for such decay and corruption arises from the 'internal principle' or nature of the entity in question.

(d) The basis of the difference between the two processes of development lies in the different character of the nature undergoing formal change. With natural species the process is one of the reproduction over time of the species; the preservation of an identical generic nature by its transmission through successive numerically distinct individuals, each of which equally embodies that single nature. The historical process, however, does not *preserve* a nature through successive generations; it *develops* a nature through successive forms. 'If we consider the genus as the substantial in this transformation, then the death of the individual is a falling back of the genus into individuality. The preservation of the genus is then nothing but the monotonous repetition of the same kind of existence.'[63]

The situation is infinitely more complicated, if not unintelligible, in Hegel's account of the process of historical change:

> a moral whole [= the state – S.M.] as such, is limited. It must have above it a higher universality which makes it disunited in itself. The transition from one spiritual pattern to the next is just this, that the former moral whole, in itself a universal, through being thought (in terms of the higher universal), is abolished as a particular [for it is elevated into the universal – ed.'s note]. The latter universal, so to speak, the next higher genus of the preceding species, is potentially but not yet actually in the preceding one. This makes all existing reality unstable and disunited.[64]

The basis of the instability here, *the contradiction, is between what exists and what is in the process of coming-to-be.*

What exists, the actual, is imperfect. But the actual contains potential: specifically, the potential for the perfect. This potential

---

[62] Ibid., 70.
[63] Ibid., 93.
[64] Ibid., 38.

Hegel describes as 'the opposite' of the actual. So the actual contains both itself and its opposite (as potential). The opposite, the potential, is not inert. It is the 'germ', 'impulse' or 'urge' within the actual which begets change towards the realisation of the potential of greater perfection. Hegel writes: 'Possibility points towards something which shall become real; more precisely, the Aristotelian *dynamis* is also *potentia*, force and power.'[65] In the Sibree edition the subsequent sentence runs: 'The Imperfect, as involving its opposite, is a contradiction, which certainly exists, but which is continually annulled and solved.'[66] The ideas Hegel is developing here have an affinity with Marx's conception of a 'driving contradiction', which is discussed below in Chapter 5 (iii).

(We also get here an indication of the proximity and the distance between Aristotle, Hegel and Marx. My understanding is that Aristotle considers essences as unities, whereas Hegel and Marx consider them as unities in contradiction. Moreover, for Aristotle, form (essence) and matter cannot come apart, whereas for Marx they can, at least in certain cases (see Chapter 5 (iii) below). Their conception of contradiction is ontological, where Aristotle's is that of a logical relation between propositions. However, Hegel does say in *The History of Philosophy* that 'with Aristotle this negativity, this active efficacy, is expressly characterised as energy; in that it breaks up itself – this independence – abrogating unity, and positing separation; for, as Aristotle says (*Met.* 7.13), "actuality separates".'[67] (The contrast is with Plato, and to his disadvantage because he does not have any 'breaking up' or 'separation'.) Where this leaves us I am not sure. A lot of work is needed before judgments can be reached with confidence about the relations between the fundamental categories of the three authors. Certainly, Aristotle has great difficulty in *Physics* 5 in accounting for change; becoming; how, in becoming, a thing can both be and not be; and in dealing with what change is between, i.e. opposites. Marx's ontological contradictions could be seen as a way out of Aristotle's difficulties.)

The reader familiar with Marx will immediately recognise the *general* relationships and movement Hegel is describing, though the content of Hegel's own version is scarcely intelligible – with universals being abolished as particulars because they come to be thought of in terms of a higher universal. The unintelligibility arises

---

[65] Ibid., 71.

[66] Ibid., Sibree's trs. (see n.40 above) 59.

[67] Hegel, *Lectures on the History of Philosophy*, trs. E. Haldane and F. Simson, in three vols, London (1894) II, 139-40.

from Hegel's idealist integument, not from the categories and their relationships. He is not talking about a real nature that undergoes dialectical development; he is 'concerned with the Spirit's development, its progression and ascent to an even higher concept of itself. But this development is connected with the degradation, destruction and annihilation of the preceding mode of actuality which the concept of the human Spirit had evolved.'[68] This is the 'dialectic of concepts' abjured by Marx in the Introduction to the *Grundrisse*.

(e) Hegel's account of the process of development as it occurs in his view that 'world history represents phases in the development of the principle whose content is the consciousness of freedom',[69] has a number of queer features which centre on the supposed transitions between stages. Each stage of the realisation of the consciousness of freedom, as it exists in the Spirit of some people or nation, 'has its definite, peculiar principle ... this principle defines the common features of its religion, its peculiar constitution, its morality, its system of law, its morals, even its science, art and technical skill'.[70] In its period of vitality it, 'the people', is driven along by the 'tension between its potential and its actuality'.[71] The tension is abolished by the realisation of the full potential of its essence or principle, and 'activity of Spirit ceases ... the living substantial soul is ... no longer alive'. What ensues is 'the life of *habit* ... which brings about natural death. Habit is tensionless activity. Only formal duration is left to it ... thus peoples die a natural death ... its institutions are without necessity, just because the necessity has been satisfied.'[72]

If, at this point, the spirit of a people wanted something new 'it would have to be a higher, more universal, idea of itself transcending its present principle'. Where would this come from and how? Hegel simply asserts that it does happen. 'Such a new principle does indeed come into the spirit of a people which has arrived at its completion and actualisation. The universal spirit does not merely die a natural death; it does not simply vanish in the senile life of mere habit.'[73] But why not? And how does it arise phoenix-like from the ashes of 'the life of habit'?

Hegel's answer, when it comes, is that thought *has* to find a new

[68] *Reason in History*, 38-9.
[69] Ibid., 70.
[70] Ibid., 79.
[71] Ibid., 90.
[72] Ibid., 91.
[73] Loc.cit.

principle. '*The resolution of existence through thought is at the same time necessarily the arising of a new principle.*'[74] This miraculous solution is not so surprising. Though peoples may die a natural death, thought, in Hegel's system, never can. For Hegel's history is not a history of peoples, or of their 'national principles'; it is a 'history' of Thought. Thought is the birthplace of the new principle 'for thought is the universal, the genus which preserves its identity' through all the change, the comings-and-goings of peoples, constitutions, empires, religions, skills, etc. Actual history merely exemplifies the 'dialectic of Thought'. It does so for the simple reason that that is how Hegel constructed his system. If history had not exemplified Thought in one way, it would have done so in another; anything could in principle count as an exemplification. For the categories of Hegel's history are not extracted from history itself; that is, they are not constructed on the basis of a study of real history with a view to explaining the actual historical motion. Rather, the categories of history are imported from *The Science of Logic*, and history is then 'shown' to instantiate them. Marx notes precisely this in the *CHDS*: 'He simply holds fast to one category and contents himself with searching for something corresponding to it in actual existence.'[75]

Hegel is quite clear that as regards world history 'the analysis of its stages in general belongs to Logic'.[76] Hegel did not discover by investigation of history that history is the process of 'development of Spirit's consciousness of freedom', and that in this process there is 'a series of ever more concrete differentiations as involved in the concept of freedom'.[77] He knew it in advance, for 'the logical and, even more, the dialectical nature of the concept in general, the necessity of its purely abstract self-development, is treated in Logic. There it is shown that it determines itself, posits its own determinations and in turn abolishes them (transcending itself), and by this very process of abolition and transcending gains an affirmative, ever richer and more concretely determined form'.[78]

Hegel's account of history, the state, etc., arises, not from a study of history, the state, etc., but from a pan-logic to which everything must conform *a priori*. It is then a question merely of looking at history to see how it conforms. (Of course, he knew a great deal of history, so that in composing his *Logic* he had some idea of what it was that had to conform to it, or of what it would have to

[74] Ibid., 93 (original italics).
[75] Marx, *CHDS*, 109.
[76] Hegel, op.cit., 70.
[77] Ibid., 78.
[78] Ibid., 79.

accommodate.) This is the primary criticism which Marx makes of Hegel in the *CHDS*, and it is the terminus to which all his other criticisms tend. As he says: 'Hegel's true interest is not the philosophy of Right but logic',[79] for in Hegel 'the various powers are not determined by "their own nature" ... Similarly, their *necessity* is not to be found in their own essence ... Rather, their fate is predestined by "the nature of the concept", it lies sealed in the holy archives of the Santa Casa of the *Logic*.'[80] Hegel stands the relation of the universal to the particular on its head because he does not make real, existing natures his starting point, as Aristotle had. Rather, he begins with an abstraction of thought, and then elides the possibility that something (say, for example, 'executive power') may *fail* to be realised, 'may fail to express its specific nature',[81] and so assumes that it finds its realisation and simply casts around for one and 'takes an empirical instance ... which can be said to realise this' category. The one he picks on for the concept of the state, is, as Marx observes, 'the Prussian State, just as it is – lock, stock and barrel'. And so Marx concludes, 'Hegel thus provides his logic with a political body; he does not provide us with a logic of the body politic'.[82]

(v) Marx: 'setting Hegel on his feet'

(a) Inverting the universal and particular

It is precisely this logic, or science, of the body politic that Marx himself is after. In that endeavour, the *CHDS* achieves a great deal more than the negative task of clearing the decks of Hegel's idealism, in order then to be able to set about the positive task of constructing a science of the body politic. It sets about the positive task alongside the negative one. Indeed, the positive and constructive task dominates the negative and critical one. Nor does the critical task approach anything like a repudiation of Hegel, for the general theoretical structure is accepted, but at the same time it is reoriented at the most fundamental level of ontology. Real natures are made the starting point.

Hegel's procedure had been to ignore the specific natures of the parts or items composing the whole (as the 'executive power', for

---

[79] Marx, *CHDS*, 73.
[80] Ibid., 70.
[81] Ibid., 109.
[82] Loc. cit.

example, represents a part of 'the state') and to ignore their specific courses of development. That he should so proceed is a consequence of his ontological starting point. For that empirical realism, Hegel substituted an idealism in which a nature and its supposed development are derived from a system of logic, external to the subject matter and imposed upon it, which lays down 'the dialectical nature of the concept in general, the necessity of its purely abstract self-development', etc.[83]

Marx rejects the idealist starting point and procedure, but he does not reject Hegel's thought root and branch. He rejects it as a fantastic inversion of the truth, not as a falsehood. He retains the potent categorial structure developed by Hegel, which can enormously advance the empirically based investigation of the 'body politic', the human social organism, its nature and movement, and the nature of its parts.

Throughout the *CHDS* Marx illustrates Hegel's perverse and incredible inversions. He points out, for example, that the correct relationships are that 'the political state cannot exist without the natural basis of the family and the artificial basis of civil society. These are its *sine qua non.*' And yet in Hegel's accounts of relationships like those between such realities as the family, civil society and state, they are reversed so that 'the condition is posited as the conditioned, the determinator as the determined, the producer as the product'.[84] Marx observes that the 'family and civil society are the preconditions of the state: they are its true aspects; but in speculative philosophy it is the reverse.'[85] In speculative philosophy

> ... what takes place does not result from the *particular* nature of the family etc., and the particular nature of the state, but from the *universal* relationship of *freedom* and *necessity*. We find exactly the same process at work in the *Logic* in the transition from the sphere of Essence to that of the Concept.[86]

Marx's reactions to Hegel's phantasmagorical constructions are always the same. He does not ditch Hegel. He retains, for example, such organic relationships as 'the condition' and the 'conditioned', but he reverses their direction. There is no need to add further illustrations, with which the text is replete. In reversing them he is following through the consequences of Feuerbach's objection that 'in

[83] Hegel, *Reason in History*, 79.
[84] Marx, *CHDS*, 65.
[85] Ibid., 61-2.
[86] Ibid., 64.

Hegel, thought is being; thought is the subject, being the predicate'. Marx reproduces this more or less verbatim in the *CHDS*: 'The crux of the matter is that Hegel everywhere makes the Idea into the subject, while the genuine, real subject ... is turned into the predicate. The development, however, always takes place on the side of the predicate.'[87] But Marx develops the insight in his own way. As the last quotation suggests, Marx wants Hegel set on his feet; reconstructed on the foundation of Aristotelian natures which are 'genuine' and 'real', which are 'the true aspects' of the material whole, and in which the real development actually takes place.

Hegel's idealist starting point not only represents an absurd ontology, it also precludes scientific understanding and explanation of the natures of the things one is talking about. One explains nothing about the nature of an item – say, the political constitution – by pronouncing it to be 'the differentiation of the Idea into its various elements'. Marx makes the point that one can make such a statement without knowing 'anything at all about the *specific idea* of the political constitution; the same statement can be made with the same truth about the organism of an animal as about the organism of the state.'[88] The scientific task is to identify the entity, organism or part in question, whatever it may be, to investigate it and determine its specific *differentia* and explain its essence:

> Our general definitions do not advance our understanding. An explanation ... which fails to supply the *differentia* is *no* explanation at all ... the real subjects ... are and remain uncomprehended because their specific nature has not been grasped.[89]

The general cannot be determined in advance and foisted off on to some particular or another. Rather, the particular must be investigated with a view to determining what truly is the general within it.[90]

Marx accepts Hegel's organicism as against the mechanistic materialism of the eighteenth century which he attacks in the *Theses on Feuerbach*, while rejecting the idealist integument as

---

[87] Ibid., 65.

[88] Ibid., 67.

[89] Loc. cit.

[90] The Hegelian procedure is frequently adopted in 'Marxist' analyses of the nature of the USSR. Those advancing the 'state-capitalist' theory, the 'degenerate workers state' theory, or the theory of the socialist 'base' with bourgeois 'superstructure', commonly begin with knowledge-in-advance of which categories will apply in the analysis of the empirical material.

non-explanatory and banal. 'The argument that the different members of an organism stand in a necessary relation to each other derived from the nature of the organism is a pure tautology.'[91] A *materialist* organicism requires that the 'various powers' of a thing be determined and explained by the essence underlying them, which powers express or manifest that essence; it also requires that the *necessity* in the line of development and in the typical activity (*ergon*) of an essence should be located in that actually existing essence, and not be derived from the 'nature of the concept',[92] or from 'the *universal* relationship of *freedom* and *necessity*'.[93]

Marx is, therefore, seeking to transpose Hegel into the form of Aristotelian materialism without losing what Hegel has gained. The centre of this attempted transposition is the reversal of the relation between thought and being as it appears in Hegel; that is, to replace Hegel's starting point in 'the Mystical Idea' with the Aristotelian starting point of real existing things with real natures which have to be discovered by investigation. 'If Hegel had begun by positing real subjects as the basis of the state he would not have found it necessary to subjectivise the state in a mystical way.'[94] His repeated complaint is that Hegel is not really interested in explaining the nature of the social-historical organism, the natures of its constituents and their real determinations. Hegel's interest in those things is only to 'reveal' them as aspects of his 'logical, pantheistic mysticism', as Marx calls it. For example, in Hegel 'the essence of the determining characteristics of the state is not that they define the state, but that they are capable of being viewed in their most abstract form as logico-metaphysical determinations'.[95] This is how Hegel gets on to his head, and Marx identifies it as his 'fundamental defect'. 'Because Hegel starts not with an actual existent, but with predicates of universal determination, and because a vehicle for these determinations must exist, the mystical Idea becomes that vehicle.'

Marx's remedy is 'to regard the universal as the real essence of the finite real, i.e. of what exists and is determined'.[96] What is wrong with Hegel, and what is needed to put him right, is a straightforward matter of replacing an idealist ontological starting point with a materialist one more in the manner of Aristotle's conception of essence. In Hegel, simply, 'the true way is turned upside down. The

[91] Marx, *CHDS*, 66.
[92] Ibid., 70.
[93] Ibid., 64.
[94] Ibid., 80.
[95] Ibid., 73.
[96] Ibid., 99.

most simple thing becomes the most complicated and the most complicated becomes the most simple. What should be a starting point becomes a mystical result and what should be a rational result becomes a mystical starting point.'[97]

To understand Marx's essentialist materialism, and to discriminate it from reductive materialism (itself a form of atomism, see Chapter 7 (i) below) which has bedevilled Marxism, it is necessary to appreciate the full significance of Marx's insistence on regarding 'the universal as the real essence of the finite real'. It means (a) that there are real natures or essences which are not 'reducible' to 'simples', (b) that coming to identify them and know them involves tracking down what is general, universal or essential in the phenomena or 'finite real', and (c) that that has to begin with an investigation of the facts of the finite real itself in order to *discover* (it cannot be known *a priori*) what is truly the general within it, so that (d) the finite real, the reality itself, can then finally be comprehended in the light of the general, the universal or the essence, that the empirical investigation turned up.

Once that is grasped then it is clear that it is no more than a partial truth to characterise Marx's method as a unilinear passage from 'abstract' to 'concrete' or 'particular', as many Marxist writers are inclined to describe it. This latter conception is commonly favoured by dogmatists, whose usual intention (conscious or unconscious, depending on whether they are dishonest or honest dogmatists) is to interpret some entity or phenomenon in terms of abstractions chosen in advance, and then to 'find' among the real facts manifold confirmations of their 'theory'. (Such a method is nowhere commoner than among those defending one or other of the traditional theories about the nature of the USSR.) Not surprisingly, observations about the affinity between Marx and Aristotle are seldom welcome in such quarters. Marcel Reding's attempt[98] to demonstrate that affinity was described by an official Soviet commentator as an attempt 'to "supplement Marx" with the purpose of hoodwinking the working people'.[99]

Marx's search for a theory of history that was *materialist*, a description by which he came to set great store, meant the search for a rejigging of *Hegel's essentialist theory of history* into a non-reductive materialist form and away from Hegel's idealist form. It did not

[97] Ibid., 99-100.

[98] Marcel Reding, *St. Thomas Aquinas and Karl Marx*, Graz (1953).

[99] In the notes supplied for the Moscow edition of Plekhanov's *Fundamental Problems of Marxism*, Lawrence and Wishart, London, n.d., 101.

mean casting around for some other theory of history altogether, one that was materialist. For the generation of Marx and Engels, 'the theory of history' means Hegel's theory of history. Hence the content and importance given by Marx and Engels to the specific description of their theory of history as 'materialist' derived directly from their object of giving content in terms of real human social existence to the Hegelian dialectic of essence, form, 'principle', etc., and of defining a materialist basis with which to replace Hegel's inverted starting point of the Idea. A 'materialist' theory of history meant to them precisely a realist version of, and therefore an *inversion* of Hegel's theory. A careful author like Colletti has sought to cast doubt on the 'inversion' thesis of Marx's relation to Hegel, because he sees it as one of the roots of the later distortions of *diamat*. We shall return to this matter in the next section.

(b) *The concrete universal: the real starting point for history*

So in Hegel 'what should be a starting point becomes a mystical result and what should be a rational result becomes mystical starting point'. The question is, then, what should be the starting point in the attempt to comprehend human history? Marx's theoretical direction can now be only towards identifying a concrete universal, a universal which is, as he put it, 'the real essence of the finite real, i.e. of what exists and is determined'. Marx is already defining a position on this in the *CHDS*, earlier than most commentators have noticed and much closer to Hegel. 'The state is an abstraction. Only the people is a concrete reality.'[100] Marx argues that the basic reality with which to begin in the consideration of the historical development of the state, the executive power, the monarch, the bureaucracy, etc., is the existence of people. The significant point, in Marx's view, is that 'monarchy cannot be explained in its own terms; democracy can be so explained. In democracy no moment acquires a meaning other than what is proper to it. Each is only a moment of the *dêmos* as a whole ... democracy is the essence of all political constitutions, *socialised man* as a particular constitution.'[101]

The expression here is peculiar. It is the expression of the democratic republican revolutionary opposed to the Prussian autocracy who emerges, full of shame at Germany's backwardness, in the letters to Ruge written between the composition of the *CHDS*

[100] Marx, *CHDS*, 85.
[101] Ibid., 87-8 (italics added).

and the *Critique of Hegel's Philosophy of Right*. It is in the latter that
Marx first appears as the proletarian revolutionary based on the
wage-workers as the universal class. Despite the unusual expression,
however, the direction of thought is clear. There are only people and
the social-historical forms they engender. Everything in human
history is the product of humans, of their conflict and co-operation.
Any particular form, of state, for example, or anything else that is
social (such as the value-form, as Marx later came to see), merely
expresses 'socialised man' as he has made himself up to that time,
and has that as its essence.

This concrete starting point for theoretical history is the result of
Marx's coming to terms with the 'speculative philosophy' of history.
It remained with Marx as the bedrock insight of all his later thought
and its importance cannot be overstated. He noted that 'the
importance of Hegel's *Phenomenology* ... lies in the fact that Hegel
conceives the self-creation of man as a process ... that he therefore
grasps the nature of *labour* and conceives the objective man ... as the
result of his own labour'.[102] That same starting point is announced
in *The German Ideology*:

> The first premise of all human history is, of course, the existence of
> living human individuals.[103]

He described, in this familiar passage, his historical method as
starting

> from the real premises and does not abandon them for a moment. Its
> premises are men, not in any fantastic isolation or rigidity, but in their
> actual, empirically perceptible process of development under definite
> conditions. As soon as this active life process is described, history
> ceases to be a collection of dead facts as it is with the empiricists
> (themselves still abstract), or an imagined activity of an imagined
> subject, as with the idealists.[104]

To be sure, Marx later warned in the *Grundrisse* against the
apparently correct concrete starting point of the 'population', and
argued that it is actually a mistaken one if taken simply on its own,
for 'the population is an abstraction if I leave out, for example, the
classes of which it is composed'.[105] But his target in that criticism

[102] *EPM*, 385.
[103] *GI MECW* V, 31.
[104] Ibid., 37.
[105] *Gr.*, 100.

was specifically the form in which political economy developed as a science. The sort of mistake he is pointing to could not have been any sort that Marx might himself have been making in 1843 at the time he wrote the *CHDS*. And the reason has to do with his relation to Hegel. The general dialectical and teleological framework is preserved in the conception of a fundamental essence in human history (the 'socialised man' of *CHDS* who becomes more precisely identified in the *EPM* as the concrete universal of human labour), which passes through a series of specific forms (which he comes to identify as organic social wholes in which a particular form of supply of human social labour is predominant) each having specific laws or realisable potentials of development, and culminating in the attainment of socialism where the fullest potential of the essence is realised in a form of society adapted by man to himself. (Cf. Chapter 6 (ii) and (iii).)

Hegel turns the efficient causation of human desire, interest, aspiration and will into a mere tool for the realisation of a non-human or supra-human purpose, that of Reason. Ultimately, Hegel can give no reason why the one should be efficacious as the efficient causation required for the attainment of the other. He cannot explain why the final and efficient causation should mesh together, and simply insists that they do and must because 'Reason governs the world'. In Marx it is clear how human hopes, desires and will can, where and when they are able, be the efficient causation within the teleological movement, where and when that is able to be moved towards the realisation of one or another human social potentiality.

The immediate consequence of his insight that the starting point proper for history is the fact that there are only people is that Marx now needs to develop categories and abstractions from that basis within which to comprehend the historical movement and its forms. This he proceeds to do in the *EPM* through to the *GI* and beyond. The course, however, is set. Contrary to the judgment of Ernest Mandel that even the *EPM* provides only the motivation rather than the framework for Marx's pursuit of his later course, it is clear that the broad categorial structure is already established in outline in the *CHDS*. The point of getting this judgment right is not to establish in which work, or in which month of which year, Marx made which discovery. The point is to arrive at a proper evaluation of what the fundamental categories of Marx's systematic thought are. What turns out to be crucial to that evaluation is Marx's relation to Aristotle and Hegel. That relation exists at the level of philosophy and ontology, and it is settled by Marx in large part in the *CHDS*.

Marx has arrived at his starting point, and he has done so through a critical appropriation of Hegel. He has Hegel's dialectical process of history in which, through a series of stages each with its own 'principle' or law, an essence undergoes changes that realise its potentialities. The realisation that the *dêmos* is the real content of social categories and historical forms, that 'socialised man' is their essence, together with the accompanying inverted form of the Hegelian view that history is the process of man's own self-creation (or self-realisation as a social animal), comes inevitably to be focused on the category of social labour. Conjointly they compose the theory of history that impelled him into political economy, and that provided the basis from which he was able to begin the critical comprehension of classical political economy in the *EPM*. Where Hegel had seen the truth as lying uniquely in 'the union of the *abstract universal* with the particular',[106] Marx sees the truth to lie in the union of the particular with the *concrete universal*, i.e. human labour and the historical forms under which it is conducted.[107] Marx's arrival at the labour theory of value is now a question only of thoroughly following through the consequences of his view of human history. Since there are only people and their activities (concrete, useful labour, and labour time), all particular historical forms in which people labour, and all the categories specific to those historical forms can only have as their essence people and their labour. There is no other content to be had by any category subsequently realised in history, including value whether the money-form, price-form, or capital-form. To consider otherwise is to enter a world of nonsense in terms of the theory of history; a world the specific quality of whose nonsense Marx later denominated 'fetishism'.

To fetishise is simply to misunderstand the social forms produced in the historical development of human social relations as if they were entities in their own right, rather than to understand them correctly as forms taken by an underlying essence. Much of the opposition to the labour theory of value that has recently arisen among Marxists is really no more then an expression of the opposition between atomism and essentialism. Authors such as Steedman and Lippi[108] want a technical problem relating magnitudes, rather than an essence-appearance (or essence-form) relation, to which they would deny validity, and for which they lack

[106] *Reason in History*, 31.
[107] See Chris Arthur's 'Dialectics and labour', in *IMP*, Vol. I.
[108] I. Steedman, *Marx after Sraffa*, London (1977); Marco Lippi, *Value and Naturalism in Marx*, trs. Hilary Steedman, London (1979).

the requisite philosophical understanding. (Cf. Chapter 6 (iii) below.)

Marx's essentialist methodological basis has eluded many who are better equipped to detect it. It has, indeed, become an enormous lacuna in the present understanding of Marx's thought. This appears nowhere more clearly than in the treatments given of Marx's relation to Hegel, with which we are still dealing at this point. In the remainder of this section (b) I shall develop further the theme of Marx's debt as an essentialist to Hegel and Aristotle, and at the same time illustrate how and why that essentialism has become a lacuna. This can conveniently be done by hanging the discussion on the work of Colletti, which has been both scholarly and extensive.

Colletti justly observes that 'the true importance of Marx's early criticism of Hegel lies in the key it provides for understanding Marx's criticism of the method of bourgeois economics (and this is why he could recall and confirm it after he had written *Capital*)',[109] as he did in the *Afterword to the Second German Edition*. This is a sound judgment, but Colletti fails to make it good by being specific about, and showing, just *what* the connection is between Marx's evaluation and reconstruction of Hegel, and his criticism of the analytical method of classical political economy at its best. (The connection is discussed below in Chapter 3 (i).) It is surprising to make such a judgment and then fail to make it good; it is doubly surprising when Colletti can also rightly note the backwardness that has remained in 'the study of Marx's work' precisely on 'the connection between his critique of Hegel and his critique of the methods of political economy'.[110] He says nothing about the nature of the connection, but passes uninterruptedly into a discussion of the essentialism of Marxist method in political economy compared to the well-known ahistorical nature of empiricist model-building. The connection lies in the theory of history, its starting point, the relation of the general and the particular, necessary and accidental change, the real natures of history's successive organic social wholes, and their common nature as realisations of potentiality in the teleological process of the coming-to-be of human society as an essence. But Colletti says nothing about any of it. Why?

It cannot be imagined that a commentator as acute and learned as Colletti can really have failed to see what is so obvious from even a cursory reading of the works in question. The presumption must be that he passed it by in silence. Perhaps he did so out of

[109] Colletti's *Introduction* to *KMEW*, 24.
[110] Ibid., 25.

embarrassment at the scope of the teleology; at the sheer depth of Marx's debt to Hegel, so indefensible in terms of what Colletti has come to accept in other of his works; and because of his hostility to the idea that there is any great substance in the 'inversion' and 'rational kernel in a mystical shell' thesis about the relation of Marx to Hegel, in which he is inclined to locate some at least of the seeds of the later sinister tomfoolery of *diamat*.

Much though his antipathy to *diamat* is to be endorsed, Colletti throws out the baby with the bathwater when he extends it to cover the inversion thesis. That thesis is not only justified, as has been argued above, but Marx repeatedly announces it himself. For example, he writes in the *EPM* that in the *Phenomenology* 'all elements of criticism are contained within it, and are often *prepared* and *worked out* in a way that goes beyond Hegel's own point of view'.[111] It is untrue to claim, as Colletti does, that only Engels and the *Doktorklub*, but not Marx, saw in Hegel a categorial structure that could give very different results from those Hegel himself arrived at. Whatever roots we are to find for *diamat*, the inversion thesis cannot be among them.

The only way to handle embarrassment is to go through the offending item in detail and either locate its source or discover that there need be no embarrassment. Silence is no response. Indeed, it is imprudent, for when Colletti goes on to show how Marx's essentialism enabled him critically to comprehend classical political economy, the reader is left puzzled about where this essentialism has sprung from and what its exact nature and meaning is. These are just the issues on which Colletti has remained silent in not dealing in detail with the relation between Hegel's *Philosophy of History* and Marx's *CHDS*.

The lacuna appears even more obviously when Colletti expounds Marx's view on the apologetic aspect of political economy. As he points out: 'What economists do, says Marx, is to substitute for the *specific* institutions and processes of modern economy *generic* or universal categories supposed to be valid for all times and places ... After which – as the "more or less conscious aim" of the operation – the concrete is smuggled in as a consequence and a triumphant embodiment of the universal.'[112] This is fine; of course the universal advanced by political economy is in reality nothing more than the particular form represented by market economy. But if that is a false universal, which is the true one? Colletti immediately *mentions* it

---

[111] *KMEW*, 385.
[112] Colletti's Introduction to *KMEW*, 27-8.

himself; ' "Labour" in general is, in Marx's words, "the universal condition for the metabolic interaction (*Stoffwechsel*) ...".'[113] But he does not explicitly *identify it as* the universal, the essence or substance of the historical movement, which in the very same quote Colletti is using Marx goes on to describe as the historical universal of all phases of history, i.e. of all specific forms of the human social organism: 'The labour process *is* therefore independent of every form of that existence, or rather it is common to all forms of society in which human beings live.[114] Even less does Colletti explain how this fundamental categorisation of 'universal' and 'particular' has arrived, or in what specific form it is utilised by Marx, and by what means he identifies what is 'specific' and what 'generic'.

Colletti has passed uninterruptedly from Marx's settling of accounts with Hegel, about which he says nothing, to Marx's analysis of the character and content of bourgeois economics. The passage from the one to the other remains unremarked and unexplained. The connection and its explanation lie, as we have seen and will see in greater detail later, in Marx's *theory of history* (and theory of science) which he hammered out in coming to terms with Hegel's philosophy and theory of history; in his realisation that all the forms that enter into human history are just so many products of the *dêmos*, 'socialised man', and his activities. The theory of history, however, involves teleology, and Colletti's uncertainties about the latter beget his resounding silence about the former. The same coyness about historical teleology appears repeatedly in his works. For example, at a point in *From Rousseau to Lenin* where it would have been very apt to develop the relation between teleology (or finalism) and efficient causation, he ducks out, saying confusedly: 'This is not the place to examine ... this relation finality/causation ... and how the Marxist concept of the "social relations of production" therefore implicitly contains a logic of scientific enquiry.'[115] The same embarrassed confusion reappears repeatedly in the later work *Marxism and Hegel*.

Colletti seems prepared to allow final causation or teleology a place only in the consideration of individual human actions, that is, in particular cases of individual people acting intentionally. He steers clear of considering what place it might have in collective human action over time, that is, in the historical process. And this despite the fact that it has a primary location in Marx's theory of history. The

[113] Ibid., 27.
[114] *Cap* I, Pelican, 290.
[115] L. Colletti, *From Rousseau to Lenin*, London (1972), 68.

reason for this lies in Colletti's complete confusion over the question of Marx's theory of history as a theory of a scientific character. The source of that confusion lies in his rejection of the conceptions of science and scientific law which he thinks he finds in the leading authors of the Second International, and in his subsequent failure to find a more adequate conception of science and law. The basis of that, in turn, is his failure to appreciate the distinctive character of the system of categories of essentialist philosophy in which an acceptable account of science and law is to be found.

(c) Propelled into political economy

By the time Marx writes the *EPM*, only a matter of months after the composition of the *CHDS*, he is extracting the last there is to be got out of Hegel, and is well advanced in laying down the basic groundwork from which the rest of his life's work was a development. The two main themes of this groundwork are: first, that human social labour is the essence of all socio-historical forms, economic, political, etc.; that these forms cohere as social organisms that have a nature which develops with necessity along a certain line unless it is obstructed dramatically, and that the development of that fundamental essence *is* the historical process, and its *telos* is communism (or the society of freely associated producers, as he preferred to call it later in his life). Secondly, communism is at the same time the *telos* of the development of human beings as a natural kind, for their specific nature is social and can therefore only be realised in the development of society within the movement of history. The two processes are, therefore, identical.

(1) Marx is already clear that human social production under capital (or under 'private property' as he then sometimes put it) is a social organism with laws of motion whose operation is a necessary expression of the nature of the beast. For example, he describes accumulation and capital concentration as inevitable expressions 'if capitals are allowed to follow their own natural course', and the same goes for competition.[116] His objections to the method of political economy in dealing with such categories are already the same in nature as those that appear in *TSV*: that it is 'analytical', and does not deal in the categories of essence and necessity, but in the category of accident. He explains that political economy explains competition 'in terms of *external* circumstances. Political economy

[116] *EPM*, 300.

teaches us nothing about the extent to which the external and *apparently accidental* circumstances are only an expression of a *necessary development*. We have seen how exchange itself appears to political economy as an *accidental* fact.'[117] Similarly, while the analytical method is sufficient to the task of identifying laws, 'it does not comprehend these laws, i.e. it does not show how they arise from *the nature* of private property'.[118] For Marx, laws express natures, and development of natures is not accidental but necessary.

It must be understood that by 'the nature of private property' here, the nature or essence Marx is referring to is the capital/wage-labour relation: that is, the specific historical form in which labour is socially supplied. Thus, he is saying that the laws arise from, and express, the essence or central social relation of the social organism. This is quite obvious on a careful reading of the *EPM*. He writes that 'the relation of the worker to labour creates the relation of the capitalist to that labour ... Private property is therefore the product, result and necessary consequence of alienated labour',[119] which here means wage-labour. He complains that political economy cannot conceive of labour in any form other than that taken by it in the bourgeois social organism: 'In political economy labour appears only in the form of wage-earning activity.'[120] It is made clear all over the place that 'the nature of private property' (from which the laws arise) is to be identified with that specific historical form of supply of human social labour, but it is particularly clear when Marx writes: 'To say that the division of labour and exchange are based on private property is simply to say that labour is the essence of private property.'[121] In the few months since the insight in the *CHDS* that the *dêmos* is the essence of all historical social forms, that insight has been much developed and applied.

The basic philosophical categories of analytical atomism, and their application in political economy which shows itself in the way that the categories of political economy are orthodoxly handled, make it impossible for political economy 'to grasp the interconnections within the movement' of history.[122] For example, it is led to set up oppositions where there are none, and where instead there is a connection to be detected which is potentially explanatory. In such a

---

[117] Ibid., 323 (italics added).
[118] Ibid., 322.
[119] Ibid., 331.
[120] Ibid., 298.
[121] Ibid., 374.
[122] Ibid., 323.

way, for example, it is led to see no more relation between monopoly and competition than an exclusive opposition, for in political economy 'competition, craft freedom and division of landed property were developed and conceived only as *accidental* ... consequences of monopoly, of the guilds and of feudal property and not as their *necessary*, inevitable and *natural* consequences'.[123] One is reminded of Sir David Ross's amazement that Aristotle should have seen monetary exchange as a development of non-monetary exchange, rather than, as he thought more reasonable, in opposition to it and driving 'barter' out of the field.

(2) The basis from which Marx is beginning his appropriation of political economy is his theory of history and its essence, human social labour and its forms. The essence of bourgeois society is the form in which human labour is socially supplied, namely wage-labour. 'The relation of the worker to labour creates the relation of the capitalist to that labour'; and 'capital is the power to command labour'.[124] (Or as Marx later crucially refined it in *Capital* by bringing in the category of surplus, or unpaid labour: 'Capital, therefore, is not only, as Adam Smith says, the command over labour. It is essentially the command over unpaid labour.')[125]

Marx is explicit that this form of supply of social labour is a necessary teleological phase in the development of social labour *per se*, in the overall movement of humanity towards the *telos* of a form of society (or form of supply of labour) made by man for himself, and which fully realises the potentials of humanity's social nature: 'It is precisely in the fact that the division of labour and exchange are configurations of private property that we find the proof, both that *human* life needed *private property* for its realisation and that it now needs the abolition of private property.'[126]

The labour theory of value is beginning to emerge out of the theory of history also. Marx locates Quesnay and the physiocrats half-way between mercantilism (wealth = precious metals) and Smith (wealth = capital). The strengths and weaknesses of the physiocrats, as Marx describes them here, tell something about the formation of his specific version of the labour theory of value and how he will differentiate it from the classical version. In the physiocrats 'the subjective essence of wealth is already transferred to labour. But at the same time agriculture is the only productive labour'.

---

[123] Ibid., 323 (italics added).
[124] Ibid., 331; 295.
[125] *Cap.*I (Moscow) 500 (italics added).
[126] *EPM*, 374.

Correspondingly, the physiocrats regard land as part of nature rather than as capital. The import for classical political economy is clear. The specific form of labour supply in bourgeois production is wage-labour, and the reverse side of this form of supply of labour is that wealth takes the form of capital. In other words, we are already within measurable distance of the criticism Marx later makes of Ricardo's view of value in *Capital* and *TSV*, viz. that he fails to notice that only *in a particular form of its supply* does labour constitute the substance of value. The basis for such a criticism is laid even though the category of value is not yet a fully developed part of Marx's armoury of abstractions. The reason is that he is thinking, in Hegelian terms, of historical stages in the process of realisation of an essence, but cast in his own terms where the stages are different forms of supply of human social labour.

Once one has understood Marx's theory of history, even here in the *EPM* just after its first beginnings, it is clear that the labour theory of value must follow as a conclusion. Once the essential truth has been perceived that 'there are only people', and that in the social realm 'each form is only a moment of the *dêmos* as a whole', then any specific *form of wealth* has labour as its essence and results from the command over labour. Value is one such form, and therefore has labour as its essence. Marx even says as much at the end of the second *MSS*: 'Capital = stored up labour = labour'; and a little later: 'the essence of wealth is ... *labour in general*'.[127]

Neo-Ricardians such as Steedman[128] do not have a theory of history. For that reason the labour theory of value is a closed book to them. There are differences within the neo-Ricardian school, of course. Steedman is a British innocent as regards history. Marco Lippi, on the other hand, is less innocent, and he sees that if the what-is-left-of-Marx-now-that-there-has-been-Sraffa line is to be successfully followed out, there is need to cut Marx's theory of history out of the picture altogether. That is indeed the aim of his incoherent book *Value and Naturalism in Marx*.[129]

(3) The question of Marx's expression cannot be given the attention it properly deserves: namely, none at all. It has to be looked into because of the repercussions that Althusser's work has had. His

[127] *EPM, KMEW*, 341 and 344 respectively.
[128] I. Steedman, *Marx after Sraffa*, London (1977).
[129] M. Lippi, *Value and Naturalism in Marx*, trs. Hilary Steedman, London 1979. One of the outstanding sources of incoherence in the book is that in arguing his principal thesis that Marx's theory of history is to be discarded because it is 'naturalistic', Lippi fails to give any account (much less any adequate account) of what 'naturalism' is supposed to be or of what he supposes to be wrong with it.

political onslaught on Marx's 'early work' has had consequences that should have been avoided. Althusser suggested that before the *GI* Marx used a concept of practice that was an ' "ideological" and universal concept of Feuerbachian practice'.[130] There is, however, no ground whatever to see anywhere in Marx's *juvenilia* (or whatever term of opprobrium one prefers) any notion of the ahistorical 'essentialist anthropology' attributed to him by various authors, among them Norman Geras.[131]

Mandel makes a comparable error of judgment in suggesting that 'the Marx of 1844 still retains, in part, such a metaphysical conception of labour', viz., an anthropological and unhistorical conception of labour simply as something necessary for survival.[132] The error of judgment involved here is to see an opposition between labour as a concrete universal, and labour as subject to historical modifications in its form of supply. There is no such opposition; Marx's essentialist philosophical method requires that there be both, and its application which is the heart of his conception of history requires that there be both. If 'labour in general' figures in Marx's early work, so too does its historically specific form of 'wage-labour', and the latter is presented as a particular historical form of the former universal. Likewise if the historically particular 'wage-labour' appears in the developed and 'mature' *Capital*, so also does the universal. It appears, for instance, in chapter 7 section 1 on 'The Labour Process', where Marx deals with 'the labour process independently of any specific social formation'. This will be dealt with in greater detail below in Chapter 5 (ii).

Mandel's evaluation of the *EPM* is poorly judged, and its weakness appears in the title of the chapter in which he deals with the question: 'From the *EPM* to the *Grundrisse*: From an Anthropological to a Historical Conception of Alienation.' With diplomatic skill and his familiar sponsorship of things transitional, he considers that 'the *EPM* constitute a transition from the first to the second, with the anthropological conception surviving here and there'.[133] But there is no such survival, and consequently no such transition.

Part of Mandel's view that the *EPM* are transitional is the they 'represent   at   most   the   motivation   of   *Capital*,   not   its "framework" '.[134] This is a more subtle question that requires more

[130] L. Althusser, *For Marx*, London (1969), 229.

[131] N. Geras, 'Marx and the critique of political economy', in *Ideology in Social Science*, ed. R. Blackburn, Fontana (1972), 289.

[132] E. Mandel, *The Formation of the Economic Thought of Karl Marx*, New York and London (1971), 169.

[133] Ibid., 163.

[134] Ibid., 167.

refined argument than there is space for here. But one of the substantial issues involved in it cannot be avoided, and that is the use Marx makes in the *EPM* of '*Gattungswesen*' or 'species essence'. Mandel takes the view that Marx's treatment of alienation in the *EPM* stops short of developing into Marx's theory of history ('historical materialism'), and diverges into a discussion in which 'alienated labour is contrasted to the qualities of generic man, as a "species being" ... and alienation can be understood at first sight, if not as *externalisation* in the Hegelian sense then at least as the negation of an "ideal human being" such as never existed.'[135] Mandel adds that Marx was later resolutely to abandon 'the concept of generic man, the "species being" '. This is actually a misreading of the relevant passage in the *GI*, but more importantly it betrays misunderstanding of Marx's theory of history and his conception of the role of man in the historical process.

(4) To see this we must turn to the second of the themes mentioned at the beginning of this section: the identity between the twin teleologies of the historical process of the coming-to-be of human society itself and of the realisation of man's nature in it.

(i) Marx's overall view of the historical process is that it is the process of development, or *genesis*, of human society through particular forms towards its fullest and highest form, in which its inherent potentials are fully realised. That is to say, the historical process is a teleological process whose subject is human society, and the *telos* to which the process tends is communism. 'The entire movement of history is therefore the actual act of creation of this communism – the birth of its empirical existence – and, for its thinking consciousness, the *comprehended* and *known* movement of its *becoming*.'[136] History is the process of coming-to-be of human society. Its essence is human labour, and its different 'principles' are the social forms in which that labour is historically supplied. History, in Marx's view, does have an end or *telos* towards which it tends, however horribly that may jar on latter-day atomist sensibilities. Though, of course, as one must always add in order to give least offence to delicate intellectual sensibilities, it is an end that is *frustratable* anywhere along the line. It can be frustrated, for example, by the working class failing to act, or acting with insufficient resolution. It can also be frustrated by the delicate defenders of civilisation, provided they can master their sensibilities for the greater good and find mercenaries from classes other than their

[135] Ibid., 161.
[136] *KMEW*, 348.

minority class to make heads roll.

(ii) Marx also has a view of man as a natural kind; a species of the mammalian order, whose essence is differentiated from others of that and other orders by the essential properties of being conscious and social.[137] If communism is the fullest historical realisation of the potential of human society, it is at the same time for man 'the first real emergence, the realisation ... of his essence as something real'.[138]

Thus, the realised human society is a society of realised humans. The full realisation of the potentiality inherent in human society as an essence, is at the same time the society in which the potentiality of the social essence of the human natural species is fully realised. A fully realised human essence, and the fully realised essence of human society, are products of one and the same process. Indeed they are one and the same thing, and Marx warns that it is 'necessary to avoid once more establishing "society" as an abstraction over against the individual. The individual *is* the *social being*.'[139]

Man, and the form in which he supplies his social labour, are not only the *starting point* of history, they are also, in their finished and fully realised form, the *product* of the process of historical development. Man makes history, but history equally realises man's essence and thus makes him: 'both the material of labour and man as subject are the starting point as well as the outcome of the movement ... So the social character is the general character of the whole movement; just as society itself produces *man* as *man*, so it is produced by him.'[140] Marx acknowledges Hegel's contribution in conceiving 'the self-creation of man as a process'; a process of history in which man is 'the result of his own labour' and in which man achieves through the historical process the 'realisation of himself as a real species being'.[141] Hegel had indeed written that 'the criterion

---

[137] His view is remarkably Aristotelian. Aristotle thought that the *differentia specifica* of the human 'soul' was consciousness or reason or capacity for deliberative desire, *proairesis*. He also thought the human animal to be the *zôon politikon*, that is, the creature whose full potential could be realised only within the *polis*. Marx's Aristotelianism is unsurprising. It is well-known that he made an extensive study of Aristotle in preparing his *Doctoral Dissertation*, and his footnotes show just how extensive it was. In the present connection, however, it is most telling that Marx made the first German translation with commentary of *De Anima*, the work in which Aristotle has most to say about the specific essence of the human kind. The translation, in Marx's handwriting, is in Amsterdam. It appears that he had intended publishing it. I am indebted to Heinz Lubasz for this information. This work of Marx has been included in the new *MEGA*.

[138] *KMEW*, 395.
[139] Ibid., 350.
[140] Ibid., 349.
[141] Ibid., 385-6.

of Spirit is its action, its active essence. Man is his own action, the sequence of his actions, that into which he has been making himself.'[142]

Thus when Marx speaks of 'species being' (*Gattungswesen*), he is speaking of the real essence or nature of the mammalian species to which we belong, and not, as Mandel thinks, of 'an "ideal human being" such as never existed'. Marx sees this essence as containing potentialities that are realisable only historically, *pari passu* with the development of human society, for the specifically human is the social. Man's process of 'realisation of himself as a real species being ... is only possible through the co-operation of mankind and as a result of history'.[143] Thus Marx ties the process of history indissolubly to man's real essence as a mammalian species. *Gattungswesen* is not a youthful, romantic aberration, but a vital element in the foundation of his theory of history. The human nature of society, and the social nature of man, cannot be tugged apart. The 'mature' Marx repeats his youthful self when he observes in the *Grundrisse* that 'the human being is in the most literal sense a *zôon politikon*, not merely a gregarious animal, but an animal which can individuate itself only in the midst of society'.[144] The essence of this mammalian species is realised only in the degree to which the essence of society has been realised. The identity of the two processes is crucial to Marx's view, and is got badly wrong by scholars who seek to divorce them as many have.[145] The identity is implicit in the sixth of the *Theses on Feuerbach* where Marx says of 'the essence of man' that 'it is the ensemble of social relationships'.

It is true that Marx speaks of the alienation of wage-labour as consisting partly in its separation of co-operative species life from individual life, and in perversely making the former a mere means to the latter rather than an end in itself. But this is not to be understood as a judgment against wage-labour from the standpoint of 'an "ideal human being" such as never existed'. The essence of the human species is not understood by Marx only in terms of what has existed, but also in terms of what its realisable potential is; and this, as we shall see in Chapter 7 below, is an application of the general analysis of identity or essence as dynamic, and unspecifiable without invoking change and potential. So when Marx writes, for example, that the essence of the estrangement of wage-labour lies in 'the fact that the human essence *objectifies* itself in an *inhuman* way, in opposition to itself', the point being made is that the progressive character of the

[142] *Reason in History*, 51.
[143] *KMEW*, 386.
[144] *Gr.*, 84.
[145] E.g. Mandelbaum, *HMR*, 186.

social organism based on the supply of human labour in the form of wage-labour is contradictory. It advances towards the joint realisation of the potentials of human society and human nature, but in a form that glaringly reveals that those potentialities have not yet been realised. In seeing what those potentials are and that communism will realise them, we are able to judge what now exists as *inhuman*.

3

The Coming-to-be of Capital

(i) The 'analytical method' of classical political economy

It is commonly recognised that in *Capital* Marx went beyond the achievements of classical political economy. How he did it, however, and what was involved in doing it successfully, have been appreciated only partially. The bit that has been overlooked is the bit that forms the basis of his dialectics. We must look first at that partial understanding, and then at what is required for its completion. The *historical* aspect of Marx's 'historical-genetic' treatment of the categories of political economy has been appreciated, but the theoretical import of the *genetic* treatment as involving the essentialist categories of essence, form, law and necessity has not.

Marx does not stress it much himself because he wrote within an ambience, and for an audience, which in large part took naturally and for granted the use of essentialist and dialectical categories. It is generally the case that authors do not go out of their way to expand upon what is going to be taken for granted by their contemporary audience. It is also generally the case that what is going to be taken for granted includes the most fundamental things of all, namely, the general way of going about things and the categories to be used. But these matters change, and since Marx's time the intellectual idiom has changed dramatically towards atomism, as we noted in Chapter 1 (iv). Taking these considerations together they amount to this: that readers of Marx in the present period face great obstacles to understanding which were not faced by most of Marx's contemporaries; the misunderstandings that those obstacles are likely to occasion do not concern merely bits and pieces here and there, but the most fundamental ground rules of intellectual operations.

Marx recognised that classical political economy, in contrast to vulgar economy, had provided the analysis which was the necessary basis for critical understanding to begin. He called it 'the necessary prerequisite of genetical presentation',[1] that is, of a dialectical presentation of the finished critical science (*Kritik der Wissenschaft*). What it lacked was an understanding of, and ability to explain, the categories it had abstracted from its study of the system of market economy. This is what Marx supplied with his 'genetical presentation ... of the understanding of the real, formative process in its different phases'.[2] Classical political economy proceeded to analyse 'the forms of human life' along 'a course directly opposite to their real development'. It does this because it begins *post festum*, having the results of historical development already to hand, and proceeds uncritically taking 'the forms which stamp products as commodities' for granted as natural and 'seeks to give an account, not of their historical character ... but of their content and meaning'.[3] Where classical political economy attempts explanation of its categories, the result is inadequate or silly. For example, Smith's account of exchange as a natural propensity to truck and barter, which is greatly inferior even to Aristotle's account.[4] Or again, the 'insipid childishness', as Marx put it, of the accounts offered of the so-called 'primitive accumulation' which explain it in terms of the parable of 'the two sorts of people; one, the diligent, intelligent, and above all, frugal elite; the other, lazy rascals, spending their substance, and more, in riotous living.'[5]

In the better accounts given of Marx's method in recent years, these familiar passages from Marx are understood in a particular way. Marx's advance over classical political economy is seen as consisting in his being historical where classical political economy had been ahistorical. Such a view is to be found in Paul Sweezy's *The Theory of Capitalist Development* and in Rosdolsky's *The Making of Marx's 'Capital'*. Sweezy writes: 'Marx's method, says Lukács, "is in its innermost essence historical". This is certainly correct.'[6] Moreover, Sweezy regards the *critical* element in Marx as arising immediately out of the *historical* approach Marx has to the categories of political economy. He says that 'a consistently historical approach to social science ... leads to a critical approach'.[7] Sweezy is expressing what is

---

[1] *TSV* III, 500.
[2] Loc. cit.
[3] *Cap.* I, Pelican, 168.
[4] *Politics* 1.8-10. A. Smith, *Wealth of Nations*, Pelican (1970), 117.
[5] *Cap.* I, Pelican, 873.
[6] P. Sweezy, op. cit., New York and London (1968), 20.
[7] Ibid., 21.

still a common view of what is fundamentally distinctive about Marx's method, and of wherein its real strengths lie. The view is not altogether wrong; it is incomplete.

What is missing from it is a satisfactory appreciation of Marx's criticism of what he calls the 'analytical method' of classical political economy. Here Marx's criticism goes beyond saying that the shortcomings of classical political economy were that it was ahistorical and uncritical, and that for that reason it could only regard the categories of market economy as natural. In considering its 'analytical method' Marx is reaching deeper; he is uncovering the reason why classical political economy had those shortcomings. They were, he says, 'a necessary consequence of its *analytical* method'.[8]

We can best get at what Marx had in mind by the 'analytical method' if we look at two crucial categories about which Marx thought that that method had led Ricardo astray: money and crisis. We will then be in a position to see what is wrong with it, why it fails to produce understanding and, more important, what is needed instead of it if proper understanding is to be attained.

Concerning money, Marx writes that Ricardo, in occasional passages, 'directly emphasises that the quantity of labour embodied in a commodity constitutes the immanent measure of the *magnitude* of its value ... only because labour is the factor the different commodities have in *common*, which constitutes their uniformity, their substance, the intrinsic foundation of their value.' But having got so far, Ricardo could get no further:

> What Ricardo does not investigate is the *specific* form in which labour manifests itself as the common element of commodities. That is why he does not understand money. That is why in his work the transformation of commodities into money appears to be something merely formal, which does not penetrate deeply into the very essence of capitalist production.[9]
>
> ... for him the decisive task is the definition of the magnitude of value. Because of this he does not understand the specific form in which labour is an element of value, and fails in particular to grasp that the labour of the individual must present itself as abstract general labour and, in this form, as *social* labour. Therefore he has not understood that the development of money is connected with the nature of value and with the determination of this value by labour time.[10]

[8] *TSV* III, 500.
[9] Ibid., 139.
[10] Ibid., 137.

(The question of how and why, under capitalism, the labour of individuals has to be mediated by a form in order to become part of social labour is discussed in Chapter 6 (iii) below.)

Elsewhere Marx puts it another way: 'Following Say, Ricardo writes: "Productions are always bought by productions, or by services; money is only the medium by which the exchange is effected".' Marx comments here that Ricardo strips away all that is specific to the capitalist form of production, or surplus extraction, by talking not of 'commodities' but of 'productions'; not of 'wage-labour' but of 'services'. And he adds: 'It is quite consistent that *money* is then regarded merely as an intermediary in the exchange of products, and not as an essential and necessary form of the existence of the commodity which must manifest itself as exchange-value, as general social labour.'[11]

Marx's criticisms go very deep. Though it is true that Ricardo is being quite unhistorical, that in itself is not enough to explain what is really wrong with what he does. Certainly, Ricardo does not understand that only in a specific social form of its supply does labour produce value. But this is not just a historical point about there being, or having been, different forms of supply of surplus-extractable labour; it is also a point about the nature of labour and its product when surplus labour is extracted in the form of surplus value, i.e. that they have the value-form, that they are exchange-values. Ricardo never realises that there is such a thing as the value-form, and for that reason he fails to understand what money is, namely, a development of the value-form. This is not just a historical point either. A history of money would not of itself reveal what money is. It would not reveal money as an aspect of the process of *genesis* of a real nature or essence, the value-form, viz. an independent expression of value. Money is a riddle, says Marx, and the key to the riddle lies in coming to understand 'the simple commodity-form' which is 'the germ of the money form'.[12] The germ itself contains a riddle, the key to which is coming to understand the relative and equivalent forms of value. What we are dealing with here is a real essence which undergoes (provided it is not frustrated by accident) a process of *genesis* through various forms from 'The Elementary or Accidental Form of Value' through to capital, the circuits of industrial capital, etc. That line of development, presented as such in the opening sections of *Capital* I, is in the nature of the beast, the value-form, and is a line of necessary change.

[11] *TSV* II, 501.
[12] *Cap.* I, Pelican, 163.

Without the value-form, it is quite impossible for Ricardo to realise what Marx explains 'must never be forgotten, that in capitalist production what matters is not the immediate use-value but the exchange-value and, in particular, the expansion of surplus value. This is the driving motive of capitalist production, and it is a pretty conception that ... abstracts from its very basis and depicts it as a production aiming at the direct satisfaction of the consumption of the producers.'[13] The ultimate source of Ricardo's shortcomings lies in his lacking the philosophical equipment needed to get to the bottom of things and to discern the value-form, and in his having to make do instead with 'analytical method' which was too superficial to cope.

A merely historical account of how money, division of labour, etc., arose would not reveal the essence of the market system. Neither would it directly give the critical element in Marx, for it does so only mediately through the categories of essence and form, and the accompanying categories of necessity and law. That 'rational dialectic' which Marx describes as 'in its essence critical and revolutionary' is a 'scandal and abomination to bourgeoisdom'.[14] The abomination has its source in fear. Fear not of what accidentally might occur, but of what is necessarily ahead unless accident obstructs or adequate obstructive action is taken.

The difference between a dialectical essentialist account and a historical one is that a merely historical account of how the categories of market economy came into being leaves us with only the negative point that they are not natural and inescapable. We can infer from this that they may be escaped. But nothing need follow about how they might be escaped, or about the necessary form of their supersession. The genetical, or essentialist, account reveals precisely that. It opens up the perspective that the value-form, as an essence, not only has a *genesis* or coming-to-be, but a typical life process also, and a process of decay and passing-away; that the form of society which fully realises the value-form must, of its nature, develop into another form of society. As McBride notes: 'Marx's "critiquing" of political economy, then, had the ... purpose of showing ... that the actual system contained tendencies that were at once potentially destructive of the existing system itself and potentially generative of a new, non-primitive system.'[15] Marx himself agreed that the scientific value of his enquiry 'lies in

[13] *TSV* II, 495.
[14] *Cap.* I, Moscow, 29.
[15] L.W. McBride, *The Philosophy of Marx*, London (1977), 16.

disclosing the special laws that regulate the origin, existence, development, death of a given social organism and its replacement by another and higher one'.[16] That is not a description of a history.

Concerning crisis, again Marx puts down Ricardo's failure to handle the phenomenon adequately to his failure to comprehend the value-form. Classical political economy had sought to devise a representation of the system as a whole which was free from inconsistency and contradiction. Of course, that is usually a perfectly proper thing to do. Nobody wants to waste time on a theory that is self-contradictory. In this case, however, it is not a proper thing to do, because the contradictions in question are real constituent elements inherent in the nature of the reality being theorised. That being the case, they are not to be dealt with as one deals with formal logical contradictions between propositions p, and not-p, that is, by removing one or the other. (The question of contradictions existing in reality is discussed in Chapter 5 (iii) below.)

Marx was able to accept the existence of these contradictions, and was able to explain how such things were possible and how they worked, because he based his understanding on the category of a whole entity in movement. Allen Wood puts it well:

> An organic whole is essentially made up of different ... reciprocally negating processes, which constitute the thing ... the conflicting elements are not incompatible in the sense that they cannot co-exist for a time in the thing. But they are incompatible in the sense that the opposition between them undermines the stability of the structure, and eventually destroys it, along with the contradictions which constitute it. The ... opposite elements in an organic whole are reciprocally dependent and cannot exist without one another.'[17]

'The world trade crisis,' Marx writes, 'must be regarded as the real concentration and forcible adjustment of all the contradictions of bourgeois economy.'[18] He explains that there are many aspects of

[16] *Cap.* I, Moscow, 28.

[17] Allen Wood, *Karl Marx*, London (1981), 202.

[18] *TSV* II, 510. Mandel treats crisis as functional to the system, in his *Marxist Economic Theory*, London (1968), 349. But crises do not occur *in order that* the self-expansion of value can start up again. They are, as Marx treats them, *crises of the society*, not cycles in an economic mechanism. There is no historical guarantee that the bourgeoisie will survive a given crisis. Just because the bourgeoisie has so far managed to survive a few should not be read back into history as a false theory of the nature of crisis. This is not an uncommon sort of weakness. Marx clearly considered that working-class upheaval was on the cards from 1848 onwards, and this is something for which McBride seeks to excuse Marx, op. cit., 14.

crisis, and these can be investigated in each sphere of the economy. Beneath these phenomena however, there are certain general forms of crisis inherent in the nature of the system which are realised in actual crises. For example, the very process of accumulation itself, the turning of money into new capital, constantly encounters obstacles: '*production on an expanding scale* ... forms an inherent basis for the phenomena that appear during crises', for it gives rise to disproportions between sectors of the economy which have to be evened out:

> All equalisations are *accidental* and although the proportion of capital employed in different spheres is equalised by a continuous process, the continuity of this process itself presupposed the constant disproportion which it has continuously, often violently, to even out.[19]

Or again, there are 'contradictions inherent in the circulation of commodities, which are further developed in the circulation of money'.[20]

> The first metamorphosis of one capital (M-C) must correspond to the second metamorphosis of the other (C-M); one capital leaves the production process as the other capital returns into the production process. This interweaving and coalescence of the processes of reproduction and circulation of different capitals is on the one hand necessitated by the division of labour, on the other hand it is accidental.[21]

These processes can get fouled up; indeed, 'the circulation process as a whole or the reproduction process a whole', 'the unity of its production phase and its circulation phase' can get fouled up.

These, and other, general forms of crisis uncovered by Marx, all derive commonly from the fully developed value-form itself. They arise from the fact that the product of labour, and the form of supply of social labour itself, are *exchange-values*, and crisis 'results from the impossibility to sell'.[22] 'Crisis is the forcible establishment of unity between elements that have become independent and the enforced separation of elements that are essentially one'.[23]

Of course, the abstract forms of crisis inherent as possibilities in

---

[19] *TSV* II, 492.
[20] Ibid., 512.
[21] Ibid., 510.
[22] Ibid., 509.
[23] Ibid., 513.

the fully developed value-form (capital), do not explain why crises occur.

> The *general possibility* of crisis is the formal *metamorphosis* of capital itself, the separation, in time and space of purchase and sale. But this is never the cause of the crisis ... If one asks what the cause is, one wants to know why *its abstract form*, the form of its possibility, turns from possibility into actuality.[24]

The causes and occasions can be many and various: e.g. a rise in raw materials. That does not concern us here.

What concerns us is that the (actualisable) potential for crisis is inherent in the nature of the fully developed value-form and its contradictions. The value-form is fully developed, as we shall see later in Section v of this chapter, when it is universalised over the whole of society, and the very supply of human social labour itself takes on the value-form as a saleable commodity. There is then a social organism in which surplus labour is pumped out of one class by another, not through forms of unfree labour (debt-bondage, chattel-slavery or serfdom), but through the relation of capital and wage-labour. That gives a division between investment and consumption, and therewith the major elements of crisis. (a) Investment can outstrip consumption and lead to underconsumption; (b) increased investment, with constant production in Department II (or with a growth slower than in Department I), leads to disproportions between Departments I and II; (c) increasing investment in fixed capital, giving a rising organic composition of capital, leads to a declining rate of profit. The point is that all of these have their basis in the fact that labour is socially supplied in the form of wage-labour, i.e. in the value-form.

Ricardo never understood that form, and hence could not understand crisis. He was not looking for 'the nature of value'. Classical political economy was not looking for a unity between the categories on the basis of an essence which underwent changes of form in attaining its higher realisations in the categories abstracted to (in part correctly) by classical political economy, which essence, when fully developed, was multiply contradictory. It was, on the contrary, seeking to demonstrate an abstract unity, and a mutual consistency between the categories *as concepts*, 'by means of analysis' which, by 'reductions', stripped away their historically specific forms. Marx described the enterprise thus:

[24] Ibid., 515.

Classical political economy seeks to reduce the fixed and mutually alien forms of wealth to their inner unity by means of analysis and to strip away the form in which they exist independently alongside one another ... it is not interested in elaborating how the various forms came into being, but seeks to reduce them to their unity by means of analysis, because it starts with them as given premises.[25]

Marx's point clearly is that classical political economy with its 'analytical method' could not recognise the contradictions as real, and so was not seeking to explain that the incompatibilities were made compatible in reality through their interweaving, changes of form, and sometimes by forcible and violent readjustments, within the continuing movement. Movement allows incompatibles to survive together, at least for a while. If movement of the organic social whole is omitted, then the incompatibilities if considered statically can be reconciled only by constructing an artificial consistency by thought operations performed on the categories considered as mere concepts, rather than as real aspects of the nature of the whole system and of its movement. A complex whole can contain contradictions *through movement*. If one thinks statically and only in terms of appearances, then these contradictions can appear only as things to be ironed out; removed by analytical procedures at the level of concepts. The dialectical essentialist method, where the identity or nature of the entity cannot be determined independently of its typical forms of movement, can admit the contradictions that exist within the complex whole. It can do so because it incorporates, rather than banishes, the *time* dimension of *movement*. It does not need to remove them because it is not embarrassed by them.

Ricardo is embarrassed by them and can respond only by 'reasoning them away'. Marx observed that 'the expansion of surplus value ... is the driving motive of capitalist production, and it is a pretty conception that – in order to reason away the contradictions of capitalist production – abstracts from its very basis'[26] or essence. 'Crises are thus reasoned out of existence' because there is no understanding of the essence, the value-form and wage-labour.[27]

From the consideration of these two examples alone, money and crisis, it is clear that the *basis* of Marx's critique of classical political economy is not simply that it is unhistorical. This is also plain in his discussion throughout the whole of *Capital* I, Part I, 'Commodities

[25] *TSV* III, 500.
[26] *TSV* II, 495.
[27] Ibid., 502.

and Money'. It is obvious that Marx's starting point and conclusion is that there is an item, the value-form, which is a real essence that is realised over time, moving from an 'embryonic form', through 'inadequate' and 'unfinished' forms, into a 'final' or 'finished form'. His discussions in *TSV* drive that fact home forcibly.

So the target of Marx's criticism of classical political economy is not simply its unhistoricalness, though that has now become the familiar target aimed at in Marxist criticism of bourgeois thinkers today, and is often wrongly believed to have been Marx's primary target. His real target is deeper and more precise. He is saying that unhistoricalness is a bad thing *because* it leads to errors that prevent thought from succeeding in its objective of understanding; that it does so because it inhibits identification of what that object should be, namely, the unearthing of a real essence which is the subject of essential transformations. The historical process itself is then comprehended, not merely as a process of undifferentiated change, but as a process of development of an essence through its essential transformations. Going about things historically is a necessary condition of success, but not a sufficient one. A historical method must be coupled with a search for the relevant real essence and its forms, which is what gives the historical enquiry its point. (The criticism of Colletti in Chapter 2 (iv b) above consisted in showing that he fails to see Marx's essentialism or 'genetical' viewpoint. It is for that reason that he fails also to explain just why history was so important to Marx.)

(ii) The starting point for the political economy of the capitalist system

Why did Marx begin his analysis of the capitalist mode of production with the commodity? The answer certainly cannot be that it was the *obvious* starting point, though it might seem to be so now. In the first sentences of the book, Marx himself suggests that it is the obvious starting point: 'the wealth of societies in which the capitalist mode of production prevails appears as an "immense collection of commodities"; the individual commodity appears as its elementary form ... Our investigation therefore begins with the analysis of the commodity.' This clearly cannot be the real reason.

Marx distinguishes two senses of 'the concrete': that experienced but untheorised reality with which we are confronted and which it is the task of theory to make comprehensible; and that same reality now made comprehensible, and thus more amenable to our control, but still there before us as concrete and experienced. The distinction is drawn in the *Grundrisse*:

> The concrete is the concrete because it is the concentration of many determinations, hence unity in the diverse. It appears in the process of thinking, therefore, as a process of concentration, as a result, not as a point of departure, even though it is the point of departure in reality and hence also the point of departure for observation and conception.[28]

Marx begins with the commodity, but not because it is the obvious concrete reality, 'the point of departure for observation and conception'. On the contrary, *his beginning with it presupposes the result of his entire analysis*. His beginning with it is the result of his essentialist dialectical categories; Marx observed that a science must be developed to a certain point before its dialectical presentation can be possible,[29] and recognised that the results of classical political economy provide the basis for the developed critical science.

It should hardly be a surprise that his choice of starting point was the outcome of the results of his theoretical work. Marx's analysis of the commodity, as it unfolds the phases of transition through which the value-form passes, reveals it to be that 'concrete' which 'appears in the process of thinking ... as a result, not as a point of departure', and not to be that other unanalysed 'concrete' which *is* 'the point of departure for observation and conception'. As he explains in a familiar passage, the method of enquiry 'has to appropriate the material in detail, to analyse its different forms of development and to track down their inner connection. Only after this work has been done can the real movement be appropriately presented.'[30] The commodity-form is made the point of departure in 'the method of presentation', because the enquiry had revealed it to be, as Marx repeatedly describes it, the 'embryonic form' of the essence whose necessary changes and realisations of potentials culminate in the attainment of the final, finished form of that essence: capital.

Why did Marx not begin with money? Because, as he says, 'the only difficulty in the concept of the money form is that of grasping the universal equivalent form, and thence the general form of value as such'. But this difficulty can be overcome, he continues, 'by working backwards to ... the expanded form of value, and its constitutive element is ... x commodity A $=$ y commodity B. The simple

---

[28] *Gr.*, 101.
[29] Marx to Engels, 1 February 1958, *MEW* XXIX, 275.
[30] *Cap.* I, Moscow (1970), 28.

commodity-form is, therefore, the germ of the money form.'[31] Hence, Marx begins with the essence in its most primitive form: the elementary commodity, or 'The Simple, Isolated or Accidental Form of Value'. The reason for the failure of classical political economy to discover the nature of money was precisely its failure to use essentialist dialectical categories, and its use of atomistic analytics instead. For that reason they were unable to discover that the riddle of money is identical to the riddle of the embryonic form of the essence, the elementary commodity-form itself which he drew out in his analysis of the Relative and Equivalent Forms of Value. 'The riddle of the money fetish is therefore the riddle of the commodity fetish, now become visible and dazzling to our eyes.'[32]

Marx found there to be a 'universal' form of the bourgeois mode of production, viz. the value-form; and he found that it has specific forms: 'the commodity form, together with its further developments, the money form, the capital form … the universal equivalent in its finished form.'[33] Thus, the unity Marx finds among the categories developed by classical political economy is not an analytical unity, where, by analytical stripping and reducing, an abstract coherence is imposed upon a set of ideas. The unity is one that Marx *discovers* in the essence or *natures of the things* studied.

This was a discovery Marx made in his enquiry. Consequently, it being the heart of the matter, this is where he starts in the 'method of presentation'. It is at the beginning of his presentation, not at the end, that he defines the problem in essentialist categories as a problem to do with the process of development of an essence:

> Now, however, we have to perform a task never even attempted by bourgeois economics. That is, we have to show the origin of this money-form, we have to trace the development of the expression of value contained in the value-relation of commodities from its simplest, almost imperceptible outline to the dazzling money-form. When this has been done, the mystery of money will immediately disappear.[34]

It must be made quite clear what the connection is between Marx's essentialist conception of science and his choice of starting point; and how and why the use of that conception of science is able to capture the reality, which atomism does not even conceive, of the process-nature of a historical development of enormous proportions.

[31] Ibid., Pelican, 163.
[32] Ibid., 187.
[33] Ibid., 174 n.34.
[34] Ibid., 139.

What Marx found in his analysis of the embryonic form, the simple commodity, was that it had an inherent fetish that was essential to the unity. He extracted this in his analysis of the Relative and Equivalent Forms of Value, where he found that the Equivalent Form was, of its nature, a contradictory unity of use-value and exchange-value. It is this that is the key to the riddle or fetish of the Money Form, for the latter is simply a more developed expression. What his discovery amounts to is that the commodity is essentially in its nature a unity of use-value and exchange-value, a unity of opposites, and that this contradiction is reproduced as an essential property of all the subsequent developments of the Form. (See Chapter 5 (iii) below.)

Use-value can exist alone. But exchange-value cannot; only what has use-value can have exchange-value. What has exchange-value, the commodity, is, thus, exchange-value and use-value brought into a unity. The commodity-form has *as its essence* the unity of the two. That is what it *is*. The commodity-form is a reality. Consequently, use-value and exchange-value, in partaking of the essence of that reality, are not mere abstractions arrived at in thought about reality, but are also constituents of reality. And so is the contradiction between them.

The commodity *is* the unity of use-value and exchange-value, in much the same way that water *is* H_2O, that light *is* a stream of photons, and that gold *is* the element with the atomic number 79. All these statements are *necessarily* true. They state truths that are true of necessity, not in virtue of any 'logical' or 'conceptual' connections, but in virtue of the essences or real natures of the entities in question. Water is necessarily H_2O. Anything that is not H_2O in its essential composition cannot *be* water, however closely it may resemble water in appearance, and the 'cannot' is ontological not epistemic. (See Chapter 7 for a further discussion of necessity, and associated philosophical categories). To be that specific unity of hydrogen and oxygen is the essence of water. We did not always know this, of course; it was a *discovery* people made about the essence of water; Marx's discovery about the essence of the commodity and money was of just the same kind. Real natures of entities do not lie around on the surface ready for our immediate appropriation. They have to be uncovered by investigation, observation and theory. To acquire such knowledge is what it is to know what things are and to understand them; Aristotle: 'There is scientific knowledge of a thing only when we know its essence.'[35]

---

[35] Aristotle, *Met.* 1031b7f.

Marx's success is due to his use of essentialist method and categories. There is a real essence underlying the entire development of market economy, and because of that fact, only the use of the categories of an essentialist philosophy is capable of penetrating and revealing that reality. This is so whether one is considering Marx's success over the riddle of money in tracking down its solution to the essential ·properties of the embryonic commodity form, or whether one is considering Marx's account of the law-governed process of the entire development, from beginning to end, of market economy.

To illustrate the unity of the essence which underlies the entire development, Marx's account of monetary crisis will serve as a single example. The undeveloped form of the contradiction between use-value and exchange-value which he found to be in the nature of the primitive commodity-form, is in essential connection with the later, more developed, contradictions of capitalist commodity production. The attainment of the developed money-form creates enough room for the contradiction immanent in the simple commodity-form to move. Further on in *Capital*, referring back to the contradiction inherent in the simple commodity-form, Marx writes: 'We saw in a former chapter that the exchange of commodities implies contradictory and mutually exclusive conditions. The further development of the commodity does not abolish these contradictions, but rather provides the form within which they have room to move.'[36] And in turn, the further development of the money-form itself begets new latent contradictions that can in the right conditions burst forth into 'absolute contradictions'. Thus, for example, when money develops beyond its function as means of circulation into a means of payment, there is a new 'contradiction immanent in the function of money as a means of payment.'

> This contradiction bursts forth in that aspect of a commercial and industrial crisis which is known as a monetary crisis … money suddenly and immediately changes over from its merely nominal shape, money on account, into hard cash. Profane commodities can no longer replace it, the use-value of commodities becomes valueless, and their value vanishes in the face of their own form of value … In a crisis, the antithesis between commodities and their value-form, money, is raised to the level of an absolute contradiction.[37]

[36] *Cap.* I, Pelican, 198.
[37] Ibid., 235-6.

(iii) The pre-history of capital:
commodities and money

What is striking about Marx's treatment of the pre-history of capital is that he does not give a pre-history. He does not examine all, or any, of the human societies that developed exchange, a form of independent expression of value (whether salt-blocks, conch shells, iron bars, etc.), or coined money. The treatment is entirely abstract, in real or apparent contrast to most of the rest of the book. Why is this? Why does Marx not go straight into the social relations of production, as he did in the earlier *Preface* of 1859? Why does he not discuss the early formation of the social relations of those pre-capitalist societies that were partly based on private exchange, in which the product of labour first acquired the early commodity-form? Why, for example, did he not discuss the palace-based cultures of the early near east where specialisation in production had developed but without private property in the product, and the transition to the fifth-century Athenian situation where such specialisation went along with producers producing privately and on their own account and marketing their product? Had he seen his task as simply to show the historical basis of the categories of political economy, that would have been precisely what he should have done.

Moreover, to have begun in that way, rather than with his problem about the 'common factor' in commodities, would have vitiated many of the now usual criticisms of the labour theory of value about machines producing value, about the reduction of skilled to unskilled labour, and sundry other manifestations of incomprehension.

In the light of what has been said above about Marx's essentialist conception of science, and in particular of social science, it is perfectly clear why we do not have anything of that sort in Part I of *Capital* I, and why we have instead what we do have. What we do have is quite clear from a brief reading and straightforward consideration of the nature of Part I, its development, organisation, content and presentation. Marx is consciously unpacking the necessary changes through which an essence, the value-form, passes in realising the early stages of its potential in its movement towards attaining its full nature and its finished or highest form: 'The Simple, Isolated, or Accidental Form of Value'; the Relative and Equivalent Forms of

Value: The Total or Expanded Form of Value; The General Form of Value; The Money Form.

This presentation of the *genesis* of an essence presupposes the results of prior historical enquiry. To have incorporated the actual history in any systematic way would have hindered the presentation of the process of *genesis* of the essence and its transformation through its early forms. It would have meant introducing 'disturbing accidental occurrences' and that would not have been to the point. It is not a historical account of that kind that Marx has in mind when he describes the methodological development necessary to go beyond classical political economy as a 'genetical presentation' which shows 'the understanding of the real, formative process in its different phases'.[38] What he has in mind is something not so different, but not the same either; a presentation of a real process of development of an essence. The closeness of the two, and the specific difference between them is captured by Engels: the dialectical method 'is indeed nothing other than the historical method, only stripped of the historical form and of disturbing accidental occurrences'.[39] A strictly essentialist presentation concentrates only on *necessary* change and abstracts from the accidental; a history fully incorporates all levels of accident, and, if well done in Marxist terms, does so without obscuring the necessary, but, on the contrary, showing how it and the accidental produce the actual historical result.

The presentation of the *genesis* of the value-form caused Marx a lot of headaches. We know that he tinkered with it repeatedly, especially with section 3 of chapter 1, 'The Value Form or Exchange Value'. He first inserted a version of this, 'The Value Form', in the first (German) edition while it was still at the printers.[40] He subsequently revised it again into the form in which it now appears as section 3 of Chapter 1.

Marx was conscious that, among other things, a finished dialectical presentation of this kind can have an *a priori* appearance:

> Of course the method of presentation must differ in form from that of enquiry. The latter has to appropriate the material in detail, to analyse its different forms of development, to trace out their inner connection. Only after this work is done, can the actual movement be adequately described. If this is done successfully, if the life of the subject-matter is

---

[38] *TSV* III, 500.
[39] Engels' review of the *Contribution*, *MEW*, XIII, 475.
[40] Since published as 'Die Wertform', in Marx-Engels, *Kleine Ökonomische Schriften*, and in English as 'The form of value' in *Value: Studies by Karl Marx*, London (1976).

ideally reflected as in a mirror, then it may appear as if we had before us a mere *a priori* construction.[41]

There is obviously a reason why the 'method of presentation' of a dialectical scientific account of something should result in a product that appears to be an *a priori* construction. (Failure to understand this reason explains bourgeois objections to the 'self-contained' and 'theological' nature of Marx's 'system'.) The reason is that having gone through the 'method of enquiry', by which he means seeking out the 'inner connection' or essence, one then has perforce to represent the movement for what it really *is*, namely, one of the development of an essence, a series of necessary changes or realisations of potential. To present the real nature of the process in this way necessarily abstracts from all the empirical material turned up and worked over in the process of enquiry, which itself resulted precisely in the tracking down, and identification, of the essence or real nature.

The presentation of such an (Aristotelian) process of *genesis* cannot easily avoid the superficial appearance of an *a priori* construction, since, in order to lay out the transformations in the form, it is necessary to abstract from the mass of data which originally revealed it in the enquiry, to strip off the 'disturbing accidental occurrences'. It is this peculiarity that Marx is referring to and explaining. He explains it in far too little detail; he gives detail enough, perhaps, for a German audience of his contemporaries, but certainly far too little for assisting the understanding of those suffering the degree of atomist contagion of the present period.

The very distinction between the 'method of enquiry' and the 'method of presentation' is one that has necessarily to force itself on someone working within the categories of essentialism and dialectics. For an atomist, there is no such distinction and everything is plain sailing. There is no essence to be discovered or abstracted to; there are no lines of development of that nature, no necessity or potentiality to be painstakingly abstracted from the fully gathered and digested empirical data, and there is no characteristic behaviour, reproduction or *ergon* of a nature to be worried about. For the atomistic social scientist, the 'method of enquiry' leads to no understanding of the real nature that underlies the phenomena or appearances, and their movement; the most that can result is the relation of accident to accident, which can be done cleverly or stupidly, but in either case cannot lead to understanding. The least that can result is the absurd explanation of the necessary (not identified as such, of course) in terms of the accidental, as in the 'Weber Thesis' about the Protestant Ethic leading by a series of 'causal' chains to the industrial revolution. There is, accordingly, no comparable 'method of presentation' other than a question of mere style.

(iv) The 'logical' and the 'historical' derivation of categories

Rosdolsky's admirable book *The Making of Marx's Capital* has a very peculiar feature, which his extensive analysis of Marx's treatment of money exemplifies throughout. He expounds Marx's theory in an unalloyed organic-dialectical manner, but shows repeatedly an inability to articulate coherently what he is doing as he does so. He can use the method, but he cannot say what it is. When he tries, he often says no more than that a dialectical treatment is a historical one. When he identifies something or other as illustrating the dialectical nature of Marx's thought, it is invariably something he identifies as 'repeated echoes of Hegel's terminology' such as 'that which repels itself from itself'. He will offer a source of reference in *The Science of Logic*, relying merely on the occurrence of terms, without any explanation of how their specific use is bound up with an entire philosophical system of ontology, metaphysics and epistemology. The need for such explanation is often covered by a reference to Lukács's supposed authority.[42]

One passage concerning the 'derivation of categories' is especially revealing. He is discussing Marx's early attempt in the *Grundrisse* to sort out what eventually appears in *Capital* as the analysis of the Relative and Equivalent forms of value. Rosdolsky criticises the earlier formulation on the ground that it reeks of a Hegelian idealist 'dialectic of concepts', and he points out that Marx was well aware of the smell and gave warning about it as a possible source of misconstruction of his meaning. Marx's warning is:

> It will be necessary later, before this question is dropped, to correct the idealist manner of its presentation, which makes it seem as if it were merely a matter of conceptual determinations and of the dialectic of these concepts.[43]

[42] Instances are given in Chapter 1 n.3 above.
[43] *Gr*, 151; Rosdolsky, *TMMC*, 114.

Rosdolsky summarises the meaning of this self-warning as 'the reader should not imagine that economic categories are anything other than reflections of real relations, or that the logical derivation of these categories could proceed independently of their historical derivation'.[44] This sounds right, but what does it mean? It is similar to the point that Colletti has repeatedly made: that Marx's categories are not just abstractions, but *real* abstractions, and they are historically specific, etc. Rosdolsky frequently speaks in this way without explanation: for example, 'the logical succession of the categories simultaneously reflects real historical development'.[45]

There are two sources of lack of clarity. First, what is the content of the metaphor of 'reflection' as a specification of the relation between economic categories and real relations? Secondly, what is a 'logical' derivation of categories, and what is the contrast with a 'historical' derivation supposed to be, particularly when it is said that the former cannot proceed independently of the latter?

It is quite certain that Marx did not have *separable* 'logical' and 'historical' derivations. Nor even did he have them in a *connected* form. What we find in Marx is what has been discussed in the preceding sections, namely, an essentialist and dialectical development, which is neither historical (though the product of historical enquiry), nor simply logical (whatever that means), but the presentation of the course or real process of development of an essence. This latter category is ontological, and nothing is illuminated or explained by discussion in terms of 'logical' and 'historical'. Rosdolsky's terms do nothing to establish or clarify the basis of the total antagonism between essentialist dialectics and atomism. They are at best nugatory in that respect, and at worst conceal the antagonism by using the eminently misunderstandable word 'logical'. That term has connotations of 'ideal' ('ideal types' and 'models') which associate well with the characteristic empiricist gap between 'truths' and the entities they are supposed to be true of. As Edgeley observes, 'materialism as an epistemological doctrine so often turns out to be a dualism, in which a materialism of the real object is combined with an idealism of theory and thought'.[46] But the ontology of real essence (the categories of dialectics), eliminates the dualism and the idealism. It is not that in adopting an ontology

---

[44] *TMMC*, 114-15.

[45] Ibid., 167.

[46] *IMP* III, 24. Some further interesting observations, relating particularly to Popper's attitude to essentialism, are in Baruch A. Brody, *Identity and Essence*, Princeton (1980), 148-50.

of real essences one *abolishes* a gap by means of a presumption. It is, rather, that one has not gone through the familiar empiricist rigmarole by which the gap is engineered in the first place. Theory then becomes, not a 'logical' construct, *but how things essentially are.*

With the category of real essence, the ontological and the epistemic coalesce. Hegel, in *The History of Philosophy*, cites Aristotle: 'thought thinks itself by participation (*metalêpsis*) in that which is thought, but thought becomes thought by contact and apprehension, so that thought and the object of thought are the same.'[47] But the coalescence of the ontological and epistemic that goes with the category of real essence has to be qualified, because there is a temporal dimension to the coalescence. Our *knowledge* of what a thing *is*, is completable only when we are acquainted with the thing in its fully developed form, or very close to it (its realised nature). Such knowledge is possible only when we are able to *observe* the fully developed item; and such observation is possible only when the fully developed item exists or has come-to-be. Only then are we in a position to abstract from the data and see the essence, its potential and necessary line of development: i.e. to *know* what the thing *is*.

A process of essential development, though it may be intellectually presented logically or illogically, is not itself 'logical'; it is ontological, that is, it has to do with the realm of being, and with the observed forms of existence of the things that there are. The relation between the dialectical categories in which the real development is presented, and the reality of the development they present, is not well expressed as a 'reflection'. The categories do not 'reflect'. The specification of the essence of a mammal does not 'reflect' a mammal; it is (or tells you) what a mammal *is*. The point about Rosdolsky's use of 'logical' is significant, not only as an indicator of his failure to get dialectical method straight; it is also an indicator of the particular way in which he has got it wrong. Rosdolsky is a Hegelian, for whom the actual has to exemplify the ideal, and this leads to a drawing apart of the 'economic' and the 'social' in his understanding of the class development.

Lack of clarity in this matter can produce disastrous misunderstandings, and quasi-Hegelianism of Rosdolsky's kind does nothing to help avert it. An example of such misunderstanding is provided by Jon Elster, who considers one of the 'three deadly sins of Marxism' to be something he calls 'dialectical deduction'. He writes that 'in *Capital*, and especially in the *Grundrisse*, Marx tried to apply

[47] Hegel, *Lectures on the History of Philosophy*, trs. in three vols. by E. Haldane and F. Simson, London (1894) ii, 147.

the mode of analysis of Hegel's *Logic* to economic phenomena, in a seemingly deductive chain. The most notorious instance was his attempt to deduce capital from the existence of money. Arguing that money is inherently expansionary, he concluded that it can only preserve itself by multiplying and hence that money 'posits' capital as its fully developed form.'[48] Marx's greatest methodological strengths can thus appear as sources of weakness. Elster accuses Marx of 'conceptual sleight of hand' in his attempt to explain that to which 'Max Weber devoted vast empirical studies – that of explaining the emergence of the reinvestment motive in early capitalism'. The nature of the misunderstanding and the comparison with Weber to the disadvantage of Marx serves to locate Elster as one of the *eclectissimi* of Anglophone Marxism. Were there any degree of clarity about the ontological nature of Marx's categories of essence and form, as denoting entities which have life-processes of coming-to-be and passing-away, such confusion as is embodied in the idea of 'dialectical deduction' would be more readily identifiable for what it is.

The best Rodolsky can do by way of explanation is to produce a passage from Engels (which was extracted above) which anyway has its own weaknesses. Rosdolsky writes:

> The logical method of approach (as Engels wrote in his review of the *Contribution* in 1859), 'is indeed nothing other than the historical method, only stripped of the historical form and of disturbing accidental occurrences. The point where this history begins must also be the starting point of the train of thought, and its further progress will be simply the reflection, in abstract and theoretically consistent form, of the course of history. Though the reflection is corrected, it is corrected in accordance with laws provided by the actual course of history, since each factor can be examined at the stage of development where it reaches its full maturity, it classical form.'[49]

This is an excellent quote for all sorts of reasons. In the few sentences that follow, however, Rosdolsky shows that he is unable to extract much from it; he can do no more than recognise the elements of truth it contains. He cites it as if it were in itself sufficient to furnish an account of Marx's method; sufficient, presumably, for every purpose, including detailed exposition, ruling out misconstructions, etc. He continues: 'That this [*sic*] was Marx's

---

[48] Jon Elster, 'One hundred years of Marxist social science', *London Review of Books*, 16 June – 6 July 1983.
[49] *MEW* XII, 475.

method from the outset can be seen best of all in the ...' and he then names works which contain 'numerous passages' that allegedly confirm what he is trying to say. But Engels' few sentences tell us little, and will convey next to nothing of any real substance to anyone who has not read *Capital* and studied it in careful detail with methodological questions in mind, and with a fair understanding of the full range of philosophical and methodological possibilities and possible misreadings. Engels' sentences are fine, however little they may explain. What is amiss is the use made of them by Rosdolsky and his belief that they settle or explain anything.

It is disappointing, in a matter so difficult as the recovery of Marx's method, and today so deeply buried beneath layers of politically motivated falsehood and nonsense, that someone of Rosdolsky's serious intent should find it impossible to do better than rely upon quotation unsupplemented by substantial explanation. He does not cite, or give references for, the 'numerous passages in the *Rough Draft*, in the *Contribution* and in *Capital*' which provide what he says they provide. If he had they would very likely settle little. Marx's method and philosophical basis is so remote from anything that is widely familiar today that quotation from his works, however detailed, comprehensive and faithful, is quite inadequate to the task of explicating it. This would probably be true even if Marx had made his methodological statements more numerous (and better directed towards later historically begotten species of misunderstanding). For what would be needed would be a work with a purely methodological and philosophical objective. Marx never wrote such a book.

Instead, Marx attained methodological and philosophical clarity for himself in the years in which he wrote the so-called 'early works' and *The German Ideology* while also developing the programme for his future work, and then left it alone, more or less. He spent the remainder of his life putting his philosophy and method to work, and refining it, in the course of striving for the paramount objective of his life (which the German revolutionaries at the time of the Cologne trials reminded him of, and impressed upon him as his first priority), namely, to provide the working class with a sound understanding of capitalism, the better to replace it in the first and only conscious revolution in human history.

It is perfectly intelligible why Marx failed, or did not bother, to write such a work. Aristotelian-Hegelian essentialist method was still the familiar idiom in his period, and not almost totally buried as it is today. (Weber fought a little war against it.) Furthermore, the work he did saddle himself with was quite enough to occupy several well-staffed research institutes of the present day for a lifetime of hard work. What is more, Marx would have been justified in thinking that the nature and content of his work were quite adequate to forestall serious methodological misunderstanding. And indeed they are, for the difficulty of his method, real though it is, is largely a relative matter. His method is not difficult to grasp in itself, but relative to, and in confused conflict with, what passes for method among diamatikers, ex-diamatikers, empiricists and the three combined, it is complex and difficult to track down and clarify.

The trouble is that Marx's method, his forms of explanation and their application in his works, amply clear though they are in principle for Adam Smith's 'ideal observers', are not read by ahistorical abstractions, but by real readers who bring to their reading a not-so-wide variety of historically and socially begotten pre-conceptions and misconceptions. Judging Marx's texts by normal scholarly standards they are as adequate as any major texts have ever been to forestall serious errors of judgment. What is different in the case of Marx as opposed to almost any other major thinker, is the potency of the reasons of direct self-interest, of intellectual, social, institutional and political comfort and tranquillity, that have operated in the direction of misunderstanding and deliberate falsification. Against that kind of motivation, no thinker could make himself clear, for in such a case misunderstanding is not a product of difficulties in the text or the subject-matter; it is a product of the class-mechanics of society. What has made the greatest difference, and what sets the dimensions of the task facing a serious author like Rosdolsky, is the fact that the problem has been unimaginably exacerbated by the consequences of the class débâcles of the 1920s and 1930s, 'socialism in one country'.

It is at this level that we should have expected a deep retrieval of Marx. Instead, when he gets off the known paths of dispute between Marxists, 'Marxists' and anti-Marxists, he passes over with a quote from Engels, which can at best cast only the faintest glimmer of light into the regions where the darkness is deepest. The grotesque misreadings of Marx that have been perpetrated, and the social, political, cultural and institutional pressures that beget their perpetuation and recommissioning, can withstand any amount of name-calling (the perpetrators and perpetuators have a respectable arsenal of epithets of their own with which to assail the dialectician), and can cope with any volume of uninterpreted and unexplained quotations (they have a fair battery of these too). Great though the value of Rosdolsky's work is, it does not fulfil its promise, because it leaves the problem of method and philosophy unresolved at the foundation, and thus leaves freedom of movement for opportunism to continue in all the familiar wrong ways.

(v) The formation of the final form
of value: capital

Marx's understanding of the *genesis*, or coming-to-be, of the capital-form is integral to, and continuous with, his essentialist presentation of the *genesis* of the value-form as a whole. Capital is the *final form* (though it itself undergoes development) attained by the value-form in its process of development. Marx writes of the more developed forms 'of the value-form, ... the commodity-form together with its further developments, the money form, the capital form, etc.'[50] Again, if we 'consider only the economic forms brought into being by' the circulation of commodities, 'we find that its ultimate product is money. This ultimate product of commodity circulation is the first form of appearance of capital.'[51]

He repeatedly goes out of his way, by his choice of expression, to emphasise the unity of the essence whose developing forms he is discriminating; or rather, to emphasise the unity that those forms have in being forms of a single developing essence. For instance, he repeatedly chooses the term 'the independent form' (i.e. of value) to express his meaning in preference to the term 'money'. To select from a multiplicity of examples where Marx labours to present the unity and hold it before the eyes of the reader, he writes of commodities, money and capital, not only as being united as forms of the same essence (value), but also as being (in their developed forms) necessarily united as forms within the process that constitutes the typical movement, behaviour or law of *ergon*, of capital, i.e. its self-expansion:

> The independent form, i.e. the monetary form, which the value of commodities assumes in simple circulation, does nothing but mediate the exchange of commodities, and it vanishes in the final result of the movement. On the other hand, in the circulation M-C-M both the money and the commodity function as different modes of existence of value itself ... value is here the subject of a process in which, while constantly assuming the form of money and commodities, it changes its own magnitude, throws off surplus value from itself considered as original value ...[52]

[50] *Cap*. I, Pelican, 174 n.34.
[51] Ibid., 247.
[52] Ibid., 255.

This passage might equally serve as a warning against atomist interpretations of Marx, such as that of G.A. Cohen, which poke genteel fun at Marxist authors who write of capital as a process or relation. We shall see in Chapter 7 how, quite generally, the process typifying the behaviour of a thing can be partly constitutive of its essence or identity. The fact is well exemplified in Marx's treatment here, as well as in his treatment of the circuits of capital in Volume II of *Capital*. There the *unity* of the different forms within the *movement* of the *whole entity* is much stressed. The commodity is seen as existing in one form only in order to move to the next, and to the one after that, in the process of capital expanding itself. One sees the same thing clearly in the treatment of crises in *TSV* II.

Aristotle held as a general principle that 'what each thing is when fully developed we call its nature, whether we are speaking of a man, a house, or a family'.[53] In thoroughly Aristotelian manner, Marx presents the final form of industrial capital as primary over earlier less developed forms of capital: 'In the course of our investigation, we shall find that both merchants' capital and interest-bearing capital are derivative forms, and ... it will become clear why, historically, these two forms appear before the modern primary form of capital.'[54] We shall see later in this section that Marx considered mere money ('money-as-money') not to have been fully comprehended until it was understood to be a lower, less developed, form of capital. The nature of money is not fully attained until it actualises its potential to become what it is capable of becoming, viz. capital.[55] Money is understandable only as a lower form of capital because that *is* what it is.

It is obvious, however, that Marx's treatment of capital is quite different from his treatment of the earlier value forms, and it is equally obvious what the difference is and why it exists. The difference is, in the first place, one of length, detail and comprehensiveness. Marx goes into great historical detail about capital and its formation, as he did not about the earlier value forms, and he analyses its 'laws of motion' in depth and at length. The reason for the difference is not just that the earlier forms were simpler, but that capital is the subject of *Capital*. Marx's interest in the earlier value-forms did not extend to the societies in which they developed. With the society that embodies that capital-form it is otherwise. Here he wants 'the illumination of the special laws that

[53] *Politics* 1. 1252b32f.
[54] *Cap*.I, Pelican, 267.
[55] *Gr.*, 251.

regulate the origin, existence, development and death of a given social organism and its replacement by another, higher one'.[56] Marx's Russian reviewer was wrong only in one detail: Marx was not concerned (in *Capital* at any rate) with just any 'given social organism and its replacement by another'. He was interested in market economy and its value-form, and its supersession by a society of freely associated producers who subordinate social wealth to themselves, rather than being dominated by it.

We were given only the barest account of the value forms up to and including money in chapter one of *Capital* I (cf. Chapter 3 (i) above). That was a rarefied dialectical account of a process of *genesis* of an essence, and was pared to the bone. The reason for Marx's chosing that severe form of presentation, as we have observed, is that the actual historical route by which, in given societies at specific times, the successive forms were attained is irrelevant to the problems that have to be solved in Part One, on 'Commodities and Money'. The problem there was to seek out what underlay the nature of capital; the solution to that lay in the problem of money; the solution to that lay in the problem of the universal equivalent form; and the solution to that lay in the simple commodity-form, specifically its fusion of use-value and exchange-value in the Equivalent Form. The object of the exercise was the preliminary pinning-down and identification of the essence of capital. The object is achieved by a tracking-down, and identification, of the distinguishable forms of the process of development of the essence. Nothing more was needed, and anything more would have got in the way of his theoretical, political and practical purpose in the book as a whole. That purpose is to analyse a society in which 'all, or even a majority of the products take the form of commodities ... [which] only happens on the basis of one particular mode of production, the capitalist one'.[57] To achieve that, as he says, he had first to undertake 'the analysis of commodities'.

But the analysis of commodities does not require a historical recapitulation of 'the special laws that regulate the origin, existence, development and death' of those social organisms in which the commodity-form first appeared, since such societies did not embody in greater part commodity relationship.

> The production and circulation of commodities can still take place even though the great mass of the objects produced are intended for the immediate requirements of their producers, and are not turned

[56] *Cap.*I, Pelican, 102.
[57] Ibid., 273.

into commodities, so the process of social production is as yet by no means dominated in its length and breadth by exchange-value.[58]

In the Ancient Asiatic, classical-antique, and other such modes of production, the transformation of the product into a commodity, and therefore men's existence as producers of commodities, plays a subordinate role ...[59]

The appearance of products as commodities requires only an elementary level of development of division of labour in society to be sufficient to complete the separation of use-value from exchange-value.[60] 'But such a degree of development is common to many economic formations of society, with the most diverse characteristics.'[61]

The same is true of money as the equivalent of commodities, as means of circulation, as means of payment, as hoard, and as world currency, for 'we know by experience that a relatively feeble development of commodity circulation suffices for all these forms'.[62] In an exceptional case, like Sparta, the particular form of class-structure for surplus extraction was threatened by money, and for that reason the money-form was resisted.[63] In general, however, the feeble development and subordinate role of commodity production and circulation meant that all those forms could be attained without putting severe strain on the fundamental class structure through which the ruling class extracted its surplus, or at any rate without imposing strains so severe that the class structure was unable to accommodate them by adapting itself somewhat.

'*It is otherwise with capital.* The historical conditions of its existence are by no means given with the mere circulation of money and commodities.'[64] With earlier value-forms and transformations, an 'insufficiency' in one form could lead to ('ripen' into) the succeeding form 'automatically'; it could pass 'by an easy transition into a more complete form'.[65] 'It is otherwise with capital', for its attainment

---

[58] Loc. cit.

[59] Ibid., 172.

[60] Cf. my 'Aristotle and the political economy of the *polis*', *Journal of Hellenic Studies*, 99 (1979), esp. 66-8.

[61] *Cap.* I, loc. cit.

[62] Ibid., 274.

[63] See J.K. Davies, *Democracy and Classical Greece*, Glasgow (1978), 55.

[64] *Cap.* I, Pelican, 274 (italics added).

[65] Both current English editions of *Capital* have been used here, since each has different strengths and weaknesses in this passage: Pelican, 154; Moscow, 67.

requires a root-and-branch reconstitution of the class structure in accordance with the requirements of value; the universalisation of the value-form; the appearance of what Marx significantly calls 'the mode of production *corresponding to capital*'.[66] It requires one historical pre-condition, 'And this one historical pre-condition comprises a world's history.'[67] The pre-condition is that 'the owner of the means of production and subsistence finds the free worker available, on the market, as a seller of his own labour power'.[68] This tumultuous class reconstitution means that 'Capital, therefore, announces from the outset a new epoch in the process of social production.'[69]

Much more human social development and development of productivity, indeed a 'world's history', is required to attain the transition to the capital-form. The barebones account adequate to the *genesis* of the earlier value forms and to tracking down the riddle of money to the simple commodity-form, is quite inadequate to account for the *genesis* of the capital-form, and for 'the historical conditions of its existence'. For this a history is needed. That is why Marx gives one, in various parts of *Capital*, but especially in Part VIII, 'The So-Called Primitive-Accumulation'. The attainment of the capital-form means the universalisation of the form of value (cf. Chapter 6 (iii) below); not only do the vast bulk of products come to assume the commodity-form leaving only marginal areas of product for direct consumption rather than for the market, but human productive capacities themselves are brought under the form of value and take on the form of a commodity. The reason why this particular transformation of the value-form, the attainment of the capital-form, is so different from all previous ones is that it alters fundamentally the form in which human social labour is supplied. (See Chapter 4 (i) below.)

The natural line of essential development of the value-form is, after a certain point, to universalise itself. This is a potential inherent in the value-form. In an earlier phase of its development 'Money *necessarily* crystallises out of the process of exchange', 'the division of labour converts the product into a commodity, and thereby *makes necessary* its conversion into money'.[70] This occurred with the extension of private production and commodity circulation in the

---

[66] *Cap.* I, Pelican, 875.
[67] Ibid., 274.
[68] Loc. cit.
[69] Loc. cit.
[70] Ibid., 181 (italics added); 203.

ancient world. So from the higher extension of commerce and of the 'commercial requirements of the new world market, which had been created by the great discoveries at the end of the fifteenth century',[71] petty commodity production and merchants' capital on the basis of a higher 'method of labour' (see Chapter 5 (ii) below), industrial capital *necessarily* crystallises. 'Commodity production is *necessarily* at a certain point, turned into "capitalist" commodity production.'[72] Elsewhere Marx observes that petty commodity production is the basis of capitalist commodity production, and that the latter 'grows on the former's tomb and nowhere else'.[73]

The development of the capital-form is a necessary change or development of the value-form, but the conditions for the realisation of this potentiality are complex and dependent on accident. The forcible frustration or termination of the necessary line of development is rich in accidental possibilities. The resilience of the old mode of production, for example, must not be sufficient to snuff out the processes leading to its own dissolution.

> To what extent it (commerce) brings about a dissolution of the old mode of production depends upon its solidity and internal structure. And whither this process of dissolution will lead, in other words, what new mode of production will replace the old, does not depend upon commerce, but on the character of the old mode of production itself.[74]

But, given the requisite material conditions, sufficient weakness or inflexibility in the old class formation and sufficient vigour in the new, and so on, if the higher form is attained, it is attained necessarily as the realisation of the potential inherent in the value-form.

(If there is as much accident in the process as this account suggests, a worry must arise about the application of necessity. That is a problem I shall leave on one side here. Another problem is whether the coming-to-be of capital is best construed as a realisation of the potential of an existing essence (the value-form), or as the coming-to-be of a new essence (capital). Where I have touched on the question of capital's coming-to-be, especially in this chapter, in Chapter 5 (i) and in Chapter 6, I have not considered these as alternatives of which at most one can be true, but as both true. In

---

[71] Ibid., 914.
[72] 'Notes (1879-80) on Adolph Wagner' in *Karl Marx: Texts on Method*, trs. and ed. T. Carver, Oxford (1975), 216 (italics added).
[73] *Cap.*I, Pelican, 931.
[74] *Cap.*III, Moscow (1971), 332.

Chapter 5 (i) the value-form is treated as both (a) the form taken by something else which is its essence, and (b) itself an essence with a *genesis*, and derivative forms that appear in the course of its development. This does not seem unreasonable, since there are two levels here: first, the fundamental essence which is human social labour; and secondly, the different forms in which it is supplied over history for the extraction of surplus labour. Forms have forms, and Marx is explicit that capital is the finished form of value. The idea that forms of an essence may themselves have a *genesis* and lines of necessary development specific to them seems sound enough, though it would benefit from a more thorough analysis than it is getting here.)

The complex process that Marx has to trace out creates problems of presentation. Given the complexity of the social movement involved in the attainment of the capital-form, and the complexity of the interrelation between necessity and accident in the most basic pre-condition (the 'so called primitive accumulation', which 'is nothing else than the historical process of divorcing the producer from the means of production'), it is not easy to see that, or to determine whether, Marx organises his treatment in *Capital* I around the question: What is it in the essence of the value-form that necessitates the development of capital and wage-labour? His presentation is in that respect deficient.

He is committed to such an account, and the quote above from the 'Notes on Adolph Wagner' shows that he knew it. But he does not give much of one in *Capital*. This is, however, a deficiency of presentation of that work. Marx had worked the problem through in the appropriate terms in the *Grundrisse*, as we shall see in Chapter 6 below, in section iii, 'the universalisability of exchange-value', but he did not incorporate this into *Capital*. 'The exchange,' he writes in the *Grundrisse*, 'of living labour for objective labour – i.e. the positing of social labour in the form of the contradiction between capital and wage-labour – is the ultimate development of the value relation.'[75]

About petty commodity production, on whose tomb and nowhere else capitalist commodity production grows, he writes: 'Of course, this mode of production also exists under slavery, serfdom and other situations of dependence. But it flourishes, unleashes the whole of its energy, attains its adequate classical form, only where the worker is the free proprietor of the conditions of his labour, and sets them in motion himself.'[76] But 'to perpetuate it would be, as Pecquer rightly

[75] *Gr.*, 704.
[76] *Cap.*I, Pelican, 927.

says, "to decree universal mediocrity" '.[77] Such decrees, were they made, would not abolish all potential for further development; they would not weigh heavily in the balance against the real forces of development leading beyond the decreed mediocrity; nor would they impart profound conviction of their rectitude to those enterprising spirits who, in being anxious to exploit the potential for exceeding mediocrity in their own case, embody those forces. Accordingly:

> At a certain stage of development, it (petty commodity production) brings into the world the material means of its own destruction. From that moment, new forces and new passions spring up in the bosom of society, forces and passions which feel themselves to be fettered by that society. It has to be annihilated; it is annihilated. Its annihilation, the transformation ... of the dwarf-like property of the many into the giant property of the few, and the ... terribly and arduously accomplished expropriation of the mass of the people forms the pre-history of capital.[78]

This is schematic rather than systematic organic-dialectical presentation. What Marx concentrates on in *Capital* are the conditions that made possible the transition to the higher form, and the *actual* course by which it was accomplished. The stress naturally falls less on the potential of the value-form to become universalised, and more on the conditions that allow the potentiality to become actual; just as, in his discussion of crises, less stress falls on the potential forms of crises which are inherent in the value-form, than on the causes which turn the possibility into actuality. (Cf. Chapter 3 (i) above.) Perhaps this properly reflects the true specific weight of the necessary and the accidental in this special phase in the process of development of the value-form, its universalisation. But it is more likely that Marx thinks the 'causes' themselves to be expressions of the developing movement of the value-form to universalise itself, than that he sees the accidental as having exceptional weight over the necessary.

In 'The Genesis of the Industrial Capitalist', for example (chapter 31), we encounter the discovery of the new world and the expansion of trade, the colonial system, public credit, international credit, the modern taxation system and the system of protection. These can scarcely be regarded as external, accidental, causes. They are themselves clear expressions of the developing drive of exchange-value towards its universalisation – or, rather, of the

---

[77] Ibid., 928.
[78] Loc. cit.

galloping commercial activity of people which was the essence of that process. What led to the explosion of such activity is not presented in *Capital* in a fully theorised form. A vital question such as 'The Expropriation of the Agricultural Population' (chapter 27), is treated in a purely empirical manner, and Marx says: 'We leave on one side here the purely economic driving forces behind the agricultural revolution. We deal only with the violent means employed.'[79]

The main point is secured, however. He arrives at that 'one historical pre-condition (which) comprises a world's history', namely, the situation in which 'the owner of the means of production and subsistence finds the free worker available, on the market, as the seller of his own labour power'.[80] By chapter 29 Marx is able to begin 'The Genesis of the Capitalist Farmer' with a characterisation of the previous two chapters: 'Now we have considered the forcible creation of a class of free and rightless proletarians', and he proceeds to the other aspect of the process with the question: if the proletariat was a class created by force, 'where did the capitalists originally spring from?'[81] Again, an empirical history follows, starting with the bailiff or *villicus* and leading through a series of intermediate forms to the farmer proper who owns capital, employs wage-labour and pays ground rent. This process is explained by Marx in terms of a series of 'factors of decisive importance': the agricultural revolution in the last third of the fifteenth century, the usurpation of common land, accidental rent customs, the fall in the value of money and price rises. By such a route, it seems, Marx reaches the conclusion: 'England, at the end of the sixteenth century, had a class of capitalist farmers.'[82]

The concern of this chapter has been to show the character of Marx's conception of science in relation to history. I have tried to do it by dealing only with his treatment of classical political economy and of the process of coming-to-be of capital. What remains outstanding is the subject matter of the far greater part of *Capital* as a whole, namely, the laying bare of the laws of development of capital itself, the tracing out of the laws of its typical movement or *ergon*, its internal contradictions as expressions of the fundamental contradictions within the simple commodity-form, and the laws of its decay and corruption.

[79] Ibid., 883.
[80] Ibid., 274.
[81] Ibid., 905.
[82] Ibid., 907.

That would raise a host of more refined problems of greater constructive interest than the uncouth problem we have been concerned with, viz. that Marx was not an atomist or empiricist; that there is a greater depth of truth in that slogan than is sometimes understood by many who subscribe to it; and that the subscriber may notwithstanding be an atomist or empiricist by reason of a lack of understanding of what essentialism and dialectics and their basic categories are, and how they are opposed to atomist-analytics.

There are two principal conclusions to be drawn. The positive one is that Marx's conception of the historical process as a 'process of natural history governed by laws' was founded on the categories of organic-dialectics and an essentialist ontology of real natures in the social sciences; that the laws he had in mind were Aristotelian-type laws of *genesis*, of *ergon*, and of decay in a whole social organism.

There is the corresponding negative conclusion. Marx's method, and the conception of science and law on which it rests, and the philosophy and ontology on which they rest, have nothing whatever in common with atomist-analytics, its conceptions of science and law, and its atomist ontology and consequent epistemology and metaphysics. Marx attacks the 'analytical method' in perfectly clear terms, though, perhaps, he does not hammer the message home with blows of a severity sufficient to drive it into the skulls of some of the *soi-disant* Marxists of the present day.

Capital does not represent a reconstruction of the entirety of human history, whose 'scientific' nature lies in showing history to be 'covered' by causal laws having the form of 'universal conditionals' relating event-types. We noted that, and why, Marx did not give a history of the societies in which the commodity-form first appeared. He left that to the professors of Marxism. That, and the set of reasons we saw for it, is as clear an indication as one could wish for, of the contrast between Marx's conception of science and his conception of how history is susceptible to a scientific treatment, and the conception of those Second Internationalists whose constant moan it was that a world history was required, not only for the completion of Marx's science, but for its vindication as science, and that consequently it would be years before there could be either.

4

The Two Turning-points of History and the Two Regulators

(i) Forms of supply of human social labour

Whenever people act together in producing what they need and want, they must somehow contrive to divide their total effort between the different activities that produce the things needed and wanted. It makes no difference in what manner they co-operate, or whether the co-operation is free or compelled.

In the best known of the letters to Kugelmann, Marx speaks of this necessity as a 'natural law' which must operate in all societies: 'That this necessity of the distribution of social labour in definite proportions cannot possibly be done away with by a particular form of social production but can only change the form in which it appears, is self-evident. No natural laws can be done away with.'[1]

In how many ways can this division of activities take place? There are only two possible forms that the product of social labour can take: either it is an exchange-value (has the commodity-form) or it is not. Correspondingly there are only two fundamental ways in which the division of activities can be achieved: first, by some sort of directly social regulation either customary or conscious, which applies in societies where the product is not an exchange-value; secondly, through the blindly working averages of the price-form, which applies in societies based on the market where the product appears under the value-form, i.e. is an exchange-value (and likewise the form of labour which produces it), and where their having that social form appears in their having the phenomenal form of a price.

No doubt history, and the imagination, can complicate this picture, for example, by showing that the decision can be

[1] Marx to Kugelmann, 11 July 1868.

unconscious and customary and thus only very loosely called a 'decision' at all, or by showing that the market mechanism can be consciously tinkered with in this way or that. None of this, however, alters the fact that there are only two fundamental forms of the product of social labour and two corresponding forms of regulation, i.e. ways of achieving the division of the available efforts, or 'the distribution of social labour in definite proportions'. Any complication can be handled only as a variant of either one form or the other; as a co-presence of both, each in conflict with the other; or as an absence of either.

Marx, accordingly, attributes only two forms to this division or regulation: the law of value and the conscious or unconscious social plan.[2] There are, therefore, only two fundamental types of society. There are those in which the product of social labour either does not take the commodity or value-form at all, or, if it does in some measure, does so only to an insignificant extent. Here the social plan is the economic regulator, either in its primitive form, or in its advanced conscious form (see Section ii below). Then there are those societies in which the commodity is the dominant form of the social product and of the form of supply of social labour, which, as we have seen, occurs only under the specifically capitalist form of commodity production (it is only when wage-labour meets capital in the market 'that the product of labour universally becomes a commodity'[3]) and here the law of value is the economic regulator.

On this perspective, world history falls into three major bands: the first, those societies prior to capitalism; secondly, the epoch of the development of the universalised value-form, capitalism, to a world level; thirdly, human society which has superseded the value-form. This was Marx's perspective, and he expresses it with unambiguous clarity in the *Grundrisse* where he writes of private production and exchange:

> Each individual prossesses social power in the form of a thing. Rob the thing of this social power and you must give it to persons to exercise over persons. Relations of personal dependence ... are the first social forms ... Personal independence founded on *objective* (*sachlicher*) dependence is the second great form, in which a system of general social metabolism, of universal relations, of all-round needs and universal capacities is formed for the first time. Free individuality, based on the universal development of individuals and on their subordination of their communal, social productivity as their social

[2] See I.I. Rubin on value as regulator, *Essays on Marx's Theory of Value*, Detroit (1972).
[3] *Cap.* I, Pelican, 274n.4.

wealth, is the third stage. The second stage creates the conditions for the third. Patriarchal as well as ancient conditions (feudal, also) thus disintegrate with the development of commerce, of luxury, of *money*, of exchange-value, while modern society arises and grows in the same measure.[4]

It is a consequence of this perspective that in all the backward and foreward movement of history, with the passage of this, that and the other social formation, there are two really fundamental turning-points. Each of them consists in a transformation in *the forms in which human labour is socially supplied*, and therewith *the form in which surplus labour is extracted*.

There are, then, three bands of history punctuated by two fundamental turning-points. Let us look first at the turning points. The first turning point is the transition from forms of unfree labour to labour supplied under the value-form, i.e. as a commodity subject to acts of sale and purchase, where social labour exists immediately only as individual labours, and becomes *social* only as abstract labour (see Chapter 6 (iii) below).[5] We saw in Chapter 3 (v) that Marx regarded this as the first great watershed in human history; the universalisation of the value-form. He speaks of it without any of his familiar irony or humour, but in frankly grandiloquent terms, rather rare for him, as a condition that 'comprises a world's history'. The second turning-point is the transition out of and beyond the value-form into the higher form of supply of human social labour, the free association of the producers consciously co-operating within a commonly agreed plan.

Both of these turning-points lead into new forms of social arrangements for appropriating the surplus. The first leads from unfree labour as the basis upon which surplus labour is pumped out (*ausgepumpt*) from one class by another, to wage-labour as a higher basis for doing the same. The second turning-point does away with class appopriation of surplus labour altogether, and replaces it with common and collective appropriation. (In each case, these transitions are made possible by an increase in the size of the surplus, which in turn is made possible by increased productivity or a higher 'method of labour'. Consideration of this must be left until Chapter 5 (ii).)

As to the three epochs, which these turning-points punctuate, they are quite clearly drawn by Marx. They are arrived at by considering the historical process in relation to a single criterion: the form in

---

[4] *Gr.* 157-8; other relevant passages are *Cap.* II, Moscow, 119-20, 483; *Cap.*III, Moscow, 786-7.

[5] See Chris Arthur, 'Dialectics and labour', in *IMP* I.

which surplus labour is extracted and appropriated. First, there is pre-capitalism, which includes patriarchal, ancient and feudal sub-forms. These are all forms of social organism in which surplus labour is extracted through 'relations of personal dependence', that is, *unfree* forms of supply of human social labour. The epoch of dependent or unfree labour has its own internal development, from debt-bondage, through chattel slavery to serfdom. The line of that development constitutes the basis of the history of the ancient world, and the key to understanding that history lies in uncovering that line of development. This has been largely accomplished by G.E.M. de Ste. Croix.[6]

Secondly, there is the epoch of universalised exchange, that is, the form of social organism based on the market, where the surplus is extracted through the supply of social labour in the form of wage-labour. Here the supplier of surplus creating labour is not unfree or personally dependent; rather, he is a free commodity owner, legally equal, and free to *contract*, with all other commodity owners. He supplies labour, not unfreely, but as a 'free' social atom, a commodity seller contracting with the commodity buyer 'of his choice'. His dependence is not personal, relating to an extracting individual; it is impersonal, relating to an entire class through a system of markets. He is, in Lenin's phrase, a 'wage-slave'. His dependence is upon a form, the value-form (or commodity-form), and this shows itself in the fact that his labour appears, not as labour, or a fragment of general social labour, but as an exchange-value which he personally owns, viz. labour-power, for which there might be more or less demand. Nobody can have a personal relation with a form, unless they are very unusual; they can have only an impersonal relationship, which is what Marx is getting at with the phrase '*sachlicher* dependence'.

Thirdly, there is the epoch of the freely associated producers, in which the surplus is not dominating them, but is subordinated to them and collectively appropriated by them.

(ii) The plan: customary and conscious

There are only two regulators, but three bands of history. The law of value is the regulator only for the middle band characterised by 'personal independence founded on real (*sachlicher*) dependence'. It follows that the other regulator, that of the social plan, is a very

---

[6] *CSAGW.*

broad category. It must cover not only the highest form of human
society, the mode of production of the freely associated producers or
socialism, but also all those prior to capitalism including the most
primitive. We must now do two things. (a) First, we must confirm
that Marx did, indeed, understand the regulator of the plan in this
broad way and made suitable distinctions for its use. (b) Secondly,
we must consider that the use of a category as broad as this invites
confusion, and so requires careful and discriminating handling such
as it has not always received.

(a) Concerning 'those small and extremely ancient Indian
communities, for example, some of which continue to exist to this
day', Marx writes that they 'are based on possession of the land in
common, on the blending of agriculture with handicrafts, and on an
unalterable division of labour'. This basis, he continues, serves 'as a
fixed plan and basis for action whenever a new community is
started'.[7] The utility of this quote does not depend merely on the
occurrence in it of the *word* 'plan'. The point lies in the entire context
of what Marx is saying about the basis of production and
reproduction of such an ancient social organism. Again, Marx writes
that we find 'in those earlier forms of society in which the separation
of trades has been spontaneously developed, then crystallised, and
finally made permanent by law, ... a specimen of the organisation of
the labour of society in accordance with an approved and
authoritative plan'.[8]

To call them both a 'plan' is to pun on the word. The customary
regulation of the earlier social organism is at the opposite end of the
historical process of the development of human social labour from the
fully conscious planned regulation of socialism. The differences
between them seem so far to outweigh the similarities that it might
seem more appropriate to avoid the pun. I have retained it, partly for
want of a term adequate to the primitive specimen, partly because
Marx himself seemed to see no great harm in the pun, but partly also
because the pun does serve to draw attention (as Marx surely
intended) to the mediated role of human consciousness in the epoch
of the market compared to its role in the epochs that precede and
follow it.

Though Marx regards as, and calls, those earlier forms of society
'specimens' of regulation by plan, developments since Marx's time
make it important to be quite clear about what such a 'plan' might

[7] *Cap*.I, Pelican, 477-8.
[8] Loc. cit.; see also 171-2.

amount to in those ancient social organisms, compared with what it means in the future society of freely associated producers, when 'free individuality, based on the universal development of individuals', stands upon the heights of productivity revolutionarily advanced by capitalism and in turn by its supersession.

In those earlier societies the regulation was customary and not conscious, and it implied very little in the way of control over nature. It also implied little insight into, and understanding of, the social relations of those participating in them, with consequently little ability to adapt those relations, or society, to the needs of man. That ability becomes historically real only with the attainment of Marx's 'third stage', the mode of production of the freely associated producers. 'Those ancient social organisms are, compared with bourgeois society, extremely simple and transparent.'[9] None the less, they fail to understand themselves, and are driven to have recourse to 'the religious reflex' for an interpretation because 'they are founded either on the immature development of man individually, who has not yet severed the umbilical cord that unites him with his fellow men in a primitive tribal community, or upon direct relations of subjection. They can arise and exist only when the development of the productive power of labour has not risen beyond a low stage.'[10]

With the attainment of a higher development of the individual and of social production the religious reflex to nature cannot endure. 'All mythology overcomes and dominates and shapes the forces of nature in the imgination and by the imagination; it therefore vanished with the advent of real mastery of them ... What chance has Vulcan against Roberts & Co.?'[11] Mastery over nature may banish the mystification of nature, but it does not demystify the social relations of commodity production, for the fetishism of commodities veils the life process of society. 'The life process of society ... does not strip off its mystical veil until it is *treated as* production by freely associated men, and is consciously regulated by them in accordance with a settled plan.'[12] 'The veil is not removed from the countenance of the social life-process, i.e. the process of material production, until it becomes production by freely associated men, and stands under their conscious and planned control.'[13]

It is only under socialism that men can come to be, and to regard themselves as being, freely associated and co-operating in

[9] Ibid., 172.
[10] Ibid., 173.
[11] *Gr.* 110.
[12] *Cap.*I, Moscow, 84 (italics added).
[13] *Cap.*I, Pelican, 173.

production. This is in contrast both to pre-capitalism where their relations are mythologised, and to capitalism where their relations are fetishised, where even a man's 'labour power takes *in the eyes of the labourer himself* the form of a commodity which is his property',[14] and where productive co-operation itself *appears* to be possible only because capital exists to make it possible by employing people (the *Arbeitgeber* of nineteenth-century German professors and of 'modern' monetarists who announce that trade unions do not make jobs).

(b) Marx's *Capital*, which must surpass even *Robinson Crusoe* as the world's most talked about and least read book, is often regarded as economics or at best as economic philosophy. It is in fact our greatest work of human self-understanding. The condition for the generalisation of that understanding to the whole of humanity, however, is the final and complete demise of the value-form. Only when human labour is socially supplied, not as concealed beneath a form, but directly as social labour, as free, conscious co-operative endeavour, will men and women really understand themselves and their lives.

There are those who are able to conclude from the fact that the USSR is not regulated by the law of value, as it is not, that *therefore* it must be regulated by the plan, and thus be a higher form than capitalism. The initial fault in the argument is one of logic. From the fact that there are only two regulators that *any* society *can* have, it does not follow that *every* society *must* have one or the other. The mere logical fallacy, however, conceals something more serious: the often overlooked historical possibility of a society which has no form of either of the regulators, and which is therefore lacking any genuine regulation. There is good reason to think that this is precisely the nature that the USSR has come to have.[15]

Such a view is capable of explaining the spectacular non-achievements of Soviet 'planning', such as the ineliminable disproportion between Department I and Department II;[16] the inability to feed its population; the mountains of waste, of unusable and defective product;[17] the inability to innovate, and the fact that it

[14] Ibid., 274 n.4.
[15] See Hillel Ticktin, 'Towards a political economy of the USSR', *Critique* no.1 (1973); and other articles by the same author cited immediately below.
[16] Ibid.
[17] Ibid., and Hillel Ticktin, 'The contradictions of Soviet society and Professor Bettelheim', *Critique* 6 (1976); 'The class structure of the USSR and the elite', *Critique* 9 (1978); G.A.E. Smith, 'The industrial problems of Soviet agriculture', *Critique* 14 (1981).

is the only society known to history in which the introduction of labour-saving techniques actually results in the employment of more rather than fewer people.[18]

These well-known features of the Soviet economy cannot be explained, as Ernest Mandel has sought to explain them, as being due to the constraints under which Soviet 'planning' operates, such that it is only a modified form of planning rather than its full form. Planning, like the law of value and indeed all Marx's categories, expresses social relations. To say at the same time, as Mandel does, both that the Soviet economy is regulated by planning and that its social relations represent no form of production by the freely associated producers (socialism), is self-contradictory. It is exactly like saying of some society that the market (law of value) is the regulator of its economy, but that the society has no form of the relation of capital/wage-labour. It simply is not possible.[19]

Those of the 'state capitalist' persuasion have been known to argue that since the USSR is not a planned economy (is not production by freely associated producers) *therefore* it must be regulated by the law of value. The same illogic, the same ignorance of the empirical reality and the same lack of imagination apply here as in the former case.

(iii) Essence and class

We have, then, two possible regulators for 'the division of labour in society at large'.[20] On the one hand the anarchic law of value, where 'there is no conscious social regulation of production. The reasonable and the necessary in nature asserts itself only as a blindly working average',[21] where 'inherent laws impose themselves only as the mean of apparently lawless irregularities that compensate one another'.[22] On the other hand the social plan.

In pre-capitalist class societies where value relations existed, they did so only peripherally to social production. The 'market', in the embryonic form of simple commodity production and circulation, existed within a social organism whose production was not regulated

---

[18] See Robert Arnot, 'Soviet labour productivity and the failure of the Shchekino experiment', *Critique* 15 (1981); Hillel Ticktin, 'The relation between détente and the Soviet economic reforms', in Egbert Jahn (ed.), *Soviet Foreign Policy: Its Social and Economic Conditions*, London (1978)50f; and *Critique* 6, op. cit., 30ff.

[19] See my 'Has Marxism a future?', *Critique* 13 (1981).

[20] *Cap*.I, Moscow, 339.

[21] Letter to Kugelmann, 11 July 1868.

[22] *Cap*.I, Moscow, 102.

by it, but by custom and direction. As Marx notes, 'the private property of the worker in his means of production' is a 'mode of production that exists under slavery, serfdom and other situations of dependence'.[23]

When it goes beyond its peripheral existence and subordinate position, however, when 'it flourishes, unleashes the whole of its energy, attains its adequate classical form',[24] it is not in order to establish itself as a new mode of production, but to establish value or the market as regulator and thus usher in capitalist commodity production: 'the latter is not only the direct antithesis of the former (sc. simple commodity production), but grows on the former's tomb and nowhere else.'[25] This is obvious enough. For value to universalise itself – that is, in particular, to extend to the form of supply of social labour itself – value relations must themselves have taken an important grip on society.

The conclusion seems to be that at the highest level of abstraction, history is to be viewed as a social process in which, at different times, either one or the other regulator of social production operates outright or largely uncontested, or operates dominantly while the other has a peripheral presence, or both operate together in a situation of instability needing resolution in one direction or the other, or neither operates in a situation of even greater instability.

Even at the highest level of abstraction, however, this formulation is misleading. Marx's view of history as susceptible to scientific treatment and presentation, in that it constituted the process of coming-to-be of an essence, is not an alternative to the view of historical change as a process of class transformation through class struggle. On the contrary, the two are indissolubly connected in Marx's view of the historical process.

One example will illustrate the relation between the two. What Marx found in the simple form of value was not only the key to *understanding* the money-form, but also one part of the impelling force that *begets* it, or in his metaphor, the germ from which it germinates. He argues that the simple form is 'insufficient', and that if there is to be historical development (i.e. development of the value-form), then it must as a matter of *necessity* be development towards the money-form. 'We perceive straight away the insufficiency of the simple form of value: it is an embryonic form which must undergo a

[23] *Cap.*I, Pelican, 927.
[24] Loc. cit.
[25] Ibid., 931.

series of metamorphoses before it can ripen into the price form.'[26]

Looking at it from the farther end of the development, 'money necessarily crystallises out of the process of exchange, in which different products of labour are in fact equated with each other and thus converted into commodities'. The historical development, the deepening and broadening of exchange activity between people that goes along with the development of private production, *develops* the opposition between use-value and exchange-value, and begets a need, a necessity, for a fuller commercial expression that will allow the separation of the acts of sale and purchase. There is a *drive*, arising from the insufficiency of the simple form, towards 'an independent form of value', money. 'At the same rate, then, as the transformation of the products of labour into commodities is accomplished, one particular commodity is transformed into money.'[27]

The development, therefore, is a necessary one arising from the internal contradiction inherent in the commodity form, and from the insufficiency of the simple form. This insufficiency, itself a product of human activity, is rectified by the daily practice and ingenuity of people who repeatedly face the difficulty of a form of exchange in which sale and purchase are fused into a single act, and they begin to act in new ways by treating one commodity in a special way. This new form of behaviour or activity is the arrival of the money-form. 'But only the action of society can turn a particular commodity into the universal equivalent.'[28] The 'insufficiency' creates 'a need ... produces a drive towards an independent expression of value which finds 'no rest or peace until an independent form has been achieved'.

There is clearly no incompatibility between seeing the historical movement as a necessary development of forms on the one hand, and as one of developing activity and social relations on the other. They are one and the same thing in Marx's conception of the process of historical change. To see the 'drive' to develop beyond an insufficient form to an adequate one is not to view the historical process in a formal way that abstracts from or omits developing commercial and productive activity among people and developing social relations; on the contrary, it is at once to presuppose that, and *make sense of it*. 'Insufficiency' is a two-place predicate. Something has to be insufficient for something else. The simple value-form is insufficient for the developing relations of private production and commodity

[26] Ibid., 154.
[27] Ibid., 181.
[28] Ibid., 180.

circulation, that is, for the progressive transformation of the products of labour into commodities and subjects of private exchange. The social activity of commodity circulation under one form grows and develops into other modified activities, and these embody the new form which supersedes the old. All Marx's accounts of the developments of new forms of value have this substantive social and historical content, and indeed, it is precisely the new sorts of behaviour, the historical content, that his accounts of the developments of forms explain, and are intended to explain.

It is inadequate to characterise the relation between the *genesis* of the value-form and the development of social relations as two aspects of a single view of history and change. For they are inseparable even in thought. The content of the form of value *is* the activity of individuals in their daily operations as members of a class, that is, their productive and exchange activity, and as the one changes so necessarily does the other. The commodity-form, real though it is as a historical form, is an expression, in terms of the social form historically assumed by the *product* of labour, of the form in which social labour is supplied. The ingenuity of people solves problems that are set for them by the form of their existing activity. That ingenuity is exercised in circumstances where the form of existing activity gives rise to problems that are inherent in the development of that form, and whose solution is itself a further and necessary development of that form itself.

Marx says that for his purposes in *Capital* he will treat the capitalist as 'capital endowed with a rational will'. Some *very* Hegelian Marxists extend this beyond anything intended by Marx, and reach the view that the individual capitalist is no more than a 'personification' of the laws of motion of capital. In consequence, the category of class is evaporated, and we are left with a mere congeries of atoms into each of which the laws are distilled. The agent of history then comes to be portrayed as an abstraction anthropomorphically endowed with personal qualities. On this view the historical process can come to be seen as a Hegelian process of the working-out of an idea; a realm of unalloyed necessity without accident.

The emphasis put upon form and essence in this book is in part a reaction to the absence of such categories in much recent Marxist literature. The position described above, however, is an overreaction to that absence. It is other-worldly to grasp the forms, and to focus upon them with such single-mindedness that one loses sight of people, arrayed in classes, acting in circumstances and within forms that are the product of necessity and accident.

5

'Methods of Labour' and the Extraction of Surplus Labour

(i) The general theory of history and the theory of the history of capital

So far we have been concerned largely with Marx's analysis of the value-form, and with the role that the categories of essentialist and dialectical philosophy have in reaching an understanding of it, of its process of coming-to-be and of human society reconstituted to the requirements of the universalised value-form, capital, or the bourgeois mode of production. This cannot be imagined to exhaust Marx's theory of the historical process, since it is only relatively recently that any sizeable part of social humanity has been subject to the rule of a class whose power flows from the private ownership of the social means of production *in the form of capital*, and who appropriate surplus labour through the form of wage-labour. Marx's theory of history, his treating 'the social movement as a process of natural history governed by laws', covers all human history and not its most recent and dynamic fraction only. We have now to look at that wider theory, to consider the relation it bears to his treatment of the bourgeois mode of production, and to consider the specific features of the latter which make it a special case of the wider theory.

In pre-capitalist class societies, human labour appears, not *under a form* (the form of value), but directly as itself. (That part of it which is unpaid surplus labour is, of course, supplied in the form of unfree or dependent labour. But this is a form of quite a different kind from the value-form.) In these cases there is, therefore, no riddle to be solved; there is no form to undergo a *genesis*, development, maturity and decay. The product of labour appears as what it is, a use-value; just as human labour appears directly as human labour. There is no form under which the product, or the labour producing it, appears. The consequence of this is that the nature of the historical process, though the same in essence as under capitalism as we shall see, requires no special scientific treatment of the kind required to come to understand capitalist commodity production. This is, in effect, the point that M.I. Finley has repeatedly made with his discusions of the ancient 'economy'.[1] The use-value does not appear under a puzzling form (analogous to the commodity, money or price forms) but merely as something someone made in the course of general social production which serves some useful purpose; there being no such form, there is no riddle that needs tracking down to any putative 'embryonic form' of the 'use-value' from which it germinated (analogous to the relative and equivalent forms of value); and the use-value does not undergo a process of universalisation in which the 'use-value' seizes hold of society and of the manner in which labour is socially supplied. In short, the laws of value-dominated society are different from those of other forms of society, and they require a different sort of treatment.

It is this difference in the natures of the social organism that explains why ancient authors on social affairs could write straightforwardly in class terms without turning a hair. Authors of the later bourgeois epoch, in contrast, have increasingly, and with increasing consciousness, denuded the discussion and analysis of social affairs of their real class content. In Antiquity there was no fetishism to conceal class relations because commodity production and circulation, though they existed, were at a rudimentary level of development and were outside the mode of surplus extraction, i.e. the class structure. Labour appears as itself, not under a form, and could thus be viewed as 'banausic', at any rate to those fortunately enough placed not to have to engage in it, and the only thing worse than engaging in it was having to work for another for wages.[2] The ways in which labour was socially supplied in Aristotle's Athens, which did not significantly include wage-labour, made it impossible for him to crack the value-relation, even though commodity circulation was sufficiently developed for him to have been able to identify the problem, and to track it down to a relation of equality between different proportions of different products.[3]

To speak of value as being a 'form' is ambiguous, and both senses

---

[1] See M.I. Finley, *The Ancient Economy*, Berkeley (1973), and his 'Aristotle and economic analysis' in M.I. Finley (ed.), *Studies in Ancient Society*, London (1974), originally published in *Past and Present* 47 (1970).

[2] Cf. G.E.M. de Ste. Croix, *CSAGW*, ch. III (vi).

[3] Cf. my 'Aristotle and the political economy of the polis', *Journal of Hellenic Studies*, 99 (1979).

are equally part of Marx's theory. We have so far dealt with it as a form in the Aristotelian sense: that is, as a form or a real nature or essence that has a line of development which, if it is not frustrated or terminated, consists in the realisations of inherent potentials. It is in this sense of 'form' that Marx's treatment of value succeeds in explaining what there had previously been failure to explain. He saw value to be a nature, and in applying essentialist and dialectical categories to it thereby achieves his results, which reached beyond classical political economy, and attains the highest point yet reached in man's understanding of himself.

Value is at the same time, however, a 'form' in the sense that it is the form taken or assumed by something else, namely, an essence which takes that form. The essence in question, which adopts the value-form, is social labour. Thus, the value-form is both (a) the form taken by something else which is its essence, and (b) itself an essence with a *genesis*, and derivative forms that appear in the course of its development.

To clarify this we must consider Marx's more general theory of history, in order to get clear about the relation and contrast between its application to pre-capitalist society and capitalist society. In other words, what sort of things are the laws of movement of human social organisms, and in what way do laws of that sort become transformed in the case of the society regulated by the law of value? It seems clear that Marx's views here show the labour theory of value to be an integral part of his theory of history, that the latter cannot be retained while rejecting the former, and that both the labour theory of value and the theory of history are indissolubly bound up with the philosophical categories of essentialism and dialectics.

(ii) Social productivity

Marx brings together the principal elements of his general theory of history in the following passage from *Capital* III:

> The specific economic form in which unpaid surplus labour is pumped out of the direct producers, determines the relationship of rulers and ruled, as it grows directly out of *production itself* and, in turn, reacts upon it as a determining element. Upon this, however, is founded the entire formation of the economic community which grows up out of the production relations themselves, thereby simultaneously its specific political form. It is always the direct relationship of the owners of the conditions of production to the direct producers – a relation always naturally corresponding to a definite stage in the development

of the *methods of labour* and thereby its social productivity – which reveals the innermost secret, the hidden basis of the entire social structure, and with it the political form of the relation of sovereignty and dependence, in short, the corresponding specific form of the state.[4]

(a) It is unequivocally clear that Marx is setting out a general relation between the level of productivity that exists (the size of the surplus, actual or potential) and the forms of extraction of surplus labour that are possible given that level.

(b) It is equally clear that the form of extraction of surplus labour constitutes the basis of Marx's category of *class*. Sociology, one of a number of toadstools that have grown upon the putrefaction of Marxism,[5] has contrived to make the category of class particularly opaque, as de Ste. Croix justly observes.[6] Whatever developments may be needed for the empirical application of Marx's conception of class, at least its basis is perfectly clear. Marx treats all class societies as in their *essential natures* social organisms in which surplus labour is pumped out of one class by another. 'The essential difference', he writes 'between the various forms of society (between, for instance, a society based on slave labour and one based on wage labour) lies only in the mode in which surplus labour is in each case extracted from the actual producer, the worker.'[7] (It is worth noting, in passing, one particularly eloquent illustration of the ravages to which Marx's work has been subject. G.E.M. de Ste. Croix's *CSAGW* is based explicitly on the fundamental insights of Marx set out above.[8] Yet another Marxist historian, reviewing the work, did not see in this the simple fact that de Ste. Croix was basing his work on Marx himself; rather, he saw it as indicating that de Ste. Croix 'has evolved his own personal brand of Marxism'.[9])

(c) If the level of productivity decides which forms of extraction of surplus labour are possible, and thus what forms of class organism it can sustain, so the nature of the class organism thus begotten and sustained decides in its turn its own kind of 'political form', 'the

---

[4] *Cap.*III, Moscow, 791 (italics added).

[5] Non-Marxist social scientists often like to put it the other way round: everything that is of use in Marx's thought has been extracted and embodied in modern social science.

[6] *CSAGW*, 43

[7] *Cap.* I, Moscow, 209; Pelican, 325.

[8] See *CSAGW*, ch. II, esp. (ii) and (iii).

[9] Christopher Hill's review of *CSAGW* in *London Review of Books*, 4-8 February 1982. For a discussion of the political and historical reasons for the kind of misunderstanding Hill's reaction represents see my review of *CSAGW* in *Critique* 16 (1983).

political form of the relation of sovereignty and dependence', 'in short, the corresponding specific form of the state'.

(d) The class relation is precisely the relation through which the surplus labour is pumped out, and, as Marx says, it 'grows directly out of production itself'. But what is 'production itself'? It looks a remarkably abstract and un-Marxian category. It cannot be anything that involves the class relation, because that relation is itself based on 'production itself', or 'grows out of' it. The class relation has to be separate also because Marx treats it as reacting upon 'production itself', having first grown out of it; the class relation grows out of 'production itself' and reacts upon it only as a secondary determination. The class relation is confirmed in its posterior position by the fact that *it* has to do the corresponding with, or conforming to, 'production itself' and not vice-versa: the class relation always and naturally corresponds 'to a definite stage in the development of the methods of labour and thereby its social productivity'.

The lines are quite unequivocally drawn by Marx. The class relation is an outgrowth of the given stage in the development of methods of labour and social productivity. There is none of the complex-dialectical-interaction-between-two-poles stuff that is familiar in some *soi-disant* Marxist work.

But if 'production itself' and 'methods of labour' do not involve the class relation, neither can they be the actual historical way in which people work at a given time. The historical labour process conducted at any time does involve the secondary determination by the class relation (where there are classes), and that relation, with or without any secondary determination it may have, is *not* involved in 'production itself' or 'methods of labour'.

These latter must, therefore, represent an abstraction both from the class relation and from the existing historical labour process. It must be an abstraction to something which Marx regards as the primary determinant of both.

It is an abstraction met with elsewhere in Marx. In the section on 'The Labour Process',[10] Marx finds it necessary 'to consider the labour process independently of any specific social formation', and he considers that this is possible because 'the fact that the production of use-values, or goods, is carried on under the control of a capitalist and on his behalf does not alter the general character of that production'.[11] He continues with an account of 'production itself' in

[10] *Cap.*I, Pelican, 283ff; and see especially 'results of the immediate labour process', ibid., 1021-2.

[11] *Cap.*I, Pelican, 283.

very general terms as 'a process between man and nature' in which man 'acts upon external nature and changes it, and in this way he simultaneously changes his own nature'. In the *Grundrisse* he notes that '*Production in general* is an abstraction, but a rational abstraction insofar as it really brings out and fixes the common element'.¹² What is at issue here is the notion of 'forces of production' as Marx uses it in the *Grundrisse*, where he also repeatedly uses the expression 'production itself'.¹³ He writes of 'all previous forms of society – or, what is the same, of the forces of social production'.¹⁴ And further, it 'has its living reality in a specific *mode of production* itself, a mode which appears both as a relation between the individuals, and as their specific active relation to inorganic nature, a specific mode of working ... the community itself appears as the first great force of production'.¹⁵

Two things are clear from the quotation from *Capital* III at the head of this section. The first is that the *differentia specifica* of class societies ('the innermost secret, the hidden basis, of the entire social structure') is the class arrangement through which a surplus is pumped out by an exploiting class. The second is that this crucial class relation always and naturally corresponds to the stage of development of 'the methods of labour and its social productivity'.

This sort of position is unpopular today with certain schools of Marxism, notably in Italy,¹⁶ which insist that class determination is primary over all other determination; that production relations are primary over forces of production, etc. The greatest impetus to this view came from Maoism, and its influence has been clear in the work of some of the most accomplished Marxists of recent decades such as Sweezy, Bettelheim, Rossanda and others. It is clear that such views had no place in Marx's thought, and they will not be discussed here. Their discussion belongs to the study of the history of misfortune of the thought of Marx, and the practical decay of the world working-class movement, which were both consequences of 'socialism in one country'. The doctrine of the primacy of production relations is understandable as a reaction against the mechanical automatism of the *histmat* account, according to which productive forces simply develop, all on their own without reference to humans and what they do. That insupportable view still exerts an influence,

---

¹² *Gr.*, 85.
¹³ Ibid., 493-5.
¹⁴ Ibid., 540.
¹⁵ Ibid., 495.
¹⁶ Not only in Italy of course. Among others, Ben Fine shows sympathy with the view when he writes: 'The articulation between forces and relations is such that the relations of production are dominant.' *Re-Reading Capital*, London (1979) 11.

even among those seeking to work their way out of *histmat*; it is clearly visible in, for example, G.A. Cohen's *Karl Marx's Theory of History*. But one does not rectify one mistake by making another. Marx, in assigning primacy to 'production itself' or 'methods of labour', is not guilty of *histmat*, or of the other heresies defined by the Maoists, Althusser and at one time Sweezy – 'the false theory of productive forces', 'reductionism' or 'economism'. He is simply *explaining*: a procedure which necessarily consists in something being explained by something else. And he is explaining in materialist and dialectical terms, which necessarily requires that one explains the conditioned by the condition, or the determined by the determinant, and not *vice versa*.

There is a problem implicit in the quotation from *Capital* III. It lies in relating the class relation 'in which unpaid surplus labour is pumped out of the direct producers', with 'the direct relationship of the owners of the conditions of production to the direct producers'. Marx writes here in a way that could suggest that these are one and the same. In fact they can be separate. Many of the owners might themselves be direct producers, and thus be strictly outside the central relation of the society, though none the less a part of the society, and may indeed represent the principal condition for the central class relation having the form that it has.

Under developed market economy, the way in which the bulk of social production is carried on coincides with the central class relation for surplus extraction, so that almost everyone is either an owner of conditions of production or a direct producer, and almost no one is both (though many may be neither). The bulk of direct production is carried out by wage-earners employed by capital, and the method by which the exploiting class pumps out the surplus is precisely through the capital/wage-labour relation. In the classical period of Antiquity, by contrast, most of the surplus was pumped out through the use of slave armies, while the bulk of social production was carried on by free peasants at or near subsistence together with some artisan craftsmen.

In this situation there is a more complex relation between the way in which the bulk of social production is carried on, and the way in which the exploiting class acquires a surplus. The two are not more or less identical as they are in bourgeois production, which in this major respect is a simpler class organism than the ancient. The complexity arises from the fact that existing methods of labour were primitive and social productivity was low, so that they were incapable in the given circumstances of yielding much of an extractable surplus. This gave two results: first, that the surplus in the classical period had to be extracted through some special social adaptation of the existing methods of labour, a *very* unfree form of unfree labour, viz., debt-bondsmen and chattel slaves; and second, that the bulk of social production was carried on outside that central exploitative class relation. In Antiquity the level of technique or productivity was low, populations small, and the majority of direct producers consisted, until around A.D.. 300, of small, free, independent producers working at or near subsistence.[17] Those realities set the conditions in which the forms of surplus extraction had to be developed.

There are fundamentally three possibilities for pumping out a surplus, as de Ste. Croix has pointed out: (i) exploitation through wage-labour, (ii) exploitation through unfree labour, which may be of chattel slaves, serfs, debt-bondsmen or any combination, and (iii) exploitation by the letting of land or house property to free leasehold tenants for some kind of rent, in money, kind, or services.[18]

In the conditions of Antiquity the third of these could not have yielded much since the peasant surplus was small or non-existent, and its extraction would have been costly and politically hazardous, as is shown by the repeated class struggles that produced the reforms of Solon and the democratic reforms of the 460s. The first manner, wage-labour, was obviously impossible. So the second, unfree labour, was the only real possibility. This form itself underwent change between pre-Solonian times and the later Roman empire, passing from forms that significantly included the debt-bondage of members of the *polis*, to forms that put a much heavier emphasis on chattel slaves from foreign sources, and finally to increased exactions upon the poor free during the first two or three centuries A.D., culminating in the enserfment of virtually the entire agricultural population by Diocletian.[19]

To come to the point, Marx's picture was this. There is a general process in which people, seeking to improve their lives, innovate and raise productivity and technique when they can. At a certain point a surplus is achieved. Early social organisms found that this surplus presented a problem for the social structure, and discovered ways of dealing with it such as protected the '*Gemeinschaft*'. In some cases the surplus was appropriated in such a way as to cement the social bond of the productive unit and to demarcate the unit's agricultural

---

[17] Cf. de Ste. Croix, *CSAGW*, ch. I (iii), esp. 13.

[18] Ibid., 53.

[19] *CSAGW*, 249-51, though this complex process remains to be analysed in full theoretical detail.

patch.[20] In other cases the surplus was appropriated for the construction and maintenance of important common productive forces such as systems of irrigation, and for the maintenance of an elite who oversaw the system. Such was the Asiatic mode of production.

The class arrangement for surplus extraction that forms on the basis of the attained level of productivity has a secondary determining effect on the first process, that relating to the growth of productivity. This secondary determination noted by Marx, may stimulate people to exercise their ingenuity towards further improvement, or it may create conditions of life in which that is not something that people can easily encompass, or in which they will not on the whole benefit from it.

If the secondary determination reacts well on the first process, and people are able to act developmentally, then that process will move forward until a point is reached where a new form of surplus extraction, i.e. a new class (or non-class, as the case may be) formation becomes possible and in due course, since the old form and its classes cannot compete, actual. In more familiar language, now rendered almost unusable by the theoretical ravages of the *Short Course*[21] and its descendants, the productive forces have burst asunder the relations of production which had become a fetter upon them.

If, on the other hand, the effect (or secondary determination) of the surplus extracting class relation is, or becomes, inimical to development in productivity and methods of labour, then stagnation

---

[20] Cf. C. Renfrew, *Before Civilization*, Penguin (1976), 146ff., where, for example, the monuments of the southern end of the Isle of Arran have been explained in such a way.

[21] 'The Short Course' is the name by which one of the most notorious of the canonical documents of Stalinism has come to be known. Its full title is *The History of the Communist Party of the Soviet Union (Bolsheviks): Short Course*, edited by a Commission of the Central Committee of the CPSU (B), under the supervision of J.V. Stalin, and published in 1938. Its best known theoretical part is chapter four, part two, 'Dialectical and Historical Materialism'. But it contains many sections of great historical interest, such as chapter twelve, part four, 'Liquidation of the Remnants of the Bukharin-Trotsky Gang of Spies, Wreckers and Traitors to the Country', where we read that 'the trials brought to light the fact that the Trotsky-Bukharin fiends, in obedience to the wishes of their masters – the espionage services of foreign states – had set out to destroy the Party and the Soviet state ... these Whiteguard pigmies, whose strength was no more than that of a gnat, apparently flattered themselves that they were the masters of the country ... The Whiteguard insects forgot that the real masters of the Soviet country were the Soviet people, ... These contemptible lackeys of the fascists forgot that the Soviet people had only to move a finger, and not a trace of them would be left.'

and ultimate collapse of the class organism will be the most likely result. Basic productive activity will continue at the previous level of development while princedoms and dynasties come and go. In this process of change, conditions of relative stability and freedom may occur at intervals in which innovation may again be worth it and a class structure and political regime comes into being which provides sufficient stability in which people may innovate and develop with some purpose, the conditions giving them reason to do so rather than not to bother. This then accelerates the development of productivity towards the point where a new form of surplus extraction is possible and new classes begin to form.

Of the two abstract pictures drawn in the previous two paragraphs something like the second rather than the first seems nearer to the actual course of history in the Mediterranean and Western Europe since Antiquity. It would be ridiculous to try to argue this here, in relation to either the collapse of Antiquity or the development of feudalism into capitalism or both. The debates have been extensive, to say the least, and it is impossible even to review them. But, paraphrasing Dobb,[22] we must have some picture of how the historical movement moves, for without one we shall not get far in finding answers to the sort of questions that need answers, nor even in identifying what sorts of question we should be asking. To sketch such a picture is the object of Section iv of this chapter, 'Europe from debt-bondage to wage-labour'.

(iii) Contradiction: form and content

(a) In any form of society in which one class pumps surplus labour out of another, its overriding and perennial problem is to maintain control over the class from which the surplus labour is pumped.

In the first instance the history of such organisms is the history of the form of surplus labour extraction. But since strife is endemic to such social organisms, their history is at the same time the history of changes in the system of control from one form to another in response to challenge. When the extractors within the organism run out of options to meet challenges, or when the challenge is so resolute as to override whatever options are at hand, the history of that organism is at the end; the control fails, the organism's heart is arrested and no longer pumps surplus labour from one part to another. Keeping the thing together, i.e. keeping control, means ensuring that the concrete labour of certain humans continues to be

---

[22] *TFC*, 169.

supplied in the social form through which a surplus may be tapped, and the difficulty in doing that arises from the persistent friction that is generated between concrete labour and that social form of its supply. The fundamental history of the particular society (surplus extracting social organism) consists in the changes, developments or adaptations that are made to ease the friction, or to dampen it when it threatens to burst into flame.

The *casus belli* in the debate between Dobb, Sweezy, Procacci and others over the transition from feudalism to capitalism was Sweezy's adoption of the Pirenne 'hypothesis'.[23] What many found objectionable in that was that Pirenne-Sweezy gave primacy in explaining the transition to an 'external factor', namely the growth in trade with the Middle East. The cause of offence was not so much the identification of the growth of trade as the 'prime mover'; rather it lay in the perception of that proposed 'prime mover' as an *external* factor. The feeling of many who opposed Sweezy was that a proper (Marxist) explanation had to be in terms of aspects *internal* to the 'mode of production'. Dobb gave this feeling its most succinct expression. He complained that the Pirenne-Sweezy explanation ran contrary to what he understood to be 'the general Marxist law of development that economic society is moved by its own internal contradictions'.[24] Now this law of Dobb is open to more than one interpretation, and not all of them are free of contamination with *diamat*. That is another question. The point at issue here is a more straightforward one. Are we, or are we not, to agree that a 'driving contradiction' is the real basis of historical change and development, and that consequently the attainment of satisfactory and fundamental historical explanation lies in correctly identifying a 'driving contradiction'? There are not a few today who would both call themselves Marxist, and regard 'driving contradiction' as a cant phrase whose use is best avoided. Such qualms, I believe, betray the shakiest understanding of the very nature of Marx's thought, and an undue and old-fashioned deference to the now decomposed canon of analytical-positivist orthodoxy.

(b) Here we run into one of the cloudiest areas of Marx's dialectical thought: the question of *contradiction*. There is little point in pretending that the term 'contradiction', and the uses Marx makes of it, are limpidly clear. There is equally little point in pretending that the question can be completely clarified here, for

---

[23] See *TFC*.
[24] Ibid., 59.

there is a great amount of clarification required on many related topics before this issue can be straightened out. There is a major set of problems here needing attention. Some clearing of the ground is possible, however.

Marx was perfectly aware of the orthodox formal logical conception of contradiction as a relation between propositions. The principle of non-contradiction enjoins that not both *p* and not-*p*, where *p* is some proposition. He did not eschew formal logic and its principle of non-contradiction; on the contrary, he frequently uses it to ensnare his opponents and to expose their errors.[25] Dialectics, in his conception, is not a super-logic that surpasses formal logic, or supplants it, as some authors have suggested it to be. Indeed he explicitly warns against just such a conception when he writes to Engels on 1 February 1858 of Lassalle's Hegelian pretensions: 'He will learn to his cost, that it is one thing to develop a science to the point where one can present it dialectically, and something else altogether to apply an abstract and ready-made system of logic.'[26]

None the less, Marx choses to use the term 'contradiction' to designate something quite different from the familiar contradiction of formal logic,[27] and it would be silly to suppose that he had nothing more than trivial reasons for doing such a thing. Coming to see what those reasons might have been is part of coming to understand what he considers dialectical contradiction to be.

Some writers are inclined to say that the commodity-form contains a contradiction: that between use-value and exchange-value. This is then linked to 'the twofold nature of the labour embodied in commodities', namely, useful labour and abstract labour. Looking at it in this way is not altogether helpful, because it does not encourage realisation of the fact that the commodity-form of the product and the abstract form of social labour that produces it, have a historical process of coming-to-be, and do not spring into the living world in their fully developed forms. In *Results of the Immediate Process of Production* Marx writes that 'the

[25] I have argued this in 'Dialectical contradiction and necessity', in *IMP*, Vol. I (*Dialectics and Method*), 5-9.

[26] *MEW*, XXIX, 275. Just how the relation between formal logic and dialectics should be understood is another problem needing attention. Geoffrey Pilling has some valuable thoughts on the question, but unfortunately he continues with traditional question-begging by speaking of 'dialectical logic'. See his *Marx's 'Capital'*, London (1980), 38-40.

[27] I thus totally disagree, for reasons that will become clear below, with the judgment of Jon Elster that 'the most important occurrences of the term (sc. 'contradiction') in the writings of Marx lend themselves to an interpretation in terms of ordinary everyday logic'. See Elster's *Logic and Society*, NY (1978), 65.

formal subsumption of labour under capital' is 'the universal form of every capitalist process of production'. He then, however, says that this formal subsumption, and capitalist production, can exist 'in the absence of the specifically capitalist mode of production'. He explains how this can be possible by contrasting the merely 'formal subsumption' with 'the real subsumption of labour under capital'. This *real* subsumption is the reconstitution the labour process, and of society, in accordance with the requirement of the self-expansion process of capital.[28] The point is obvious: it is possible, indeed it is necessary, to have individual capitalist production processes conducted in society, before society as a whole has been revolutionarily reconstituted on the basis of value.

Within this point about development, however, there lies a theoretical point. It is only when there is fully developed exchangeability (cf. Chapter 6 (iii) below), fully developed circulation and a production process fully recomposed by capital with its unbridled division of labour free from all customary constraint, that there can *be* abstract labour. The development of capital and of abstract labour goes *pari passu* with the development of the bourgeoisie and the proletariat. Thus, the contradiction of useful labour and abstract labour itself has a process of coming-to-be, just as the classes do.

This leaves us with the appearance of a problem: does the contradiction already exist before the full development of abstract labour, or does it only really arrive with the arrival of fully developed abstract labour? Some of Marx's locutions seemed designed to accommodate the apparent difficulty presented by the fact that the contradiction itself has a development. Thus he writes of the commodity-form having an 'immanent contradiction', and of this contradiction having 'developed forms of motion', namely, 'the antithetical phases of the metamorphoses of the commodity'.[29] This suggests that the contradiction is a constitutive part of the inherent nature of something (in this case the commodity-form), which, as the thing develops, expresses itself in the behaviour of the thing in different ways; as it behaves in its coming-to-be, as it operates in its mature form, and as it declines and interpenetrates with what supersedes it. This does seem close to the way Marx thought of the matter. We noted earlier, in Chapter 3 (ii), that Marx considered that the more developed forms of the commodity-form provided the more articulated conditions in which the elementary *constitutive*

---

[28] *Cap.* I, Pelican, 1019ff.
[29] Ibid, 209.

contradiction of the commodity form itself can find expression in even more developed ways: 'We saw in a former chapter that the exchange of commodities implies contradictory and mutually exclusive conditions. The further development of the commodity does not abolish these contradictions, but rather provides the form within which they have room to move.'[30]

Further light is shed by Marx's idea of an 'absolute contradiction'. This expression is met with in his discussion of the development of money beyond its function as means of circulation into a means of payment. He says that within this new function there is a new 'contradiction immanent' which '*bursts forth* in that aspect of a commercial and industrial crisis which is known as a monetary crisis ... money suddenly and immediately changes over from its merely nominal shape, money on account, into hard cash. Profane commodities can no longer replace it, the use-value of commodities becomes valueless, and their value vanishes in the face of their own form of value ... In a crisis, the antithesis between commodities and their value form, money, is raised to the level of an *absolute contradiction*.'[31]

The 'immanent contradiction', then, is something which is essential to and (at least partly) constitutive of a real nature or essence (a unity), such that the nature in question *is*, definitionally, that immanent contradiction. The immanent contradiction itself is the necessary co-presence (unity) of the two elements or poles that are actively or potentially antagonistic (opposites). 'Opposites' are those elements that form an immanent contradiction which is constitutive of the nature or essence of such a contradictory and complex unitary entity.

The life of such an entity or essence is the life of its contradiction. As the entity grows and develops in the course of its life, and as its complexity-in-unity increases, so the room for the expression of its immanent contradiction increases. As the entity attains its more developed forms, they in turn embody further contradictions. These, however, all derive from the original immanent contradiction. Thus Marx can write: 'There is an antithesis, immanent in the commodity, between use-value and value ...; the antithetical phases of the metamorphosis of the commodity are the developed forms of motion of this immanent contradiction.'[32] Here we can begin to see the basis for an account of a dialectical law: the law of the normal life of the entity or essence is the law of the unfolding of its

[30] Ibid., 198.
[31] Ibid., 235-6 (italics added).
[32] Ibid. 209.

constitutive contradiction.

In this sort of way, I believe, it should be possible to clarify satisfactorily what a 'driving contradiction' is; how such a thing does lie at the basis of historical change and development in a complex and contradictory entity such as a class society; and consequently how tracking down such a driving contradiction is the key to the satisfactory explanation of such historical change and development.

An 'absolute contradiction' is a condition in which the opposites, which compose the contradiction constitutive of the essential unity, pull apart from each other and cease to interpenetrate. The meditations holding them together in the unity break down, leaving each of them free and independent, bringing the life process of the whole entity to a standstill. (This is gone into in detail by Marx in his treatment of crisis. Indeed, his working use of the dialectical categories under discussion here is richly represented in the sections on crises,[33] and they are crucial passages for study by anyone seeking to carry matters further and deeper than I manage to do here.)

Marx's dialectical contradictions are, therefore, ontological and not propositional. That is to say, they have to do with *being*, and in particular with identifying and specifying the essence and typical life-process of particular kinds of beings. They do not have to do with the formal logical relations between propositions. Marx knew perfectly well that the point of formal logic is that it is *formal*; that is, that all considerations of *content* are set aside. Marx's contradictions are not formal.[34] On the contrary, they are arrived at by an investigation of material and historical *content*. Once arrived at, their value is that they reveal the real essences which lie beneath appearances. Their behaviour *is* what the perceived empirical phenomena, semi-analysed appearances, statistics, etc., really are. It is in virtue of this that they explain. They give the essence of some entity. That is what it means to say that they are ontological.

It is now possible to evaluate one traditional line of criticism of Marx, in all its incomprehension and superficiality. This is the line of Bortkiewicz (he has had many followers) who writes: 'We find in Marx the perverse desire to project logical contradictions on to objects themselves, in the manner of Hegel.'[35] Marx, following in

---

[33] *TSV* II, 492-535.

[34] This bears on the question of whether there can be, for Marx, any such thing as a 'dialectical logic'. I have argued that there cannot be, in 'Dialectical Contradiction and Necessity', in *IMP*, Vol. I, esp. pp. 9-14. The question is a large one, and needs much more thought.

[35] 'Value and price in the Marxian system', *International Economic Papers*, no. 2 (1952), originally published in German in 1907.

the tradition of Aristotle, Hegel and others, has developed a framework of categories adequate to deal with the ancient problem of 'the one and the many' (which so exercised the Greeks), and the problem of 'unity in difference', not to mention the problems of coming to understand the motions of market society. Bortkiewicz reacts like a pretentious philosophical novice when presented with such a category framework. His criticism, and all the others of its kind, are not based upon any serious intellectual considerations of what they have before them, but upon ignorance of the depth of what is involved. Not being especially well informed about the philosophical presuppositions and principles of his own general position, quite ignorant of those upon which Marx's position is based, and *a fortiori* unaware of where and how the two philosophical bases collide, he thus has all the necessary preparation behind him to plough merrily ahead with the tedious, familiar and incomprehending middle-brow criticism, as many have done since and continue to do to this day.

(c) The driving contradiction in capitalist society is that contradiction which is definitional of the value-form, viz. the contradiction between the form and content of the commodity-form. This contradiction is immanent in the value-form *per se* even in its primitive beginnings. It acquires its most vital social expression, however, and becomes the driving contradiction of society, when the form of supply of human social labour itself comes to adopt the value-form in becoming the commodity wage-labour: that is to say, with the arrival of market economy or capitalism. The contradiction is then fully developed into that between human social labour *per se* and its value-creating form.

This 'driving contradiction', however, is only the specific form taken within market society, of a more general form of driving contradiction that powers the movement of any form of class society. For the history of any surplus-extracting class society is the history of the friction between concrete human labour and the particular surplus-creating social form in which it is confined. The essence of the particular social organism consists in the enforced unity of those two things, which, however, can never really be reconciled, but only held together by force or by forms of mediation. The enforced unity of such opposites is the home of what Marx calls a *contradiction*. The driving contradiction of a social organism, the source of its history and the reason why is *has* a history, is identical with its real essence. For what it *is* is the co-presence, *necessary* to (=essentially constitutive of) that specific form of organism, of two elements that are *necessarily* opposed. What the extractors seek to do is to maintain the contradiction in some form; the other side of the class struggle is that the suppliers of surplus labour are constantly challenging the contradiction, forcing changes in its form and occasionally seeking to abolish it.

That is why Marx divided the world history of class extraction of the surplus into the two great social forms or epochs noted earlier in Chapter 4 (i): the epoch of the extraction of surplus labour through 'relations of personal dependence', and the epoch of such extraction through relations of 'personal independence founded on objective dependence'. *The driving contradiction in societies of either form is that between concrete labour and the form of its supply for surplus extraction* (not necessarily the same as the way the bulk of production is done). For capitalism, the essential contradiction is between concrete labour and its abstract form; for pre-capitalism it is between concrete labour and its unfree form. This is the theoretical core of Marx's view that history *is* the history of class struggle.

De Ste. Croix has begun to recover that view after its loss for several decades, and it lies at the heart of his *Class Struggle in the Ancient Greek World*. In basing his account on the extraction of surplus labour, he is basing himself on class struggle. He reminds us that 'on 17/18 September 1897 Marx and Engels – thinking back to the *Communist Manifesto* and beyond – wrote to Bebel, Liebknecht and others: "For almost forty years we have stressed the class struggle as the immediate driving power of history." '[36]

(d) It is sometimes thought that on Marx's account of the commodity-form, the form itself is a unity of opposites; that the essence of the commodity-form is the unity of use-value and exchange-value, together with the fact that the relation between use-value and exchange-value is contradictory. This way of putting it could be misleading. It suggests that the contradiction inherent in the commodity-form lies in the *content* of that form, which in turn will be construed as two poles that constitute the unity, viz. use-value and exchange-value. This seems an unhelpful way of looking at it.

The contradiction is better located between the form and the content. On this view we should have to say that the *content* is the use-value,[37] the simple product of human labour, and the *form* is its

---

[36] *CSAGW*, 47.

[37] Rosdolsky draws attention to the misreading of the *Contribution* which has lead Hilferding, Sweezy and others to consider that use-value lies outside political economy. He points out that in Marxian political economy use-value plays a more significant role than in previous economics because 'use-value itself – as the use-value of a "commodity" – possesses a historically specific character' notably in its role in the relation between the relative and equivalent forms of value. The point makes no

exchangeability. A thing's having the value-form, or commodity-form, is simply its having the socially and historically acquired quality of exchangeability (see Chapter 6 (iii) below). Thus, we should not say that the unity that constitutes the value- or commodity-form is a unity between two poles of its content, exchange-value and use-value. We should say that the unity constitutive of its nature is one of content and form: its being a use-value and its taking the value-form. Its inherently contradictory nature lies not within its content, but between its content and its form, and its unitary nature lies in this unity of form and content.

It is necessary to analyse the commodity-form in this way, if we are to avoid detaching its reality as a historical form of the product of labour, from the basis that explains how the product can assume such a form, viz. the social form of supply of labour. The contradictory nature of the commodity-form is no more than an expression in terms of the product of labour, of that fact that the labour producing it is twofold in nature: its content is actual concrete labour, and its form is the social form in which it is supplied for the extraction of surplus labour (which in its developed form is abstract labour). Marx identifies 'the contradiction immanent in the commodity' as one 'between use-value and value'; and he immediately glosses this as the contradiction 'between private labour which must simultaneously manifest itself as directly social labour, and a particular concrete kind of labour which simultaneously counts as merely abstract universal labour'.[38] Thus the contradictory nature of the commodity-form, together with all the further contradictions that arise with its later and more developed forms (including crisis) can be seen to have their basis in the driving contradiction of the society: that between labour and the form of its supply for surplus extraction.

(e) It is necessary to distinguish 'immanent contradictions' from the *actualisation of contradictions*. The former have to do with the form and content that constitutes the essence of something. The contradictory nature of something, however, is quite a different matter from the actualisations or realisations of that constitutive contradiction as they occur in the life-process or *ergon* of the entity. These episodes in the life of the entity are consequences or necessary

---

difference to my argument here, and it is mentioned only to obviate possible confusion. The quote cited by Rosdolsky in *TMMC* 76, is from *Marginal Notes on A. Wagner, MEW*, XIX, 371.

[38] *Cap.* I, Pelican, 209.

expressions of its being of a contradictory nature. They are realisations of the nature of the entity, or more precisely they are realisations of the immanent contradiction constitutive of that nature. They are what they are because of the nature of the immanent contradiction, and their occurrences arise from it. Obviously it is not all the myriad actualisations of the immanent contradiction that are constitutive of the nature of the value-form.

Marx's view seems to be that the immanent or constitutive contradiction represents not only the nature of the entity, but also the *potential* for the contradiction's own actualisation, as the occurrence of *actualised* contradictions in the subsequent life of the entity. The fact that an entity is in its nature contradictory shows itself in the fact that in the development and life-process of that entity it suffers episodes of crisis arising from that contradiction. Because it, has a constitutive contradiction in its nature, it is prone in its life to suffer such episodes. This is to reaffirm in another way the suggestion made in (b) above, that the life-process of such an entity is the life of its contradiction.

Caution is necessary with Marx's term 'potential contradiction'. That a contradiction is potential does not mean that it might not come to pass, or that if it does then it does so only accidentally or as a matter of chance. To say that the contradiction constitutive of the entity is also the potential for the occurrence of actual contradictions (including 'absolute contradictions'), is to say that it is in the nature of the entity that its typical life-process will be marked by the occurrence of such actual contradictions. It is not a matter of accident that a thing's potentialities are realised; on the contrary, it is in principle a matter of necessity. A truly miraculous matter of chance would be that such a contradictory entity might live its life without realising its potential. That, indeed, would be impossible, for it would mean that it was not living its life; or not living.

It is true that in some parts of his writings on crises Marx appears, or may be thought, to give more weight to the contingent or accidental than he does to the necessary and essential. He writes that the separation of (or contradiction between) sale and purchase, the contradiction inherent in money as means of payment, etc., 'are merely *forms*, general possibilities of crisis, and hence also forms, abstract forms of actual crisis'. And he goes further: 'These forms alone ... do not explain ... why the potential contradiction contained in them becomes a real contradiction.'[39] 'In investigating why the general *possibility of crisis* turns into a *real* crisis ... it is ... quite

---

[39] *TSV* II, 512.

superfluous to concern oneself with the forms of crisis ... This is precisely why economists like to suggest that this *obvious* form is the *cause* of crises ... But it cannot be said that the *abstract form of crisis* is the *cause of crisis* If one asks what its cause is, one wants to know why *its abstract form*, the forms of its possibility, turns from possibility into actuality'.[40]

This hard-headed insistence, as against the economists, on delving beneath the obvious forms in order to find the real cause, even though that might be something contingent like a bad harvest, can be misunderstood. It would be misunderstood if it were thought to be a theoretical retreat in the search for explanation, from the necessary or essential and back into 'the wealth of contingent factors'. The truth is the reverse. This becomes clear when Marx complains 'how insipid the economists are who, when they are no longer able to explain away the phenomena of overproduction and crises, are content to say that these forms contain the possibility of *crises*, that it is therefore *accidental* whether or not crises occur and consequently this occurrence is itself merely a matter of chance'.[41]

Moreover, natural disasters such as bad harvests logically cannot of themselves cause capitalist crises. The occurrence of a capitalist crisis requires a capitalist system in being – a condition that is by no means provided by the occurrence of natural disasters. This consideration is hardly one Marx would have been likely to overlook. The immediate cause of crisis may be a contingency, but the explanation of its occasioning a (specifically capitalist) crisis of the system must lie in the nature of the system. That is where Marx seeks his explanation: 'The *general conditions* of crisis ... must be explicable from the general conditions of capitalist production.'[42] The heading of the entire section §10 is: 'Crisis, which was a contingency, becomes a certainty. The crisis as a manifestation of all the contradictions of bourgeois economy.'[43]

In terms of commodity-producing society as a whole, the fundamental source of all contradiction lies in 'the twofold character of the labour embodied in commodities', that is, between the concrete labours of producers and the social form in which they are supplied for surplus-labour extraction, viz. abstract labour. The occurrence of a crisis, that is, the empirical refutation of Say's Law, is the realisation of the possibility of contradiction between the opposites, concrete labour and its abstract form, whose unity constitutes the specific form of the surplus labour-extracting class

[40] Ibid., 515.
[41] Ibid., 512.
[42] Ibid., 515.
[43] Ibid., 507.

organism. A crisis is the clearest possible manifestation of the independence of the form and the content, and at the same time of their unity within the system. Though Marx's discussion of crisis in Chapter XVII of *TSV* II is mainly in terms of the metamorphoses of commodities, of sale and purchase coming asunder, and of the impossibility to sell, it really comes down to the contradiction between concrete labour and its abstract form of supply. (Things are not really so very different under other surplus-extracting organisms, or what some would want to call 'modes of production'. Even for societies based on dependent labour, feudalism for instance, one can speak just as well of 'the twofold character of labour' as one can for society based on the production of values. The twofold character is simply transparent: subsistence labour on the plot and *corvée* labour on the *demesne*.)

(iv) Europe from debt-bondage to wage-labour

The ancient class organism was the city-state with slave and peasant production, and finally production by serfs. The potential for development, and the line of development of this organism was not such as could easily lead to the development of those higher methods of labour and productivity that would usher in the capital-form and its new form of surplus extraction. Rather, its line of development was towards something that would have to disappear before such a transition might become possible, viz. an imperial system.

In pre-Solonian Athens the landed aristocratic families extracted the surplus in significant part through the debt-bondage of Athenians, and it was the class struggles around this that principally produced the Solonian reforms. This, in turn, led to the greater use of chattel slaves from foreign sources. The main focus of political and institutional development from this point was similar to that of republican Rome, which Marx characterised as 'the struggle of small versus large landed property specifically modified, of course, by slave conditions' (Marx to Engels, 8 March 1855). This *stasis* was widely reproduced throughout the Greek cities, and when, in order to relieve the strife, a daughter colony was established elsewhere with land allocations to the troublesome poor free of the mother city, the same classes and the same *stasis* were reproduced, often within a generation or two of the foundation.[44]

[44] In the first pages of this section I have relied on various works, but I have relied heavily on de Ste. Croix's *The Origins of the Peloponnesian War*, London (1972) and on his *CSAGW*. I have drawn conclusions, in part from his work, about which I am confident he would wish, at the very least, to reserve judgment.

In Athens by the 460s a radical form of compromise was reached in which the *dêmos* was given a share in power without drastically jeopardising the essential supremacy of large landed property, and which provided an institutional form (democracy) within which the *stasis* between large and small landed property could largely be contained and which relegated the awful danger of either side being driven to call upon the slaves for support, a danger which still existed even though the slave mass tended increasingly to become a polyglot assemblage drawn from far and wide and thus lacked cohesion. This form was reproduced in various forms elsewhere within the Greek world in the period before the Peloponnesian war, for its advantages naturally recommended themselves to the many states whose development produced the same sort of *stasis* that had originally produced it as a solution at Athens. This tendency was strengthened by the rise of Athens towards being the Hellenic *hêgemôn*, though that is a further line of development of the ancient social organism to which we must return shortly.

Not all the states took the Athenian path, of course. Where conditions favoured them local obligarchies resisted making such concessions to the *dêmos*. In this they were usually able to look to Sparta for moral, or more material, support. For Sparta, the socio-historical freak of Antiquity, no development was possible because of her uniquely deformed class nature, and the spread of the Athenian solution was a grave threat to that. The Spartan unfree population were descendants of a *polis*, Messenia, that had been conquered and enslaved as a totality. They had a common language and culture, and continuously nursed aspirations to re-establish their own *polis*. They were a social time-bomb, and the entire internal development of Sparta was conditioned by the fact. Everything in Spartan life was subject to the overriding need to contain a uniquely dangerous helot population. The imminence of the real and perceived danger is amply revealed in the fact that each year the ephors declared war on their own servile population, so that should Spartan citizens need to shed helot blood, they might do so without incurring religious pollution. The total militarisation of Spartan citizen life was the specific adaptation required for the unusual form of the problem of control over unfree labour that characterised Sparta. That form of life was unadaptable, since it was adapted to a single condition that would not go away, and consequently any further form of development represented a threat to the essential militarisation. This adaptation made Sparta initially militarily powerful in comparison with other states that were achieving a more rounded development, and even made her *hêgemôn* over a period. Yet while she was *hêgemôn*, visiting embassies were often astounded at the primitiveness of the citizens and their life, the absence of any substantial building, the inferiority of the culture, and so forth. Since almost any change represented a threat to the class structure, there were no internal developments, and those that arose outside, such as money, were resisted.[45] Spartans, when abroad, were notorious for their avarice and for their desire for the good things of life which were available in more normally developed states.

It has been compelling argued by de Ste. Croix that the origins of the Peloponnesian war lay with Sparta, rather than with Athens as has been the commoner view. In the light of the fatal threat to Spartan social relations posed by the progressive extension of the Athenian democratic solution to the combined problem of the *stasis* between rich and poor free and of control of servile populations, de Ste. Croix's account is already the more plausible even before he goes into detailed analysis of the evidence. The conjecture might reasonably be hazarded that the Spartan 'hawks' who favoured war were the more clear-sighted, and that possibly they recognised in some way that there was a social process working its way through the Hellenic states to which they could never adapt and with which they could not co-exist, and that consequently only two possibilities existed: either that the process be halted, or that Sparta go under. At any rate, the Spartans were able to overcome Hellenic chauvinism, and, when the need was greatest, to use alliance with the pan-hellenic enemy, Persia, as the final means to put an end to that process. In doing so, the conditions were prepared for the advance of Macedonia, and eventually for the Roman imposition. Whatever tendency, or potential for development, towards a higher level of commodity production and circulation might have been latent in the Hellenic *klein Staaterei* was killed. If there was such potential, then the furious struggle put up by the irremediably backward, maladaptive and sterile Spartan social freak to prolong its own form of existence was a crucial element in the non-realisation of that potential. (Perhaps it is not altogether implausible to see a parallel with the USSR today: an ossified, maladaptive, socio-historical freak with no potential for further development within itself, acting as major contributing agency in the frustration of progressive change outside.)

However, there is reason to doubt the existence of any great potential for a higher development of commodity production and circulation. There is evidence, largely negative, that the surplus

[45] See J.K. Davies, *Democracy and Classical Greece*, London (1978), 55.

extracting class mechanism of Antiquity was unfavourable to development of technique and methods of labour.[46] In addition, there was another tendency of development of the antique class organism, mentioned at the end of the paragraph before last, working in the same direction. The *klein Staaterei* made inevitable the formation of defensive or offensive alliances, and at the same time geographical and social facts made it inevitable that certain states would tend to become dominant in such alliances, and that dominance had the potential to develop into something else. Athens, for example, developed from being a *primus inter pares* in such an alliance to being a recipient of what amounted to tribute, and to having a significant hand in the domestic politics of certain allied states, even to the point, in the case of Chalcis, of insisting that court cases of a political nature involving possible loss of citizen rights be heard in Athens rather than in the city concerned.[47] Rome and not Athens was finally to realise the fullest form of this tendency.

When it was realised, the imperial system taxed the regions and cities, so tending to reproduce those cities as centres of imperial administration and revenue-gathering. This was not conducive to their own local development, and it left them and their indigenous citizens little control over the surplus or incentive or room for development. Consequently, the imperial system that was an extension of the *klein Staaterei* of city states was a brake on the development of methods of labour and productivity. For the latter process of development to resume, and thus for the attainment of the higher forms of value, the imperial system had to go. The major tendencies or lines of development of the ancient class organism were inimical to any great extension of petty commodity production, and thus to the development of capital, which, as Marx observed, grows only on the tomb of the former and nowhere else. That class organism offered little to the peasants who were the bulk of the direct producers, and came to offer even less when, after the period of

[46] See M.I. Finley, 'Technical innovation and economic progress in the Ancient World', in *Economic History Review*, 18 (1965), 29-45. The state of the debate seems unsatisfactory. Finley, of course, argues that innovation and progress were slight. Yet he thinks 'there was a more or less continuous rise in population, probably throughout the first century after Christ', but makes little or no effort to explain how this could have been possible without some development of the kind he is concerned to deny or minimise. H.W. Pleket considers some evidence of improvement ('Technology in the Graeco-Roman world: a general report', *Talanta* V (1973) 6-47), but his discussion of it is unilluminating. J. Kalendo has argued for a 'technological revolution' in Roman agriculture between 100 B.C. and 100 A.D., *Acta Poloniae Historica* 18 (1968) and *Archeologia* 22 (1971).

[47] Davies, op. cit., 85

large-scale chattel-slavery, the ruling class inevitably directed their attentions as surplus extractors upon the peasants in the first three centuries A.D. (This course was always there as a possibility, but it was not fully realised so long as the peasant surplus was small or non-existent or too hazardous and costly to collect, and so long as the slave option was adequate.) When, finally, the 'barbarians' arrived to threaten the empire, the agricultural population could not have cared less, or even welcomed the change.[48]

With the decline of the Empire in the fifth, sixth and seventh centuries, little or nothing was lost of the productive methods and levels of technique that had been achieved. Just as people, the direct producers, seek to improve themselves and their lives when conditions of surplus extraction or insecurity do not make it pointless, so they throw nothing away without reason. Gordon Childe noted that the real basis of culture 'was no more annihilated by the collapse of the Roman empire than smaller accumulations had been in the lesser catastrophes that interrupted and terminated the bronze age. Of course, as then, many refinements ... were swept away. But for the most part these had been designed for, and used by, only a small and narrow class ... Most crafts were still plied with all the technical skill and equipment evolved in Classical and Hellenistic times.'[49] Lynn White has concluded that 'there is no proof that any important skills of the Graeco-Roman world were lost during the Dark Ages even in the unenlightened west'.[50] With 'methods of labour' and 'production itself' still intact, and the social integument of Antiquity gone, the process of development of productivity gathered pace in the new conditions and 'from the twelfth and even from the eleventh century there was a rapid replacement of human by non-human energy wherever great quantities of power were needed or where the required motion was so simple and monotonous that a man could be replaced by a mechanism'.[51]

Several of the contributors to the debate occasioned by Sweezy's reply to Dobb's *Studies in the Development of Capitalism* placed emphasis on this development of technique in their accounts of the rise of the market, and of the market-regulated society of capitalism, out of west European feudalism. Dobb's final contribution seems to lean more

[48] De Ste. Croix, *CSAGW*, ch. VIII (iii).

[49] V. Gordon Childe, *What Happened in History*, Pelican (1942 and repr.), 250.

[50] Lynn White, 'Technology and invention in the Middle Ages' in *Speculum* 15 (1940) 150; now largely replaced by his paper in Vol. 1 of the *Fontana Economic History of Europe*.

[51] Ibid., 156.

decisively in this direction than it had earlier in the debate against the Pirenne-Sweezy position. And Rodney Hilton stressed the importance of the increased control of the (increased) surplus by the direct producers, which, together with other things, gave further incentives to improved technique, which in turn intensified the differentiation of the peasantry into rich and poor, thus advancing the capital/wage labour relation.[52]

Although the debate tended to concentrate rather less on the earlier development of petty commodity production and circulation, and rather more on the transition to bourgeois relations, the general line of explanation offered by Dobb and Hilton was a powerful one.

What fundamentally powered the formation of new classes was the diffusion of technique, the new methods of labour and their higher social productivity. On top of that, accidental circumstances conspired to put peasant economy in a favourable position to fight with the lords and other extractors over the control of the surplus; the plague in particular was efficacious in this respect. The importance of the visitations of the plague, however, can be exaggerated. They seem best judged as a major but accidental accelerator of processes that were already under way. (Trotsky's observation is apt, that the 'historical process is a refraction of the historical law through the accidental'.)[53] Thus the *corvée* was already in decline by the time of the first visitation of the plague in 1349, and had largely gone by the end of the century;[54] the monetisation of relations must have had a secure hold before the plague for it to be possible for the lords to respond to the consequences the plague had for them by pursuing 'the monetary possibilities of the lord's right over customary tenants'.[55] Moreover the implication of national wage regulation after the plague would seem firm indication that a substantial proportion of labour was already supplied in the form of wage-labour.

The basis of movement was the availability of technique which allowed the peasantry to sustain its position with respect to the surplus, and to advance it over time with the increasing circulation of products in the commodity-form. Had such technique not been available, and had commodity production and circulation been correspondingly limited, the struggle over the lesser surplus would most likely have attained only the dimensions of a *political* struggle

[52] There is a little more on this in my brief 'Marxist theory and the history of the Communist movement', *Critique* 10-11 (1979).

[53] L. Trotsky, *My Life*, Pelican (1975), 515.

[54] R. Hilton, *The English Peasantry in the Later Middle Ages*, Oxford (1975), 59.

[55] Ibid., 58.

within feudalism and between *its* classes. The outcome could only have been a revitalisation of the powers of predation of the lords should things have gone their way, or a modification of the system should things have gone in favour of the subordinate. What imparted to the class struggle within feudalism the dimensions of a social revolution was, to return to the initial passage from *Capital* III, the 'definite stage in the development of the methods of labour and thereby its social productivity'.

The struggle was essentially between different ways of extracting the surplus, and hence two different forms of supply of social labour. The inability of the ruling class to extract, or to increase the extraction, of the surplus (or, looking at it the other way round, the successful resistance of the peasants, and their occasional allies such as the esquires, to the extraction), left more disposable surplus within peasant economy. Peasants were therefore able, and had incentive, to apply and develop new technique. Market economy, the production and circulation of commodities, grew, and English feudalism was inadequate to the task of preventing or drastically inhibiting it.

On the contrary, the need of the lords to counter falling revenues led them to adopt methods for increasing revenue which contributed directly to undermining the very class arrangement in which they were the extractors of the surplus. For example, with the servile refusing service, landowners were forced to take on hired labour. This added to the development of wage-labour, and at the same time increased the already growing need of the lord for money. Not unnaturally another tendency arose for the commutation to money payments of customary 'fines' for permissions to marry and so on, heriots and labour service; and a further tendency for landowners to lease out all or part of their *demesnes*.

In short, in order to sustain themselves as a ruling and surplus extracting class, they were driven in various ways to contribute both (1) to the undermining of the specific forms of surplus extraction upon which they were constituted as the exploiting class, and (2) to the development of the new forms of surplus extraction and hence to the revolutionary class recomposition of society. The very relations that were in the process of being superseded were themselves, therefore, the medium, in which the new forms and relations spontaneously developed and moved. Although, from the viewpoint of later development, the old relations appear as (and were) barriers to the new, they were at the same time the medium of the coming-to-be of capital. Marx said as much: 'These limits became barriers only after the forces of production and the relations of intercourse had developed sufficiently to enable capital as such to emerge as the dominant principle of production.'[56]

The general picture of the forces operating is reminiscent of that 'drive' which Marx describes as forging restlessly ahead in conditions of elementary commodity circulation until an independent form of value, money, is attained. Here also, so many part-processes were going on which imparted the dimensions of a 'drive' of the money form towards the capital form. The superiority of the new mode of surplus extraction was asserting itself, as Preobrazhensky described it, in molecular fashion at points throughout the society;[57] the old modes of surplus extraction were powerless to compete, were compelled to adapt in order to continue in any form at all, and in due course came to constitute within the developed capitalism the peculiar rent form examined by Marx in volume three of *Capital*

The historical process throughout has been the formation of classes on the basis of the form of surplus extraction 'corresponding to a definite stage in the development of methods of labour and thereby its social productivity', and the working through of the potentials of those class organisms in the process of class struggle. Once capitalist relations are attained, however, the form in which the class struggle exists and asserts itself changes dramatically. This is necessarily concomitant with the quite new forms taken by the laws of this human social organism, compared with those of previous ones.

To begin with, the general process, underlying Marx's view, in which people seek to improve their lives when they can, insofar as it relates to technique and productivity, now takes the form of an 'objective' law of an 'objective' economic system. With the new form of supply of human social labour, embodied in the circuit of industrial capital (in which the men·and women of the producing population are dignified as 'LP')

$$M - C \overset{\nearrow MP}{\underset{\searrow LP}{}} \ ... P ... C - M$$

with 'the reciprocal compulsion which the capitals within it practise upon one another, on labour, etc. (the competition among workers is only another form of the competition among capitals)',[58] the relations between individual capitals and the relations between

[56] *Gr.*, 650.
[57] E. Preobrazhensky, *The New Economics*, Oxford (1965 and rept.), 82 int. al.
[58] *Gr.*, 651.

capital and wage-labour force the process of increasing the relative surplus ahead at breakneck speed. The increasing productivity aspect of the human endeavour to improve becomes a function of capital and of the class of capitalists, and at a certain point becomes contradictory because the surplus extracting class relation makes the fruits of improvement potential rather than actual for the direct producers. (Though as technique advances and labour becomes increasingly co-operative, both at the level of the individual enterprise and internationally, the potential for direct appropriation of the surplus by the direct producers becomes an increasingly realisable potentiality.)

Furthermore, the mode of social control changes. There is no need to labour the familiar point that all previous surplus-extracting class relations were transparent, and the surplus extractors maintained the subordination of the surplus producers largely, if not altogether, by direct force operating through 'law'. Under the law of value, the exploitative class relation becomes opaque; ostensibly the categories and relations of the economy appear 'natural', in fact they are historical with a fetish appearance as natural. At the level of appearance, subordination in the form of legal bondage is overcome, and the direct producer is legally free; but only to become, in Marx's terms, 'objectively' dependent within a market economy which operates systematically to the disadvantage of the worker.

> It is not individuals who are set free by free competition; it is, rather, capital which is set free. As long as production resting on capital is the necessary, hence the fittest form for the development of the force of social production, the movement of individuals within the pure conditions of capital appears as their freedom; which is then also again dogmatically propounded as such through constant reflection back on the barriers torn down by free competition.[59]

The truth of the latter comment has held to the present day. Devotees of market economy seem never to tire of reminding us proudly that slavery was abolished.

(It is such an appearance of freedom that von Hayek, and other anachronistic heralds of the market such as Friedman and Rawls, are concerned to uphold. They are greatly assisted in their chosen tasks by the disastrous aftermath of 1917, 'socialism in one country', which has numbed the human imagination, and hindered the aspiration of many workers in advanced countries for any higher

[59] *Gr.*, 650.

form of freedom.)

Capital is, as we have seen, the final form of a real nature. And the form of society corresponding to capital has laws of *ergon* and development in a way that previous social organisms did not. With human labour socially supplied under the value-form, as a commodity, its social character is transferred to its own product, and we have 'material relations between persons and social relations between things'; 'a definite social relation between men, that assumes, in their eyes, the fantastic form of a relation between things'.[60] Thus, the laws of *ergon* and the social development of the class organism appear in the fantastic form of law-like relations between the categories of political economy and their magnitudes. When the forces of production and the relations of intercourse have developed sufficiently to enable capital as such to emerge as the dominant principle of production, 'the inner laws of capital – which appear merely as tendencies in the preliminary historic stages of its development – are for the first time posited as laws; production founded on capital for the first time posits itself in the forms adequate to it ...'[61]

[60] *Cap.*I, Moscow, 78, 77.
[61] *Gr.* 650.

6
History as Change and History as Progress

(i) Necessities in the historical process

Chapter 1 began with the complaint that Marxists had, whether through oversight or dereliction, neglected the category of necessity. We now have, it seems, a super-abundance of necessities.

In the analysis of Marx's conception of the historical process we have found necessity operating at four levels.

(a) The primary level is the indubitable, if rather indefinite, tendency of human beings to improve their lives and themselves where and when they can.[1] This tendency we saw not to be a function of human 'individuals', nor a function of 'society' considered as a totality abstracted from and set above human individuals. Marx warned against 'once more establishing "society" as an abstraction over and against the individual. The individual *is* the *social being*.'[2] Rather, it is a tendency that is both individual and social, and its being both is a consequence of Marx's conception of the specific kind of mammal human beings are, our specific 'species being' or *Gattungswesen*; we are 'not merely a gregarious animal, but an animal which can individuate itself only in the midst of society'.[3] Moreover, the realisation of the fully developed nature or *telos* of the human species ('the realisation ... of this essence as something real'),[4] is at the same time the realisation of the *telos* of society as something real, an organism whose constituents are themselves whole organisms, namely, human beings. The full realisation of the essence of society is identical with the full realisation of the essence of man as a mammalian species whose *differentia specifica* is to be social.[5]

[1] See Chapter 2 (v) (c) (4) above.
[2] *EPM*, 350.
[3] *Gr.*, 84.
[4] Ibid., 395.
[5] See Chapter 2 (v) (c) (3) above.

(b) In the improvement of life the most decisive aspect is the development of the 'methods of labour' or the level of productivity. This fundamental insight was appreciated in the original Marxist tradition, and Trotsky exemplified it clearly in writing that: 'Every class society has been formed on the basis of definite modes of struggle with nature, and these modes have changed in accordance with the development of technique. What is the basis of bases – the class organisation of society or its productive forces? Without doubt the productive forces. It is precisely upon them, at a certain level of development, that classes are formed and reformed.'[6] Productiveness of methods of labour governs the formation of the class organism, and the development of such productiveness governs its transformation into another class organism. It thus governs the form of supply of social labour and with it the mode of surplus extraction. (On the other hand, it should not be overlooked that there is a 'secondary determination' of class structure back upon the methods of labour and 'production itself'; this was discussed in Chapter 5 (ii) above).

(c) The third layer of necessity exists in the specific class organism, or forms of control and extraction of the surplus, that come into existence. These social organisms have their own potentialities and limitations which constitute necessities in, and limitations which impose themselves on, both the development of those entities and the ways in which they can and cannot handle the accidents and fortuities that may befall them.

(d) The fourth layer of necessity in the historical process is that involved in the development of human society from its beginning towards its *telos*. In this development, society passes through the three bands of history Marx outlines: (i) the earlier social forms based on relations of personal dependence or unfree forms of labour; (ii) the 'second great form' which is a general system of social metabolism and universal relations of personal independence founded on objective dependence; (iii) free individuality, or the relations of the freely associated producers.[7]

The four layers of necessity clearly interlock in Marx's conception of the historical process. The first three are related in a fairly straightforward way. Man's efforts to improve his life as in (a) mean above all his co-operative efforts to develop his relations with nature, that is, to secure an increased and more stable subsistence. This clearly leads into his efforts to develop his methods of labour as in

[6] L. Trotsky, *Problems of Everyday Life*, NY (1973), 228.
[7] *Gr.* 157-8; see also the discussion above in Chapter 4 (i).

(b). The consequent level of productiveness decides the scale of the surplus and with it the forms in which it may be extracted, that is, the class structure as in (c). Much remains to be said about these connections, but it is the fourth layer of necessity that most needs attention.

(ii) The society of universal relations

Mankind emerges from his pre-history only when he takes *conscious* control, collectively, of social production and reproduction.[8] This is the point of historical development at which the *telos* of the nature of the human species and the *telos* of society are jointly realised.[9] The end state of human social pre-history is established. So is its beginning state which Marx identified in *The German Ideology* with the familiar words:

> Man can be distinguished from animals by consciousness, by religion or anything else you like. They themselves begin to distinguish themselves from animals as soon as they begin to *produce* their means of subsistence ... By producing their means of subsistence men are indirectly producing their actual material life.[10]

This is the first movement of the generic nature of the human species *and* of human society. The beginning-state and the end-state of the process of coming-to-be of the social animal and of his society are in place. But what of the process itself which leads from one to the other?

It must be a process that generates the conditions required for the realisation of man's potential to take mastery over his social existence. For such control to be possible social existence itself must have been developed to a level, and into a form, that makes it potentially controllable by man himself. This form must be one of real and universal social interconnections, which has superseded all local barriers and all material and subjective parochial limitations. As Marx observes, people 'cannot gain mastery over their own social interconnections before they have created them'. To create them to a degree that is potentially controllable they must have overcome 'merely local connections resting on blood ties, or on primeval,

---

[8] See Chapter 4 (i) above.
[9] See Chapter 2 (v) (c) (4) above.
[10] *MECW* V, 31.

natural or master-servant relations'.[11]

The reasons for people's inability to understand their relations with nature and their social relations in pre-market societies have already been discussed. Romantic reactionary opponents of the market, like Carlyle and Müller, yearned for a return to an 'original fullness' supposedly exhibited by man in earlier epochs. Marx's more sober evaluation is that man seemed to be more individually developed because he had not yet worked out his relationships in their fullness. He comments that the bourgeois viewpoint has never advanced beyond the antithesis between itself and the romantic viewpoint 'and therefore the latter will accompany it as legitimate antithesis up to its blessed end'.[12] A fitting comment whose truth is borne out by some of today's fans of William Morris, supporters of the Braverman thesis and some in the Green Parties.

Marx well understood the fascination that some periods of our human past can exercise over us. The archaic and classical Greeks, in particular, exercise a potent attraction. This fact and the reasons for it have to be understood, however. Marx felt the attraction, but he also sought to bring into conscious awareness the reasons why he felt it. He asks himself why we are so deeply attracted by Greek art, and by epic poetry when the press has wiped out the singing, the telling and the other conditions of epic poetry. He finds the answer in the relation of the adult with the child. One cannot become a child again, and yet one adores the child and tries to reproduce its veracity at a higher level. 'Why should not the historical childhood of humanity, its most beautiful unfolding, as a stage never to return, exercise an eternal charm? ... The charm their art has for us does not conflict with the immature stage of society in which it originated. On the contrary its charm is a consequence of this and is inseparably linked with the fact that the immature social conditions which gave rise, and which alone could give rise, to this art cannot recur.'[13] The romantic feels the charm, but lacks an adult comprehension of his feelings. He then proceeds to form a 'theory' based on his feelings.

The high level of development of social interconnections that makes control of them possible is reached through the development of commodity production and exchange up to the level of the world market. In his discussion of the price-form in the *Grundrisse* Marx treats the 'lists of current prices' as a palpable index of the attainment of universal social interconnections.[14]

---

[11] *Gr.*, 161-2.
[12] Loc. cit.
[13] *Gr.*, 111.
[14] Ibid., 160-1.

This development of universal social interconnections in the world market occurs, however, in the form of a contradiction, and the contradiction contains the conditions for going beyond the world market. The contradiction in the development is this: On the one hand, with the development of the world market there is an increasing all-round interdependence in production and consumption; 'the general social bond' of this world social metabolism. On the other hand, this increasing interdependence develops in the alienated form of operators on the market who are mutually independent and indifferent. The *de facto* universal interdependence of each on all within 'the general social bond' based on universal exchange-value contradicts, and is contradicted by, the independence and indifference of the individual operators one to another.

The contradiction intensifies as the system develops. For that reason increasing attempts are made to overcome it so that 'institutions emerge whereby each individual can acquire information about the activity of all the others and attempt to adjust his own accordingly, e.g. lists of current prices, rates of exchange, interconnections between those active in commerce through the mails, telegraphs, etc. (the means of communication of course grow at the same time)'.[15] Thus the formation of the world market contains the contradictions between the '*connection of the individual* with all' and 'the *independence of this connection from the individual*'. The market further develops the contradiction and in the process gives rise to attempts, such as the fabled 'lists of current prices' to subordinate the independent system to the individual again. Marx judges that these aspects have 'developed to such a high level that the formation of the world market already at the same time contains the conditions for going beyond it'.[16] Having created universal social interconnections in an alienated and fetishised form, the world market furnishes the possibility of having universal social interconnections without the alienated form, i.e. the possibility of mankind gaining conscious control over the universal social interconnection he has created, i.e. the society of freely associated producers producing according to a commonly agreed plan.

Marx has pointedly formulated the task in *The German Ideology*:

In the present epoch, the domination of material conditions over individuals, and the suppression of individuality by chance, has assumed its sharpest and most universal form, thereby setting existing

[15] Loc. cit.
[16] Loc. cit.

individuals a very definite task. It has set them the task of replacing the domination of circumstances and of chance over individuals by the domination of individuals over chance and circumstances.[17]

(iii) The universalisability of exchange-value

Socialism could arise only on the basis of the fully developed market. This is clearly Marx's view. Socialism presupposes as a prior condition a degree and universality in the development of wealth which could have been the result only of 'production on the basis of exchange-value ... whose *universality* produces not only the alienation of the individual from himself and others, but also the universality and comprehensiveness of his relations and capacities'.[18]

We may wonder whether the value-form is the only route through which men might have developed the universality of social interconnections to the high level where they can be turned over into socialism. Maybe another course might have been possible. Some may consider that this must remain speculation. It will be argued below that Marx was right to identify private production, or the production of exchange-values, as the *only* course with this potential.

The value-form seeks to universalise itself. That is to say, the social action of people acting under value relations, once they have been developed to a certain point, tends to, or induces them to, generalise those relations and to effect a reconstitution of society into a new class formation for surplus extraction whose finished form is the world market or the universality of social interconnections. The value-form has within it the potential for universalising itself and taking hold of society as a whole and reconstituting every aspect of life to its own requirements. (See Chapter 3 (v) above.) Once it has done so and developed to the level of the world market, then we have the universality and comprehensiveness of man's social interconnections and capacities developed to the point at which man, having developed them, can replace their control over him by his control over them. Production under the value-form, commodity production, has in its nature a tendency towards such universal relations as a realisable potential, and indeed as the natural aim or *telos* of its own process of development, if it is not frustrated.

It is, as a matter of fact, through the market that man has achieved universal relations. It is, to that extent, idle to speculate whether there might have been some other mode of production with

[17] *MECW* V, 438.
[18] *Gr.*, 162, italics added.

the nature of possessing a dynamic developmental process with the same *telos*. What we *know* is that the form of supply of human social labour corresponding to the commodity-form of the product did have such a potential, and realised it in its universalisation over society and the world.

What we now need to see is how production and consumption based on the value-form has that potential. On this question, the *Grundrisse* is more explicit and profound than *Capital*, which is in comparison a textbook and one which has proved misleading to many. Marx lays out the argument in the 'Chapter on Money' in the *Grundrisse*.[19]

The cornerstone of the argument is the 'law of nature' he refers to in the most famous of the letters to Kugelmann (see Chapter 4 (i) above), which in the *Grundrisse* he expresses thus: 'Economy of time, to this all economy ultimately reduces itself. Society likewise has to distribute its time in a purposeful way, in order to achieve a production adequate to its overall needs.'[20]

Where production is communal, directly and immediately co-operative, and where there is an unmediated unity of needs and capacities, then there is a direct 'exchange' of services, and *ipso facto* a general system of social production. Where production and exchange are *private*, however, there is no immediate co-operation with an accompanying *general* system of social production. On the contrary, there is only a mass of producers, buyers and sellers, operating individually and on their own account alone. To get a general system of social production out of this requires particular forms of 'social mediation' (as Marx calls them) which will make co-operation possible, though the forms give it a competitive and unco-operative appearance, and achieve the result only *post festum*, i.e. after, and as the outcome of, a mass of individual dealings. These forms provide the means by which private labour is welded together into a general system of social production. Necessary co-operation having been made to appear an anarchic procedure, these forms are the means by which the (hidden) reality of co-operation and general social production is asserted through the (manifest) anarchy and fragmentation of individually pursued and fragmented private production.[21]

[19] Especially from page 161 to the end of the chapter.

[20] *Gr.*, 173.

[21] I. Steedman and his co-thinkers take the system to be a mere conglomeration of atoms, which they assume will integrate harmoniously, and which they try to prove *analytically* by proving consistency between certain propositions. This will not do. It makes an ontological assumption, which there is no attempt to justify, and which is the contrary of Marx's ontological grasp of the nature of the capitalist system.

It is in the nature of private production that it is not immediately general social production, but only becomes such as 'socially mediated private labour'.[22] The mediation consists in arrangements which, when they are sufficiently developed, appear as the realities corresponding to the categories of political economy: money, circulation, price, etc. The development of private production and exchange, therefore, is identical with the development of this social mediation, whose forms or categories enable private labour to constitute general social labour.

The development of these forms, however, has as its own finished form the society of universal relations. This is precisely how Marx presents matters in the *Grundrisse*, in contrast to *Capital*. The attainment of capital (the highest form of value) and the world market, is the culmination of the development of the earlier value-forms (if they are developed rather than frustrated by the way things actually come out in the historical wash).

The system of private production requires for its perfection the *general exchangeability* of all objects. Such general exchangeability does not simply exist or arrive. One thing, a single product of labour, cannot have the character of 'being exchangeable' all on its own. 'Exchangeability' is not a quality or character that can be exemplified by one thing alone, it is a feature of a system; one thing can acquire that character progressively only in proportion as others acquire it also. Thus the general exchangeability of all objects requires all objects to adopt, in addition to their natural and particular forms, a *general form*.

Looking at it from the point of view of labour, individual concrete labours cannot be equated, and so cannot be exchanged. To become so exchangeable, individual concrete labours must become participants in general labour. In other words, the different labours must be brought together under some objective form which is adequate to make them all mutually exchangeable. But concrete labour and labour time, does not exist in such a form, i.e. one which is independent of and separate from the particular characters that it has and of the natural characters of the items it produces. Such a form must, therefore, be social and a product of history.

The 'general form' or 'adequate objective form' (as Marx calls it)

---

[22] *Gr.*, 214. 'On the contrary, the question that has to be answered is: since, on the basis of capitalist production, everyone works for himself and a particular labour must at the same time appear as its opposite, as abstract general labour – how is it possible to achieve the necessary balance and interdependence of the various spheres of production, their dimensions and the proportions between them except through the constant neutralisation of a constant disharmony?' *TSV* II, 529.

for the equation of concrete labours, and for the exchangeability of all the objects produced, is value and in particular its independent form, money. Money does not *make* them commensurable and so equatable (which was one of Aristotle's suggested solutions to the problem).[23] They are already commensurable as products of social labour, but money as a universal expression of the value of commodities which is independent of all commodities, is the required and adequate form realising the general social relation between products as products of private labour. In communal production labour is, and appears as, directly social and general, and the product has an immediate character as a part of general social production. In private production the social and general character of labour or production appears only *post festum*, after the conduct of private operations *en masse*, and the product must be transformed into *a form* in order to attain a *general* character.[24] That form is money: money is the 'adequate exchangeable form' of labour time in its private form, and 'is the medium ... in which they (exchange-values) obtain the form corresponding to their general nature'. 'Money is labour time in the form of a general object.'[25]

The development of private labour requires money as a general form, a 'social mediation', an independent expression of value, i.e. that general form which objects must come to adopt, in addition to their natural and particular forms, if they are to acquire the character of exchangeability in higher measure.

Money and exchangeability have developments of their own. For example, barter, payment in kind and feudal services do not amount to exchangeability or the circulation of commodities. The latter requires that commodities are *prices*; that there be not merely isolated acts of exchange but a constant flux of them 'proceeding more or less over the entire surface of society; a system of acts of exchange'.[26] 'To have circulation, what is essential is that exchange appears as a process, a fluid whole of purchases and sales.'[27] In *Capital* Marx writes: 'The circulation of commodities differs from the direct exchange of products not only in form, but in essence ... (it) breaks through all the individual and local limitations ... and

[23] For the detail of Aristotle's argument, and the reasons why he himself rejected it, see my 'Aristotle and the political economy of the *polis*', *Journal of Hellenic Studies*, 99 (1979), 59-60.
[24] *Gr.*, 171.
[25] Ibid., 167-8.
[26] Ibid., 188.
[27] Ibid., 196.

develops the metabolic process of human labour.'[28] *General exchangeability*, in other words, is a historical condition reached in social development, and its attainment is not given merely with the attainment of money. Marx comments elsewhere that a low level of circulation is sufficient for the emergence of money.

Money likewise has a development through various extended functions: (1) as a measure, where it is merely a particular, if preferred, commodity, gold or silver;[29] (2) 'as a medium of exchange and realiser of prices'[30] where it ceases to be a particular commodity and becomes the general commodity;[31] and (3) 'as material representation of wealth – accumulation of money'[32] not as treasure, but potentially and then actually as capital.

This general development of money and circulation constitutes the process of development of the 'social mediation' required for the development of private production. The development of each category is reciprocally conditional on the development of all the others. The developments constitute a general process of development which is itself the process of coming-to-be of the entire system of private production and exchange of which they are aspects.

Money 'as universal material representation of wealth'[33] makes possible 'the universality of the development of wealth' which is a precondition of socialism.[34] As well as the universality of wealth, it also makes possible the 'degree ... of development of wealth' required for socialism. For example: 'Money provides the possibility of an absolute division of labour.'[35] The word 'absolute' here is a rendering from the German meaning 'free', 'unrestricted' or 'unrestrained'. Marx's meaning is, therefore, that money allows the fullest development of the division of labour demanded by the forces of production (as developed, and developing, at the given time) free from social restraints and ties which money relations dissolve. (That unfettered division of labour creates real abstract general labour, by multiplying without number its detailed forms between which 'hands' have repeatedly to transit.)

He writes in the *Grundrisse* that 'patriarchal as well as ancient conditions (feudal also) thus disintegrate with the development of

---

[28] *Cap.* I, Pelican, 207.
[29] *Gr.*, 203.
[30] Ibid., 208.
[31] Ibid., 213-14.
[32] Ibid., 203.
[33] Ibid., 217.
[34] Ibid., 162.
[35] Ibid., 200.

commerce, of luxury, of *money*, of *exchange-value*, while modern society arises and grows in the same measure'.[36] And in *Capital* he writes, as we have seen:

> The circulation of commodities differs from the direct exchange of products not only in form, but in its essence ... We see here ... how the exchange of commodities breaks through all the individual and local limitations of the direct exchange of products, and develops the metabolic process of human labour.[37]

A few pages later:

> Circulation bursts through all the temporal, spatial and personal barriers imposed by the direct exchange of products, and it does this by splitting up the direct identity present in this case between the exchange of one's own product and the acquisition of someone else's into the antithetical segments of sale and purchase.[38]

These 'antithetical segments' express the contradiction which, as we saw in Chapter 5 (iii), is both constitutive of the value-form, and the source of life, social movement and development in the value-producing society which impels it towards its finished form, world market economy. The entire development is encapsulated in Marx's statement that:

> There is an antithesis, immanent in the commodity, between use-value and value, between private labour which must simultaneously manifest itself as directly social labour, and a particular concrete kind of labour which simultaneously counts as merely abstract universal labour, between the conversion of things into persons and the conversion of persons into things; the antithetical phases of the metamorphosis of the commodity are the developed forms of motion of this immanent contradiction.[39]

Marx's argument, then, is clear in its direction. The all-round development of man's social interconnections, the society of universal relations and the world market, is the finished form of the system of private labour and exchange, or 'production on the basis of exchange value ... whose universality produces not only the alienation of the individual from himself and from others, but also

[36] Ibid., 158
[37] *Cap* I, Pelican, 207.
[38] Ibid., 209.
[39] Loc. cit.

the universality and the comprehensiveness of his relations and capacities'.[40]

The crux of the argument is this: that *private production is the only form of production with this universalising tendency of development, because the universal development of social interconnections and capacities requires the dissolving effect of money to remove local barriers, and money and the other forms of 'social mediation' arise only on the basis of developing private production,* that is, on the basis of developing exchangeability up to the point of *general* exchangeability. Without the removal of parochial local barriers, social interconnections and capacities cannot move towards a universal development, and only market economy, or the 'second great form' of human social relations, has the capacity to remove them. Marx had already begun to appreciate this in the *EPM* where he wrote that '*money* must triumph over other forms of private property'.[41]

(It is worth noting in passing how little of Marx is understood by proponents of 'market socialism'. Brus, for example, regards money and price as a conventional device for consumer allocation or choice. He, Selučky and others have, in effect, regressed to a position approaching that of the 'time-chitters' with whom Marx dealt in detail in the 'Chapter on Money' in the *Grundrisse*.[42] Neither market-socialists nor time-chitters comprehend the market as a system of social relations. To regard money in such a way is like thinking of the human arm as something that might naturally come to exist as a discrete item in natural history without any connection with such a thing as the human body.)

As with *Capital* so with the *Grundrisse* it is not always immediately clear whether Marx is discussing petty commodity production or capitalist commodity production. This has been, and remains, an unnecessary source of disagreement and confusion. What is clear from the *Grundrisse*'s discussion of value, however, is that Marx is discussing categories in the context of their process of coming-to-be. It would be only a superficial reading of the 'Chapter on Money' that would fail to see that the categories under investigation are each understood to have a full realisation that is attained historically through social development, and that these full realisations are attained only with the final finished form of the whole system of

---

[40] *Gr.*, 162.

[41] *KMEW*, 340.

[42] See the debate between W. Brus and H.H. Ticktin, 'Is market socialism possible or necessary?' *Critique* 14 (1981). See also R. Selučky, 'Marxism and self-management', and the reply by H.H. Ticktin, 'Socialism, the market and the state: Socialism vs. Proudhonism', *Critique* 3 (1974).

private production – capitalism or the world market. Consequently, when discussing any of them in their earlier stages of development, it is their unfinished form that is in question; their pre-capitalist form, i.e. a stage in their development before they have attained their true nature. Money is not yet money, nor circulation yet circulation. Certainly, there are forms of money and circulation existing before the transfiguration of private production into industrial capital and world market – in the Ancient world, for example. But it is not fully, or really, yet money; nor circulation. His remarks about circulation are especially clear in this implication: you *do not have* real circulation until you have a full flux of acts of exchange over the entire surface of society; in other words, until money relations have become universal, and have dissolved, transformed or subordinated all others. Likewise with money. You *do not have* real money until it has become the universal representation of wealth and made accumulation possible (Aristotle: 'What each thing is when fully developed we call its nature'). These conditions evidently do not pertain until the advent of fully developed industrial capital.

This feature of the categories of political economy, that they have a historical development towards their fully realised nature in the attainment of the world market, creates other problems. It is possible to see what they really are only when they have reached their full development or have got close to it (cf. Chapter 3 (iv) above). This presents big problems for thinkers working in periods of history before the attainment of the finished system of world market economy. Marx had a generous appreciation of Aristotle's analysis of value and money in the *Nicomachean Ethics*. Aristotle's failure finally to penetrate the mystery of the value-form by abstracting to abstract labour Marx attributed to the existence in Aristotle's world of very different forms of supply of labour. Without something like the full and universal development of wage-labour, it was *de facto* impossible for Aristotle to crack the problem.[43]

Likewise with Adam Smith. His failure in the analysis of value, and his conception of money, lay in his failure fully to abstract from concrete labour. He further failed to see the product of labour as fully seized upon and penetrated by the commodity-form, and its contradictions of concrete/abstract labour and use/exchange-value. Both of Smith's failures are explained by Marx as a consequence of the fact that in the period of Smith capitalism had still not fully developed, but existed along with significant elements of petty commodity production, the direct production of use-values, limited

[43] *Cap.* I, Pelican, 151-2.

circulation and partial artisan ownership. Thus the incomplete historical development of the system and its categories obstructed the intellectual comprehension of both.[44] Again, the point is that the real natures of money, circulation, etc., are attained only late in the total development; in fact, they are attained only when the entire system of private production has reached its finished form.

(iv) Possible world histories

How does Marx classify societies? And how does he identify what constitutes progress in historical change? These two questions have sometimes been answered wrongly because they have been run together and given a single (false) answer. It is important to keep them apart.

Marx classifies societies in terms of the method of surplus extraction they embody, that is, by the kinds of social classes, if any, that make them up. It is within the domain of historical societies so classified that Marx discerns the three great bands of history: pre-market, market and socialism.

A separate question is how Marx identifies progress or social development within the overall process of historical change. How he does this depends on which band of history is in question. For the first band, i.e. for societies based on relations of direct dependence, progress is a function of development in the 'methods of labour' directly. For the second, viz., market society, progress is a function of the development of the value-form. Or more precisely: it is a function of the development of 'methods of labour' or productivity, not directly, but through the development of the forms of 'social mediation' which were discussed in the previous section.

Having separated the questions in this way, it is clear at once that their answers, though not the same, are connected in a number of ways. Most obviously and importantly, the two bands of history overlap and interpenetrate. So the questions are not entirely distinct either. The importance of being clear about how the two questions and answers differ can be seen from the disastrous consequences for Marxism that have in part been consequent on confusing them. The consequences are the loss of Marx's understanding of the nature of science, his understanding of law and necessity, his theory of the historical process and especially his theory of value and therefore of private production and of capitalism as its finished form. It would

[44] *Gr.*, 169.

perhaps be better to present the confusion as a consequence of those losses and as an expression of them. But it makes little difference.

The point is that if one fails to grasp Marx's essentialist and organic-dialectical method, then one can gain no real grasp of anything much in Marx. For example, if one fails to see Marx's theory of accident and necessity in history and that the necessity involved arises from the development of a real essence, then all his most fundamental and characteristic explanatory abstractions and therewith his explanations are lost. One is left with only the class organisms known to history, and must resort to rummaging in them to find some basis on which to rest an account of direction (or progress) in history. Classification and progress can then become hopelessly confused.

(That, of course, may be what is wanted. It is certainly what was wanted by the sponsors of 'dialectical and historical materialism'. There can be no doubt that the pseudo-Marxist *diamat* idea that what follows a collapse or decay must be a progressive generation (read: Tsarism to Socialism) was an effort aimed at laying claim to the allegiance of the world working-class movement for the USSR by claiming the USSR to *be* socialism. If socialism already *existed*, then the paramount duty of socialists must be to defend it. If socialism existed in the single country of the USSR, then the defence of socialism meant the defence of that country; a defeat for socialism meant a defeat for that country; a favourable trade deal for that country meant a victory for socialism, etc. Thus the 'defence' of socialism (= the USSR) must be the real substance of the fight against world capital, and must therefore be the real substance of the world class struggle, regardless of whatever struggle the working class may be waging in any other country or continent.)

If one were to compile a shortlist of sentences from world literature about which the greatest quantities of nonsense have been written, high on the list would appear the sentence from the *Preface* to Marx's *A Contribution to the Critique of Political Economy* which goes: 'In broad outline, the Asiatic, ancient, feudal and modern bourgeois modes of production may be designated as epochs marking progress in the economic development of society.'[45]

Necessity in Marx's theory of history has sometimes been, and during the apex of the reign of Moscow's nationalists over the world's official Communist movement exclusively was, understood to consist in a particular ordered sequence of class formations each historically progressive beyond its predecessors. In the canonical

[45] Op. cit., London (1971), 21.

document of 'socialism in one country', namely, the *Short Course* of 1938, we are instructed that 'five *main* types of relations of production are known to history: primitive communal, slave, feudal, capitalist and Socialist'.[46]

The point is that the interpretative inheritance of 'socialism in one country' is that the necessity in Marx's theory of history is thought to lie in an ordered sequence of stages. Today those influenced by 'socialism in one country', whether directly or indirectly, do one of three things: either they reject this inheritance and then find great difficulty in finding any account of necessity or progress in history, which they none the less want though they are left with nothing but a 'wealth of factors' and the 'endless nuances of history' from which to try to extract an account;[47] or they lose all sight of necessity;[48] or they more or less accept the inheritance and seek a 'logic' or necessity that will run through the three, five or seven stages from the beginning to the end of human history.[49]

In the much cited sentence from the 1859 *Preface* about 'epochs marking progress in the economic development of society', Marx is *not* offering a *list* of societies, procession through which constitutes progress. He is offering, as he says, 'in broad outline' those epochs within the entire panorama of human history (including its backward movements and blind alleys) 'which may be designated' as milestones within that total movement; nodes which may be seen as 'marking progress in ... development'. It is, therefore, obviously a waste of time to scrutinise this *obiter dictum* from the *Preface* with a view to finding some inherent 'logic' in the supposed list or sequence, or clarifying anything about the necessity involved in Marx's account of historical development. W.H Shaw is correct, and grasps

[46] *Short Course*, Moscow (1938), 123.

[47] E.J. Hobsbawm provides an example of this in his introduction to *KMPCEF*, 19-20, where he writes that 'the general theory of historical materialism requires only that there should be a succession of modes of production, though not necessarily any particular modes, and perhaps not in any particular predetermined order'. Apart from the vacuousness of such a 'theory of history', one wonders how he would square that with his other view that there *is* direction in history and that 'certain social phenomena cannot be conceived as appearing in history earlier than others', as he puts it in 'Karl Marx's contribution to historiography', in R. Blackburn (ed.), *Ideology in Social Science*, London (1972), 279.

[48] As G.A. Cohen tends to do in *KMTH*.

[49] W.H. Shaw seeks such a 'systematic evolutionary logic' in his *Marx's Theory of History*, London (1978) 159. He does not succeed in finding one, but he does have the merit of being unafraid of facing the problem squarely: 'For Marx there had to be some underlying developmental necessity to history or else historiography could never be scientific', loc. cit.

the bull by the horns, in insisting that Marx does see necessity in history. But he is misguided in thinking it to be located here.

As we saw in the foregoing section, the most crucial historical development in the process by which we got where we are today, the society of universal relations, is the development of private production and exchange and of their forms of 'social mediation'.

As scientific historiography, Marx's system is not based upon history considered as *the particular* manner, in all its contingency, in which the value-form happened to emerge and then to develop. On the contrary, it is, as regards the modern epoch, based upon abstracting from those contingencies to the essence of the commodity or value-form, its natural line of *genesis*, and its transformations into higher forms of the essence which, if they occur, occur necessarily as realisations of potentialities inherent in private production; or rather, in the 'social mediation' of the value-form considered itself as an essence (or as a form taken by the underlying essence of human social labour, but one which itself has a nature and development).

From the study of actual history (where 'actual' means the full historical process including all forms of contingent change as well as necessary ones) and political economy, Marx was able to extract the essence and the necessary changes, or essential transformations of form, which constitute the coming-to-be of the fully developed essence. In the light of that analysis he was able to comprehend the historical process and to identify what was progressive in it.

His scientific historiography was, thus, based on an understanding of the course and forms that development would *necessarily* have to take if there was to be progressive development. It is not primarily concerned with the particular meandering route followed by history in the course of which those forms happen to have been realised. The actual movement studied by historians can, from this point of view, be regarded merely as the vehicle in which these transformations were carried forward. It is, moreover, a vehicle that could have travelled any number of roads other than the one it actually travelled. In only some of these would the potentialities of the value-form have been realised. Not all change is progress. There does not have to be progress or development, but if there is it necessarily consists in the attainment and then the transformations of the value-form or, what is the same thing, the development of social relations or forms of social activity which those value-forms sum up, and which presuppose the adequate development of 'methods of labour'.

The basis of the science that we find in *Capital* lies in its analysis of the essence of value and of its transformations of form that lie within the complex and contingent course that history has actually taken, and which could have lain within other courses that history might have taken. Not all other possible courses, however. Among possible courses we have to distinguish those in which successive transformations (or some of them) of the essence of the value-form would have been realised, but in some manner contingently different from that in which they have been realised in actual history. The remaining possible courses are those in which the value-form and private production never came into existence at all, where there would have been change but little (or no) progress.

7

Atomism and Essentialism

(i) The two traditions

The main object of this chapter is to redeem in small part the pledges made in the foregoing chapters by expanding a little on the central categories of essentialism and upon their interconnection. There are also two secondary objectives: first to expand a bit more on what atomism involves, and secondly to bring out sharply the main points of conflict between atomism and essentialism. In this section I shall sketch in the main lines, and then look at some of the principal categories in more detail in the subsequent sections.

The most fundamental difference between the two traditions is that between their respective ontologies; that is to say, between the kinds of thing they are prepared to admit actually exist.

The atomists fall into two camps here, the first of which will be mentioned and then forgotten. First, there are the idealist atomists whose starting-point is some version of the belief that the only things we have an unqualified right to assert the existence of are the fundamental building-blocks of *knowledge*. These items are usually identified with contents of the mind of some kind, such as sensory experiences. They then see their constructive task as re-jigging the 'structure' of human knowledge on this 'secure' foundation. (Secure, that is, from the sceptic who thinks there might be some reason to doubt the existence of the world external to the mind, or at least to suspend judgment on the matter until someone comes up with some proofs. Cf. Section vi below.)

Secondly, there are the materialist atomists who accept the existence of (are prepared to admit into their ontology) ordinary things like people, buckets and spades, bacteria and voles, but who believe that the existence of these things is somehow secondary to another ontological level that is primary, viz. that of the fundamental building-blocks of the universe, matter (in this context sometimes referred to as 'primary matter'). This view I shall refer to as 'reductive materialism', as I have thoughout.

Reductive materialism has long been known to rest on a weak metaphysical basis. I will not pursue that here, however, since it is not immediately relevant to the present purpose. For those who want to pursue the issue, an article by Patrick Suppes deals excellently with the inadequacy of the reductive materialist conception of matter and with the desirability of introducing into physics an Aristotelian conception of matter, together with its cognate categories of form, potential and relative levels of matter.[1]

The major conflict between essentialism and reductive materialism is between their respective ontologies. Reductive materialism believes in an ontology of simples, of basic building-blocks lacking complexity, and further believes everything else is reducible to them. Essentialism, on the other hand, admits into its ontology what I have referred to up to now as 'organic wholes' or 'entities', and does not consider them to be reducible but rather irreducible.

The category of 'whole' or 'entity' needs some unpacking. It refers to things that are not simple but complex. The complexity in question is not mere physical complexity, such as is involved in an aggregate of simples (a pile of sand, say) where the complexity is reducible to component simples. Rather, it is a metaphysical and ontological complexity. There are several aspects to this.

First of all the entity will be made up of parts, as for example the human body is made up of a cardio-vascular system, a skeletal bone-structure, and so on. The relation between the whole entity and its parts is not the same as that between the constituent simples of an aggregate like a pile of sand. The complexity of an entity is irreducible, and it is what exists.

Entities are metaphysically and ontologically complex in a second way. Entities typically come to be, exist for a certain period and then pass away. It is part of the nature of an entity in its embryonic or immature form, to have the *potential* to become or develop into a mature specimen. Mere aggregates are not complex in that way. A pile of sand does not have of its nature a potential to become anything, though it may be made into something, but that is quite a different matter. Furthermore, mature entities have typical ways of behaving, a life-process or *ergon*. Aggregates of matter do not, do

---

[1] Patrick Suppes, 'Aristotle's concept of matter and its relation to modern concepts of matter', *Synthese* 28 (1974), 27-50

anything.

Thirdly, entities are typically of a certain kind. They do not appear as one-off jobs, but as instances of a kind or species, and their coming into existence is usually something that happens in the course of the life-process of some higher level entity such as a breeding-group or an astronomical system. The higher level entity is a presupposition of the existence of the individual, even though it is 'made up' of individuals. In general, when we are dealing with entities, the identity of a thing (what it is) is a function of species, not of individuals. We cannot ask if an individual is 'the same', full stop. It only makes sense to ask if it is the same daffodil, star or what-not.

Finally there is the question of the relation between an entity and its matter. Of course, both the entity and its parts are made up of matter, and that matter may be 'made up' (in some sense) of 'simples' (in some sense). But even if we knew everything about the different levels between the entity and its ultimate material composition, it would still not be reducible to those components. There is a category of 'form' involved which cannot be circumvented.[2] This, in turn, connects with the Aristotelian conception of relative matter; bricks, for example, are the matter of a house, and clay, the matter of bricks. There are many such levels between a human society, a human being, and the level of elementary particles, mesons, twisters and the like.

So far the examples considered in contrasting the two traditions have been taken from organic and inorganic nature. But of course the conflict extends into the social sciences too. If we simplify matters by saying that method in the social sciences involves explanation at two levels, the level of 'aggregate phenomena' and that of 'individual phenomena', then the conflict between the two traditions appears as that between (1) the atomist view that 'aggregrate phenomena' are explicable in terms of 'individual' ones (a position sometimes known as 'methodological individualism'), and (2) the view that though the relations between the 'aggregate' and 'individual' levels are not as simple and uni-directional as the first view portrays them nevertheless primacy in explanation lies with the 'aggregate' level, for example, with classes, and with capital and its forms. The first view is atomistic and reductionist, and it is vulnerable to versions of the same objections as its counterparts in the realms of inorganic nature

---

[2] C.H. Waddington offers a discussion of this in the first essay of his *The Strategy of the Genes*, London (1957), 1-10.

and of organic nature below the level of human society.[3]

In the remainder of this chapter I shall keep the exposition of the central categories of essentialism simple by considering only examples of everyday things like cats, tigers, ladders, tables and eyes. If the simplicities of atomism are not up to the job of accounting even for things like these, they will clearly be incompetent in accounting for the greater ontological complexity found at the level of human social existence and its history. There is a second advantage in limiting ourselves only to familiar things from organic and inorganic nature, and that is that it helps to show that, and how, essentialism bridges what has often been thought a gulf between the natural realm and the social realm. If it is true, as I am contending, that the basis of dialectics lies in the essentialist categories, then since essentialism bridges the supposed gulf, we may be able to get new bearings on the vexed question of whether, or how, dialectics itself applies in the natural realm. I shall not tackle that task here however.

(ii) Identity: essence and matter

How is a thing's essence to be characterised and thought of? When we ask of something 'What is it?' we are most likely asking for a partial specification of its essence, for its essence is what the thing is. It is not much help being told that it is, indeed, this very thing itself, because we know that already. The uselessness of that answer is part of the reason why dialectical thinkers have traditionally shown impatience with atomist-analytical specifications of abstract identity: A = A. This sort of thought is, indeed, a great favourite with analytical-atomists, and it is well-known in the formulation given of it by Bishop Butler much favoured by G.E. Moore: 'A thing is what it is and not another thing.'

What is associated with that approach to identity which has made

[3] Jon Elster attempts to uphold the first view, and violently attacks the second which he dubs 'methodological collectivism' and identifies as one of 'the deadly sins of Marxism', in the article referred to in Chapter 3 n.48 above. He goes on to attack the sort of view of Marx defended in this book, which he describes as Marx's 'speculative belief that history was a vehicle for the self-realisation of humanity ... the embodiment of an objective teleology'. He then curses it as a (or the) cause of Stalin's terror, labour-camps and purges, saying that it 'has led to more than a violation of *methodological* individualism: that in the name of historical necessity actual individuals have been sacrificed.' It is a fine judgment whether muddle, ignorance or slander predominates in these perorations. He might, in any case, have cursed Aristotle as the real culprit, for he held that 'A city is naturally prior to the household and to each of us, just as any organism is prior to its parts'. (*Politics* 1253a19).

it attractive is that it takes account of the sense we can have of the uniqueness and individuality of the thing in question, whatever it may be: it is *this* very thing, made up uniquely of *these* constituents; other things being made up of constituent particulars which, though they may be similar, are numerically distinct. Something like this may lie behind aspects of Wittgensteins's idea in the *Tractatus* that the generality of the predicates involved in propositions, the fact that they may apply equally properly to many distinct objects, is unsatisfactory; that such generality gets away from the real identity, the 'this-ness', of the thing, which would be adequately captured only in a language (were one only possible) such as named univocally each ontological atom or constituent particular of the thing's composition.

Certainly, many have been attracted to the reductive-materialist idea that what a thing is, its identity, is bound up above all with its material composition: this river *is* these bits of water and silt flowing past; this frog's eye *is* these molecules. A primary difficulty with that solution has always been that, even if we do identify and reidentify ordinary material items in ways that involve their physical being, we do not do so in terms of their constituent matter, and in many cases we cannot since it is in a continuous process of change. The human body is said to change all or most of its physical constituents every seven years, yet a person retains his or her identity or essence throughout.

The paradigm possessors of identity are wholes, entities or beings that endure over time. Such wholes may be made up of stuff or matter, but they are not merely aggregates of stuff. Considering only simple material items like tables, it is possible to give a theoretical explication of their identity, inasmuch as they are articulated wholes with parts, or, in Aristotelian terms, have 'form'. But with mere aggregates of stuff, like a bit of water each of whose parts is also water, no similar account is possible. Indeed, they seem not to have an identity at all, except derivatively from the case of real wholes with a principle of unity or 'form'.[4] So much the worse for the reductive-materialism of the eighteenth century criticised by Marx in the *Theses on Feuerbach*, and still in favour today with some of the zealots of atomism.

---

[4] The case is carefully argued by Eli Hirsch, 'Essence and identity', in Milton K. Munitz (ed.), *Identity and Individuation*, NY (1971).

(iii) Wholes and parts; kinds and species

It is not possible to identify something such as an eye simply in terms of its material composition. This is a quite general point about the nature of wholes and their parts. If something is part of a larger whole, as an eye is of a whole organism, then that is part of its essential nature, and we need to know more than its physical character in order to know what it is, i.e. its essence. We need to observe the functioning of the whole in order to learn what the part is *for*, i.e. what it *is*. An eye is not merely a lump of flesh but an organ of sight, and it is not correctly identified except as such an organ; that identification, and the item's identity, is possible only in relation to the whole. We can get this sort of thing wrong; lungs were once thought to be cushions for the heart, and it was a discovery that the heart is in fact a blood pump.

Apart from animate organisms, something similar is true for artifacts. Materially, a ladder is an arrangement of planks and holes. But that is not what a ladder is; nor does such knowledge give you a knowledge of what it is. Again, the point is a general one. Hegel's attack on Kant's concept of 'the concept' was that he considered Kant to have been too easily satisfied over the question of identity. The example he took was $100. Kant had been content to consider the identity of the $100 you have simply in terms of those things that you have in your pocket: 'an empirical content ... having no relationship with any other content and possessing no determinate character relative to such.'[5] Hegel's point was that $100 means nothing on its own; its possibility, existence and identity presuppose other things. This is clearly right, for it presupposes social relations in which goods are both produced and circulated in the historical form of commodities in a process in which money, as the universal equivalent, functions as an aspect. Its identity as $100, what it *is*, arises only from its being a part or aspect of a wider whole, and not from within itself, or from its material nature.

Moreover, with many kinds of things and parts of a thing, we cannot identify them as what they are by considering either them, or the whole of which they are a part, on its own. We sometimes have to consider other wholes of a similar nature. Identifying duck and drake, which may be of very different appearances, as being of the same species involves knowledge of the breeding. The same is true of correctly identifying species or sub-species. If the species tigers were to contain sub-species which do not interbreed, then you have only

---

[5] Hegel, *Science of Logic*, trs. A.V. Miller, London and NY (1969 and 1976), 88.

got part of the way in saying what they are, if you are in a position to say only that they are all just tigers. You will have got further along the way when you are able to discriminate for any individual of the species which breeding group or sub-species it belongs to. Ignorance of the latter is partial ignorance of what the thing is. Thus what an individual is, is a question of its kind or species; the particular is not independent of the general.[6] (See Chapter 2 (v a) above.)

Its being of a certain kind is not merely a matter of its appearance and morphological resemblance to others, for a thing's kind is essential to what the thing is, and its appearance may mislead as to its kind. If we were to discover that among the things we had called tigers there was a group whose anatomy was reptilian rather than mammalian, we should not conclude that some tigers are reptiles. Tigers *are* mammals, and we should conclude that some things that look like tigers are actually something else, anti-essentialist prescriptions notwithstanding. It is not appearance, but real natures that guide our drawing of species lines in the world, and our knowledge of those lines is a vital element in our ability to say what any particular thing is.

The primary subjects of discourse are wholes with real essences which we can and do come to know more about through observation, investigation and analysis. Aristotle, accordingly, took as paradigms of being, not aggregates of stuff or abstract 'things' or 'primary matter', but entities, *ousiai*, or wholes with a real unity in complexity and a life. On an essentialist ontology, the unity of the whole and its parts is, in central cases, not the result of accidental or fortuitous accretions, but the result of the increasing differentiation of an original essence. For atomist ontology, on the other hand, there are not entities such as men, stars, and trees, with natures, but abstractions denoted by the dummy-term 'thing', x, which happen to have certain 'qualities'. Real natures no longer guide our identifications of things and our classification of them into kinds and species, but rather, as Locke claimed 'the boundaries of species are as men, not as nature, makes them'.[7] The idea that such identifications

---

[6] There is a problem about determining which properties are the essential properties of an item. Baruch A. Brody suggests a solution in *Identity and Essence*, Princeton (1980), 116-33.

[7] John Locke, *An Essay concerning Human Understanding*, Peter Nidditch (ed.), Oxford (1975 and corr. 1979), 457. On the other hand Locke, despite his inconsistencies, cannot reasonably be interpreted as a standard empiricist holding only to nominal essences and rejecting real ones, as generations of empiricists have been pleased to portray him. J.L. Mackie gives a good and clear discussion in *Problems from Locke*, Oxford (1976), chs. 3 and 5.

and classifications are mere matters of convention, of how we choose (or have chosen) to carve up the world and talk about it, is difficult to defend, not to say ridiculous. (Baruch Brody offers a brief and robust treatment of it.)[8]

(iv) Essence and potential

Not only can the constituent matter of an item change; it can also change its form. The kitten becomes a cat, the sapling a tree. This does not mean that the essence itself changes. Rather it means that certain sorts of change belong to the essence. If a kitten were not going to become a cat then it would not be a kitten, for a kitten *is* an immature cat. Of course, it is a purely verbal matter that we use the term 'kitten' to *mean the same as* 'immature cat', but what is not verbal is that these things *are* immature cats. It is a question of the nature of members of that mammalian species as we have found it to be: creatures of this species, indeed normally of the entire mammalian order, start as fertilised eggs, develop in a womb, are born and then develop further along lines that are quite standard for the species into fully mature creatures of their kind. Were we to find that some of them were generated in some other way, say from eggs in a nest, or that they developed along quite different lines, say through a chrysalis state, we should have to conclude not that the term 'cat' needs redefining and broadening to include these unusual 'cats', but that these are not cats at all but things of a different species or order altogether. 'Going to be a cat in the future' is part of what it is to be a kitten now; to be a kitten now is to have the present potential to become a cat; to be an adult cat is to have realised that past potential

For radical atomists, of course, there is no such thing as an entity's real being, nature or essence. Accordingly, the potential for becoming a cat is not part of any such nature, and to say of a kitten that it is going to become a cat will be rendered false should the kitten meet with a fatal accident before reaching adult cathood. On this view it was not going to become a cat because (as it happened) it got killed, and had we said earlier that it was going to become a cat we should have done so only because we did not know what was going to happen to it. 'Going to be a cat' is not a real feature of the creature, but simply a statistical generalisation about a 'class' of creatures which we, mistakenly in this case, believed to be true of this particular creature because it resembled them.

[8] Baruch Brody, op. cit in n.6 above, 73-5.

All this is quite implausible, for the potentiality for becoming a cat is inherent in all members of the species, and is bound up with their identity as a species, and with the identity of an individual as a member of the species. If the creature did not have the potential to become a mature cat it would not be an immature cat, i.e. a kitten. Potential is a feature that the creature *necessarily* has. What is not necessary is that that potential be realised, for accidents can happen. If the creature meets with such an accident, then accidentally its potential is not realised.

(v) Chance and necessity

The atomist view fails here also in not distinguishing different kinds of change, and it does so quite consistently as a result of its denial of real essences. It is not in the nature of kittens that they meet with fatal accidents, but it is in their nature to develop into cats. One cannot say of a kitten that developed into a cat that 'it met with an accident'. Developing into a cat, unlike getting hit by a car, is necessary not accidental. It is only against a thing's essence that we are able to chart its accidents. Atomism, in effect, treats all happenings as accidental. That is part of the reason why, as we shall see, the typical account given of scientific law tends to be some version of the idea that they assert 'regularities', or constant conjunctions of 'event-types'. This is quite natural, for if there are no real natures with inherent potential for development along certain lines and with certain characteristic activity or behaviour, then one line is as likely as another. Or rather, since atomism denies the real basis for such lines of development or *genesis*, one 'event' is equi-probable with other 'events'. 'Event' is, indeed, a characteristic category of atomist metaphysics, and its special virtue is that it serves the need to have a blanket category in which to fuse, or confuse, accidental change with non-accidental change.

It is a consequence of this confusion of different kinds of change that *statistics* is required to occupy a special place in atomist methodology. Statistical statements, however, are no form of explanation at all. What is more, probability and the probabilistic treatment of 'events' is an anti-essentialist ruse which rebounds on the atomist. For atomism needs to have ways of abstracting from the accidental. That is why, in order to overcome its own limitations, it introduces such strange and abstract creatures as 'perfectly weighted coins', 'unbiased roulette wheels' and the like, together with *a priori* legislation about how these creatures behave 'in the long run'.

Making presuppositions about the behaviour of these creatures 'in the long run' is tantamount to presupposing laws of nature that go beyond the finite data available. Thus, it is an irony of atomism that it can really commit the offence which it falsely alleges against essentialism.

In atomist historiography, the confusion between the two kinds of change shows itself in the nescient belief that all 'events' are unique, and that each historical development needing explanation (and they are all believed to need it equally, none more than others), is to be explained in terms of a 'wealth of factors' to which there is no particular limit and among which there is no particular priority. Any essentialist or organicist historian seeking a deeper level of explanation and law is faulted, not because he makes mistakes, but for the very nature of his enterprise. (Thus atomism obstructs more serious intellectual endeavour, for which reason it is justly called nescient.) He will be accused of cramming history into preconceived categories, or of forcing a framework of theory on to a congeries of 'events' whose richness and infinite variety makes such attempts pretentious and false. Such humility in the face of 'events', such becoming modesty about the limited powers of the human reason, sometimes show a truer face in outright hostility to theory as such. Nescience of this kind suggests perhaps that it is found preferable *not* to understand, and so not to seek understanding, and to belittle those who do. If atomism once served to promote change in the heroic period of the dismantling of feudalism and of bourgeois construction, it now obstructs change by seeking to obstruct our view of the basis of its necessity. The intellectual spokesman of a declining ruling-class, the promotion of whose interests no longer promises anything in the interests of the under-class or of mankind, must speak with such a voice, if they must speak.

On an Aristotelian ontology, however, chance and fortuity are not elevated into the major category under which all sublunary happenings fall. Aristotle considered chance happenings to be exceptional, and that what is not exceptional, what happens 'always or for the most part', cannot be fortuitous.[9] What happens always or for the most part does so *phusei*, 'by nature'; and this is so because there is some entity or system which, in virtue of its real nature, has a particular form of life or way of behaving (its *ergon*), and it is this that we are in fact observing in the set of events that happens always or for the most part. We come to understand those sets of events by coming to understand the real nature or essence of the entity that

[9] *Physics* 2. 196b10ff.

produced them.

Entities typically *grow*. They develop along certain lines typical of their kind or species, from an embryonic form to a mature one. Development, both embryonically and genetically, is a matter of increasing differentiation of a whole, not of contingent and extraneous additions. Were any item not so to develop, from what we believe to be a non-accidental cause, then it would not be a thing of just that kind.

(vi) Real necessity

Such changes as growth, and those mentioned above as typical behaviour (*ergon*), are understood by Aristotle as necessary changes. They are 'internal motions', arising from a thing's essence, and realising its potentials or expressing its nature. (Forms of explanation, it should be noted, very characteristic of Marx.) Such changes are contrasted with accidental changes, which are 'external motions' and result from chance.

When Aristotle says, for example, that the growth of an entity constitutes *necessary* change, the necessity involved is not 'logical', or *de dicto* necessity. It is not being said that any entity that does not so change fails to satisfy a logically necessary condition for being *called* a something or other. What is in question is a real necessity, a necessity *de re*, about the being of the thing, and what it is in its essential nature.

Atomist philosophy rejects real, or *de re*, necessity. But as Milton Fisk has argued,[10] this rejection is less a conclusion of arguments against *de re* necessity than an unavoidable consequence of adopting an atomist ontology which is incapable of supporting such necessity. The classical empiricist argument against there being an objective necessity in a physical connection was given by Hume. It is that we cannot know what we are talking about when we either affirm or deny such a *de re* necessity, because it is not possible for us to acquire the 'idea' of it. This verdict follows as a conclusion from the classical empiricist doctrine that all ideas derive, in one or other of the ways he allows, from impressions of sense, together with his view that there is no impression from which the idea of a real necessity could be derived. What, then, lies at the root of this position, and of the rejection of real necessity, is simply the adoption of an ontology in which impressions are the primary entities of the knowable world.

---

[10] See Milton Fisk, *Nature and Necessity*, Bloomington and London (1973), 4.

The motive for adopting this ontology is, as was suggested in Section (i) above, a proper concern with the avoidance of error, improperly magnified into an obsession by taking seriously the sceptical arguments advanced by Descartes in the *Meditations* and handed down by long tradition to Russell, Ayer and others of atomist persuasion.[11]

When Marx attributes necessity to historical developments, usually developments of form, he is using such a notion of real necessity, and it is of a piece with his entire essentialist theory that he should. Real necessity is incompatible with determinism, for determinism, in the modern forms in which it has become familiar since the reductive-materialists of the eighteenth century, rests on laws conceived of as universal regularities of event-types. The Aristotelian and Marxian conception of law does not relate 'event-types'; more importantly it is not universal but specific to a given real nature and the necessary tendencies associated with it; and most importantly it cohabits with the category of accident in a way that hardly lends itself to grand determinist designs, in spite of what has usually been written and said about Marx's grand design.

Determinism does not arise for Aristotle because his conception of law allows for the frustration or abortion of a development, and, in his conception of it, necessity is a function of form and essence, not of matter, which he regards as the realm of the accidental. He does not have the view that events fall under 'lawlike generalisations' of universal application of the form $(x) (Fx \rightarrow Gx)$, that is: for all things, if a thing is F then it is also G. This is for two reasons: first, because he does not see 'events' (or 'impressions of sense') as the ontological data requiring explanation; second, because he puts specific things, entities, wholes, in that primary place, and so dispenses with the abstraction 'all things' (x).

So with Marx: laws are effectively definitional of a thing's nature, and they explain what happens in the world, not by trying to predict 'events' on the basis of other 'events' ('initial conditions') together with universal regularities, but by uncovering what some entity's *ergon* and tendencies of development or potential are, and seeing how it can be expected to act or develop and probably will, unless interfered with. The interferences are the realm of the accidental,

---

[11] In some cases there is a suspicion that the refusal to have anything to do with real necessity is a secondary party in partnership with a deep preference for a necessity that will have a bit of mystery in it. The theology of Dummett seems a case in point. In seeking for something for mankind to be less than, it is hoped that something of the kind may be found in logic and 'logical necessity'.

and can be dealt with and evaluated only in relation to a prior understanding of the realm of necessity of form and essence, in relation to which they are the accidental. As Aristotle pointed out, there can be no science of the accidental.[12]

In history, the importance of the accidental cannot be exaggerated. Its significance and comprehension, however, is possible only in relation to law and necessity. The interweaving of the accidental and the necessary would be a fascinating aspect of Marxist historical writing if there were a wider and deeper appreciation of what law and necessity mean in history.

(vii) Essence and time

Aristotle's conception of Being is dynamic, as we have seen. An essence is a locus of change and motion. Explaining this to be Aristotle's basic viewpoint, a recent author was conscious that he would appear 'thoroughly unaristotelian' to many in the community of Aristotelians.[13] Time, however, is fundamental to Aristotle's categories. Atomist thinkers have often favoured reducing time to epistemic ordering-relations of 'earlier than' and 'later than' between 'events'; or, as it has recently been put: 'Temporality is understood in this ... tradition as abstract and formal, not as concrete historical time.'[14] Aristotle, on the contrary, makes time ontological as a function of the movement and change of real existents: 'Time is the number of motion.'[15] Without the reality of change, there would not be so much as the idea of time according to Aristotle.[16] The proximity of Aristotelian and Marxian categories is revealingly illustrated in Trotsky's observation that '... existence is itself an uninterrupted process of transformation; time in consequence is a fundamental element of existence. Thus the axiom "A" is equal to "A", signifies that a thing is equal to itself if it does not change, that is, if it does not exist.'[17]

Classification, saying what something is or specifying its essence, involves change. As we saw in Section iv above, some sorts of change

---

[12] *Met.* 6. 1026a33ff.

[13] S.R.L. Clark, *Aristotle's Man: Speculations upon Aristotelian Anthropology*, Oxford (1975), 114.

[14] Hans D. Sluga, *Gottlob Frege*, London (1980), 3. Sluga also notes on page 2 that 'anti-historicism has been part of the baggage of the tradition since Frege.'

[15] *Physics* 4. 219b2.

[16] Ibid., 211a11ff.

[17] L. Trotsky, *In Defence of Marxism*, NY (1973), 49.

are essential features of a thing's nature, and are thus vital to determining what it is.

There is another dimension of change in relation to essences, however, which leads us beyond anything we can learn from Aristotle. Aristotle believed essences themselves to be fixed and unchanging. Linnaeus in the eighteenth century believed the same. His system assumed the immutability of species, and was therefore limited to the description and the classification of plants according to their appearances. This is aptly described by Trotsky as 'the infantile period of botany'. He adds. 'Only decisive repudiation of the idea of fixed species, only the study of the evolution of plants and their anatomy prepared the basis for a really scientific classification.'[18] Without a knowledge of how existing species of organisms came into being, how they relate to extinct species, how extinct species relate to each other and to other existing species, we cannot have full knowledge of what present species and existing things are; no matter how high the 'standards of excellence' attained in the *description* of their present *appearance*.

This consideration has its place in social science also. We considered in Chapter 3 the evolution of value from its embryonic form as the simple commodity through to its later forms; the necessary appearance of an independent expression of the value of commodities, money; and money itself as an undeveloped form of capital. But in whatever detail one may analyse the laws of motion or laws of *ergon* of capitalism, its essence will not be fully grasped unless it is seen that that essence contains the potential to develop into something else. One will not fully grasp the nature of capitalism, without having identified the necessities within it which constitute its potential to become something else.

(viii) Teleology and explanation

It is obvious that many of the categories fundamental in the organic and dialectical thought that goes with an ontology of real natures are teleological. We have seen how the essence of something, an eye, a ladder or $100, is bound up with its being part of a larger whole, and such things typically have a purpose, end or *telos*. We have also seen how the essence of an entity or species can be bound up in part with its natural line of development, or the realisation of its inherent

[18] Ibid., 51-2.

potential. Such a process of change introduces teleological notions like an 'aim', '*telos*' or 'finished form'.

Even in these more penetrating post-positivist days, the admission of teleology is still usually sufficient reason for many people to dismiss a position without more ado. Notwithstanding the demise of positivism and the unredeemed promises of reductive-materialism, it is still widely believed that efficient causation alone is the foundation of all genuine science and of any acceptable explanation, and that teleology is pre-scientific, possibly animistic, and even perhaps theological.

This state of affairs is based upon two connected sets of misconceptions. It is based in part upon a popular mythology that has come to surround Aristotle's teleology, and in part upon a zealous faith that the solvency of reductive-materialism is sufficient to redeem the promissory-notes it has issued like confetti and drawn upon the bank of atomism. In this section we shall look at the first of these, and then consider the second in the following section.

Aristotle's understanding of the natural order in teleological categories was put to work by the Schoolmen of feudalism as a usable framework within which to expound the then Christian view of the world of creation as purposive, the social order as an expression of divine wishes, etc. Modern thought is often seen as inaugurated by a break with belief in a divine teleological cosmology. Until recently it was common for Democritus and the ancient atomists to be held in higher scientific esteem that Aristotle, and this position is only now beginning to change. Of course, Aristotle was one thing and feudal Christianity another, but the distinction tended not to be too well marked. Early modern atomists found Aristotle impossible to take. Hobbes, for example, could write: 'I believe that scarce anything could be more absurdly said in Natural Philosophy, than that which is now called Aristotle's *Metaphysiques*; nor more repugnant to Government than much of what he hath said in his *Politiques*; nor more ignorantly, than a great part of his *Ethiques*.'[19]

Messrs. progressives, liberals and free-thinkers of anti-clerical taste, heroically fighting the battles of 1789 in the gentler circumstances of twentieth-century Bloomsbury and other locations, did not allow themselves to be intimidated from saying what needed to be said about Aristotle. Bertrand Russell, for instance, sticking up for Anaximander for having prefigured Darwinian evolutionism in holding that men are descended from fishes, could write: 'But

---

[19] *Leviathan*, Oxford (1909), 522.

Aristotle and the Church banished such theories until the eighteenth century.'[20] (Hegel wrote of Aristotle that 'no philosopher has had so much wrong done him by the thoughtless traditions which have been received respecting his philosophy'.[21] The observation, true at the time, now has wider scope in virtue of the appearance of yet more 'thoughtless traditions' unforeseen by Hegel.)

In spite of all this, however, it is simply not the case that Aristotle's teleological categories, ontology, metaphysics and theory of science constitute a purposive cosmology with a 'guiding intelligence', or anything much like it. The mythology still runs deep, however, and even Aristotelian scholars are affected by it. Mansion, for example, sees Aristotle's treatment of chance as an obstacle to his teleology, and Hartman considers it to be in systematic contradiction with it. Both see the treatment of chance as an admission on Aristotle's part that cosmic teleology is imperfect and subject to disturbances from matter. In fact there is no cosmic teleology, and the theory of chance or accidental change is, as we have seen, an integral accompaniment of the teleological category of motion which distinguishes necessary and accidental change.[22]

One favourite occasion for anti-teleological commonplace is Aristotle's theory of *ergon*. According to Aristotle, all full entities, and many items that are entities derivatively, such as artifacts, have an *ergon*. This is usually translated as 'function' and gives rise to standard objections. For example, Aristotle considers that the builder and cobbler have characteristic *erga*, and he asks: 'Are there acts and *erga* of builder and cobbler, but not of man? Is man born to be inactive? Or rather, just as eye and hand and foot and in general every part clearly has an *ergon*, should we not suppose that man has an *ergon* on top of these?'[23]

A standard pattern of response is to say, as Hardie does, 'The obvious answer is that one may not, unless one is prepared to say that man is an instrument designed for some use ...'[24] The use of the teleological category of *ergon* is thus seen as propelling one into a cosmic teleology in which everything that has an *ergon* must be the artifact or tool of some maker or Maker, and the *ergon* or 'function' is the purpose which the Maker intended that item to serve. This is not

[20] *Human Knowledge: Its Scope and Limits*, London (1948), 47.
[21] *Lectures on the History of Philosophy*, trs. Haldane and Simson, London (1894), vol.2, 118.
[22] This is well argued by W. Wieland, 'The problem of teleology' in *Articles on Aristotle*, vol.1, eds. J. Barnes, M. Schofield and R. Sorabji, London 1975.
[23] *NE* 1097b28f.
[24] W.F.R. Hardie, *Aristotle's Ethical Theory*, Oxford (1968), 23.

far short of a travesty of Aristotle.

The translation of '*ergon*' as 'function' is inadequate. As Clark has argued, 'the ergon of a variety of living creature, tool or organ is the particular form of life, of activity which "makes sense" of its structure. A part of an animal that seems to us to be superfluous, odd, deformed is suddenly explained when we see how it is generally, normally, characteristically used. This of course is perfectly compatible with its original production by random mutation.'[25] Properly understood, the *ergon* of a thing, creature or system is, as we have seen, often an indispensable determinant in our efforts to find out what the item really *is*, and to reveal its nature.

Some, of course, may still want to read Aristotle as a cosmological teleologist and find reason to interpret him in that way. That issue need not be argued, for the important point here is that such an interpretation is not inherent in, and does not follow from, the teleological categories of essentialism and an ontology of real natures. It would be external, and have to be superimposed.

This is clear even in Aristotle's case from his use of '*ergon*', which relates it to a thing's nature, what it *is*, and not to the designs of a guiding intelligence. The *ergon* of an eye, for instance, is said to be sight (*NE* 1. 1097b24f), and that of the vegetable soul 'to reproduce and feed' (*De An.* 415a25). Thus, the *ergon* is the characteristic activity, not the intentions of a designer. Moreover, the very same features can constitute also a thing's *telos* or final cause, for sight is also the *telos* of the eye (*De Gen. An.* 778a33f.) 'Each thing's *ergon* is its *telos*' (*EE* 1219a8), 'for the *ergon* is the end, and the activity the *ergon*' (*Met* 9.1050a22). The 'form' or *eidos*, *telos* or end or final cause, *ergon* or 'function', and *to ti en einai* or essence of a being are the same thing, for 'a thing's nature is its end or final cause' (*Phys.* 2. 194a28f).[26]

(ix) Efficient causation and teleology

The atomist ontology of reductive materialists makes it difficult for them to accept teleological categories, since an ontology of real natures (which underlies and requires those categories) poses inconvenient obstacles in the reductionist's course towards the long-promised reductions. If he is impatient, not perhaps to get to the promised land but at least to sustain belief in its possiblity, he will

---

[25] Clark, op. cit. in n. 12 above, 16.
[26] These observations are Clark's, ibid., 16 int.al.

want to circumvent rather than face up to these inconveniences. Thus Bertrand Russell, again fearlessly fighting the battles of the eighteenth-century materialists, can write:

> There are some who hold that the fundamental category of biology should be that of 'organism', and that, on this account, biology can never be reduced to chemistry and physics. This view is derived from Aristotle, and was encouraged by the Hegelian philosophy ... It is, to my mind, an erroneous view, and one which, insofar as it prevails, is a barrier to scientific progress.[27]

He then proceeds to deal with it in the following way:

> Let us first try to state the logical essence of the theory. It holds that the body of an animal or plant is a unity, in the sense that the laws governing the behaviour of the parts can only be stated by considering the place of the parts in the whole ... The eye is merely a transmitter and transformer of radiant energy. But the 'organic' view would hold that the way in which the eye deals with radiant energy cannot be understood without taking into account the rest of the body, and of the body as a single whole ... Speaking generally, scientific progress has been made by analysis and artificial isolation.[28]

There are a number of misunderstandings at cross-purposes here (assuming that Russell is attacking an Aristotelian position, as he seems to suggest he is; though it is possible that he has some other target mainly in mind like Henri Bergson and the vitalists). But what really seems to be worrying Russell is that if we were to follow the organic view (as he portrays it) in investigating how the eye deals with radiant energy, then we would not be led to do the obviously right sorts of things with a view to discovering the mechanisms of efficient causation in the eye. He thinks this first, because he believes that teleological and holistic categories are antagonistic to efficient causation; and secondly, because he believes in any case that the investigation of efficient causal mechanisms constitutes the whole of science. Consequently, he believes 'organicism' to be a barrier to scientific progress, and he would be right if the two preceding beliefs were right, but they are both wrong.

A final cause is not an agent as an efficient cause is; if it were, then it could only be such incoherently for it would be an agency in which the future acted upon the past. But the account given of necessary

---

[27] *Human Knowledge* (cf.n.18 above), 48.
[28] Ibid., 48-9.

change in earlier sections, although teleological, involves no such incoherent agency, and, far from excluding efficient causality, presupposes it. If an embryonic member of a species contains a potential to develop along a certain line characteristic of its species towards a finished form, it does so by means of efficient causality, not contrary to it or in spite of it.

Teleological explanation, therefore, does not replace efficient causal explanation, though it may suggest where they are to be sought. It is natural that atomists should want to eliminate teleology, for not only does it have no place in any form of their programme, but to anyone who has swallowed the incoherent basis of that programme and been lured by its preposterous promises, teleology must itself appear to be preposterous. The only way sense can then be made of it is to try to reduce it to efficient causality, and that is indeed the most serious sort of attempt that has been made to achieve its elimination. Such attempts have been conspicuously unsuccessful.[29]

Not only need there be no conflict in practice between efficient and final causality, but the two are even mutually supportive. We have seen that a part of a creature or system that seems superfluous is explained when we come to see how it is used (what is is *for*) in the life-activity or *ergon* of the creature or system. It is also obvious that this is perfectly compatible with its having been produced by random mutation. There is no conflict. Beyond that, the interrelations of final and efficient causality can become more complex. The fact that the part produced by the efficient causality of mutation did not lapse, but was perpetuated in the genetic line, is explained by the fact that it served an end. The changes effected by mutation do not occur in order to serve some end; but the fact that they do serve an end may explain why they do not lapse, when they do not lapse.

(x) Law

Still worse for the apostle of reductive-materialism is the fact that a teleological notion is required to account for efficient causality. The Humean idea of efficient causality is that it is a matter of regularities or uniformities of events, of invariable succession of one event-type by another event-type. Geach, however, rightly points out that true causal statements do not state what *de facto* always happens, but only

---

[29] See E. Nagel, *The Structure of Science*, London (1961) ch. 12; and see Clark's criticisms in op. cit. in n. 12 above, 53-4.

what happens if nothing interferes.[30] The notion of a tendency (potentially frustratable) has to be brought in here, and it is a teleological notion. A tendency expresses the nature of an agency as characteristically expressing itself in certain behaviour. What actually happens in the world, in all its complexity, is the resultant of the conflicting tendencies (laws of *genesis, ergon* and decay) of real natures. To understand what happens is to understand those natures and their tendencies, and to see how their conflicting operations resulted in what happened. If one begins from an ontology of real natures then it is natures and not 'events' that are primary.

Mackie has attempted to reply to Geach. To do so, he distinguishes between 'a full complex physical law, which would state what always does happen, and the law as so far known, which tells us only what would, failing interference, happen'.[31] Here, the Humean conception of laws of efficient causality as statements of invariable succession is redeemed, not with reference to any existing laws purported to be of that kind, but by issuing yet another promissory-note: that one day there will be laws that do state invariable successions. Even if one is able to stretch the imagination of what a future form of law might be to its limits, and thereby follow Mackie in imagining it to be none other than the Humean regularity, the fact of interference will have to be accommodated. At the moment we accommodate them with the laws we have, by saying that these laws do not tell us what *does* happen, but what *would* happen so long as there was no interference. If we believe in the perfectibility of Humean law, then we believe in the future possibility of a law stating what does happen, which does not contain in its formulation a general exclusion clause covering all possible interferences indifferently. The only way of excluding a clause which excludes interference as a category, is to include in the law an individual exclusion clause for each possible interference. The labour of producing such a formulation, which would need to be indefinitely long, would recommend itself only to someone whose idle curiosity was tireless, or to someone who was already convinced that the form of law had to be Humean.

Building on the category central to atomism, the 'event', does not lead us far towards understanding what there is, or even towards making much sense of much of our common talk about things. Yet one of its leading exponents, Davidson, can confess that 'the

---

[30] G.E.M. Anscombe and P.T. Geach, *Three Philosophers*, Oxford (1963), 102-3. See also Geach's 'Teleological explanation', in *Explanation*, ed. S. Körner, Oxford (1975), esp. 93-4.

[31] J.L. Mackie, *The Cement of the Universe: A Study of Causation*, Oxford (1980), 76.

assumption, ontological and metaphysical, that there are events, is one without which we cannot make sense of much of our most common talk ... I do not know of any better, or further, way of showing what there is.'[32]

The period of opposition to the war in Vietnam was marked by great movement and imagination in American thought. It was during this period that work appeared in an arcane region of philosophy which had the consequences of partially dislodging atomism from its position as the only certified and accredited mode of conducting intellectual operations, and of reopening the ancient conflict between essentialism and atomism.[33] Since conditions of career normality were restored in America, atomism has partially recovered. But although the rate of development of essentialism has slowed and its best-known recent rediscoverers have decelerated the process of drawing out its consequences almost to a standstill, it has not disappeared. The conviction remains in many minds that atomism is fundamentally flawed and peculiarly infertile.[34] J.L. Mackie, a philosopher whose inclinations were towards some form of atomism, was compelled in his honest fashion to accept conclusions which could only have been awkward for him. 'There is in principle,' he wrote, 'a choice between an ontology of persisting things and one of events and concatenations of events.' This choice, in his view, is already implicitly made in our ordinary language, and 'the concept of persisting things' is 'psychologically almost irresistible'. It would be strange, however, if prejudice arising from ordinary language were to be thought the end of the matter. Mackie rightly went further: we go on using the category of changing and persisting things because, in

---

[32] D. Davidson, 'Causal relations', in *Causation and Conditionals*, ed. E. Sosa, Oxford (1975), 94.

[33] The work referred to was mainly in the philosophy of logic and was particularly associated with Hilary Putnam and Saul Kripke whose most efficacious piece was *Naming and Necessity*, originally published in 1972, and later in revised and enlarged edn., Oxford 1980. There had been defenders of essentialist positions before this but they were few. Notable among them was Irving M. Copi, whose 'Essence and accident' is (among his many other works) important; it is found in *Aristotle*, ed. J.M.E. Moravcsik, NY 1967, London 1968.

[34] Hans Sluga seems to reflect something like this when he observes concerning the procedures of analytical philosophy: 'One might, of course, argue that this procedure is designed to proceed systematically from simple to more complex cases. Eventually, it will therefore reach the analysis of the most difficult philosophical texts. But there is little evidence in the actual progress of the discussion to encourage such hopes. After eighty years of debate linguistic philosophers are still not agreed on the semantics of simple proper names. How long would it take to construct a semantics of philosophical discourse?' Op. cit., n.14 above, 4.

his term, it is 'appropriate'. To what is it appropriate? Mackie was compelled to say: 'the world as it is lends itself to description in these terms.'[35]

The world as it is: in this phrase lies the recognition of the primacy of ontology over epistemology. Our language, and our talk about events, is possible only because the world as it is is a world containing entities that persist through change. This philosophy, however, has still to be carried through to its conclusion. Essentialism is a long way from being sufficiently developed, and further still from being developed into a dialectical form. Contradiction has yet to be developed as an ontological category. The philosophy and categories that Marx took for granted, and which constitute the foundation of his method, have been lost, and they need to be both regained and developed.

[35] *Problems from Locke*, Oxford (1976), 171.

Glossary

Atomism
The metaphysical system (or set of them) whose ontology (q.v.) admits only, or gives primacy to, atomistic 'small-bits'. There are two principal varieties of atomism, accordingly as the atoms are considered as physical or as epistemological, that is, as atoms of matter or as atoms of knowledge. Hume was an epistemological atomist; his ontology admitted only 'atoms of experience', or 'impressions of sense' (more recently commonly referred to as 'sense-data'). In this, or things very like it, he has been followed by most forms of empiricism (q.v.). On this sort of view only those ideas or propositions that stand in a fairly direct relation to immediate sensory experience can be considered as partaking of genuine knowledge. Physical atomism considers that phenomena and things are properly explicable only in terms of their ultimate material constituents. The version of atomism that appears in the social sciences is 'methodological individualism'. See Chapter 7 (i).

Contradiction – see Chapter 5 (iii).

Diamat – see **Histmat**

Efficient causation
Aristotle identifies causes of four kinds: efficient, formal, material and final. In recent times, particularly in periods when positivism has been dominant, only one of these has been considered seriously scientific, and that is efficient causation. This is usually thought of as what is involved in chains of events in which each event in the chain 'causes' the one succeeding it. The relation between any two such events has been the subject of much debate since Hume. Hume's successors have attempted to devise accounts of scientific laws as statements of mere *regularities* between events, i.e., as statements that

assert no more than that certain sorts of events are, or just happen to be, constantly conjoined in our experience of the world. These endeavours have encountered many difficulties (see Chapter 7(x); for example, it has proved hard on this approach to distinguish between a law of nature and a generalisation whose truth is merely accidental, such as 'All the screws in Smith's car are rusty'.

Empiricism
A family of philosophical theories which put great emphasis on epistemology at the expense of other sorts of considerations. These theories share a general disposition to tie a tight bond between what can be known (or properly considered to be knowledge) and what can be directly experienced through the senses. Classical forms of empiricism consider that even talking about 'what can be experienced through sensation' is rather profligate, since it implies the existence of a 'what' that is the external object of inner sensory states; accordingly the purists consider that what can be known and what exists are limited to mental states, and if anything else is to be said to be known, or to exist, it must be a justified hypothesis about, or a valid inference from, mental states. Being an empiricist is not to be confused with being *empirical*. Being empirical is having due regard to the facts, investigating them thoroughly and reviewing them comprehensively, before hazarding a theory, hypothesis or interpretation. One does not need to be an empiricist in order to be empirical, and being empirical does not mean that one is an empiricist. An Aristotelian essentialist is empirical, since essences are discovered by observation and investigation; but he is not an empiricist, and would not support the theoretical baggage of empiricism.

Epistemology
Epistemology, or the theory of knowledge, is the study whose object is to determine what can count as genuine knowledge and as truly known, and to determine the criteria by which such knowledge can be discriminated from error, mere belief, prejudice, supposition, etc.

Ergon
Usually translated as 'function', which is not quite adequate. The Greek word means literally 'work'. It conveys the idea of the typical behaviour of a kind of thing: behaviour of a kind that expresses the essence of the kind of thing it is. It is closely associated with a thing's end, aim or *telos*. Thus the *ergon* of capital is what Marx lays out in his treatment of the circuits of capital in *Cap*.II, and its *telos* (in so far

as it is distinguishable) is self-expansion. It is in this sense that we can speak of some of Marx's results as giving the laws of *ergon* of capital.

Essence

A specification of the essence of an entity specifies those characteristics that make it the kind of thing it is (or the very thing it is) and without which it could not exist or be what it is. The essence of an entity is not something lying around on the surface which simply has to be apprehended, nor can it be got from a dictionary definition. It has to be discovered by means of observation, investigation and analysis of facts. For example, part of the essence of gold as we presently understand it is that it is that element having the atomic number 79. We did not always know this; we discovered it. It *was* part of the essence of gold before we knew it to be so, and would still have *been* part of that essence even if there had never existed any intelligent creatures like humans to discover it. Other entities, such as forms of human society, also have essences which have to be discovered. See also **Teleology.**

Final causation

A final cause is not a 'cause' at all in any recognized use of the term. The final cause of a kind of thing is that end or state towards which it tends to develop by its nature, if it is not interfered with. The tiger moth larva will develop into a tiger moth, if its development is uninterrupted, and this is its final cause. The final cause of the value-form is capital. That is, given 'The Simple or Accidental Form of Value' (*Cap*. I, chapter 1, section 3(a)), then if it develops, its final form will be capital. (See also **Telos.**) A kind of thing (capital, for example) may have forms subsequent to its final form (or final cause), but these will be forms of its corruption, its decay from its fully finished form, and its interpenetration with what supersedes it.

Histmat and Diamat

Abbreviations of East-European origin which refer to the versions of 'historical materialism' and 'dialectical materialism' which were authorised as orthodox in the Stalin period. Their original canonical adumbration is to be found in *The History of the Communist Party of the Soviet Union (Bolsheviks): Short Course*, edited by a Commission of the Central Committee of the C.P.S.U. (B), 1938. The best known, and theoretically most significant part, is chapter four, part two: 'Dialectical and Historical Materialism.'

Materialism, reductive or otherwise – see Chapter 7 (i).

Metaphysics

As employed here it means enquiry into the most fundamental categories used in thought and science. In this sense, even the Logical Positivists had a metaphysics (since they had a theory about which were the fundamental categories), notwithstanding the fact that in their conception of philosophy, metaphysics was the prime enemy, and in their vocabulary the word 'metaphysical' was the ultimate insult. They understood metaphysics to be a variety of philosophy which claimed to be able to make the world intelligible at a level deeper than science could ever penetrate. The two senses of the term should be kept apart; only the first is used in this book.

Nature or **real nature** – see **Essence**.

Ontology

The realm of *being*, or of what is or exists. It should be understood in relation to epistemology (q.v.) which concerns the realm of *knowledge*, or of what is known. The philosophical vogues of recent decades, which have influenced conceptions of methods in the social sciences, have had for the most part a very restricted ontology which has been fused with their atomist epistemology (q.v.). That epistemology has set tight constraints on their preferred ontology, with the (desired) result that non-atomistic entities (e.g. social classes) came to seem problematical unless they could be reduced to the permitted atoms (individual agents), or in some way construed in terms of them alone.

Teleology

Often thought of as a theory that sees the world as the artifact of a God or Guiding Intelligence and each thing in the world as existing and behaving in the way that it does as a fulfilment of his purpose. That is not the theory of teleology adopted in this book (see Chapter 9 (viii)). Here it is a theory about how the real nature (essence, q.v.) of a whole entity is to be identified; how its development from immature, to mature (*telos*, q.v.) and declining forms is to be explained; and how its characteristic behaviour (*ergon*, q.v.) is to be explained in a law-like fashion. A whole entity can be anything from an amoeba to a form of human society, or an astronomical system.

Telos
The form, state or condition towards which an entity develops by its nature, unless its development is interrupted (either by external accident, or, in the case of a nature which contains a constitutive contradiction, by the way in which that contradiction develops). The *telos* is the final form attained in an entity's process of development.

Select Bibliography

Addis, L. 'Freedom and the Marxist philosophy of history', *Philosophy of Science*, vol. 33, nos. 1-2 (1966)

Althusser, L. *For Marx*, tr. Ben Brewster, Penguin, Harmondsworth (1969)

Althusser, L. *Lenin and Philosophy and other Essays*, tr. Ben Brewster, London (1971); second edition (1977)

Althusser, L. and Balibar, E., *Reading Capital*, tr. Ben Brewster, London (1970)

Anderson, P. *Passages from Antiquity to Feudalism*, London (1974)

Anscombe, E. 'Causality and determination', in Sosa, E. (ed.), *Causation and Conditionals*, Oxford (1975); originally published by Cambridge University Press (1971)

Anscombe, E. 'Aristotle', in Anscombe, G.E.M. and Geach, P.T., *Three Philosophers*, Oxford (1963)

Aristotle *De Anima, The Works of Aristotle*, vol. 3., ed. W.D. Ross, tr. J.A. Smith, Oxford (1931)

Aristotle *Metaphysica, The Works of Aristotle*, vol. 8, ed. and tr. W.D. Ross, Oxford (1908)

Aristotle *Politics*, entitled *The Politics of Aristotle*, tr. with introduction, notes and appendices by Ernest Barker, Oxford (1946) repr., with corrections (1952)

Aristotle *Ethica Nicomachea, The Works of Aristotle*, vol. 9., ed. and tr. W.D. Ross, Oxford (1925)

Aristotle *Physics, The Works of Aristotle*, vol. 2., ed. W.D. Ross, tr. R.P. Hardie and R.K. Gaye, Oxford; and tr. W.D. Ross, Oxford (1936)

Aristotle *De Motu Animalium*, entitled *Aristotle's De Motu Animalium*, text with translation, commentary and interpretive essays by M.C. Nussbaum, Princeton, NJ (1978)

Aristotle *De Generatione Animalium, The Works of Aristotle*, vol. 5., tr. A. Platt, Oxford (1912)

Arnot, B. 'Soviet labour productivity and the failure of the Shchekino experiment', *Critique* 15 (1981)

Arthur, C. 'Dialectics and labour', in Mepham, J. and Ruben, D-H. *Issues in Marxist Philosophy*, vol. 1., *Dialectics and Method*, Hassocks (1979)

Arthur, C. 'Hegel, Feuerbach, Marx and Negativity', *Radical Philosophy* 35 (1983)

Ayer, A.J. *The Foundations of Empirical Knowledge*, London (1940)

Benton, T. *Philosophical Foundations of the Three Sociologies*, London (1977)

Bettelheim, C. *Les Luttes de classes en URSS*, Paris (1974)

Bettelheim, C. *The Transition to Socialist Economy*, Hassocks (1975)

Bhaskar, R. *A Realist Theory of Science*, Hassocks (1978)

Bhaskar, R. 'Scientific explanation and emancipation', *Radical Philosophy* 26 (1980)

Binns, P. 'The question mark over Marx and Aristotle', *Times Higher Education Supplement*, 29 April (1977)

Bohm, D. and Hiley, B. 'On the intuitive understanding of non-locality as implied by quantum theory', *Foundations of Physics* 5 (1975)

Bohm, D. *Causality and Chance in Modern Physics*, London (1957)

Bolton, R. 'Essentialism and semantic theory in Aristotle', *Philosophical Review* 85, 4 (Oct. 1976)

Bortkiewicz, L. von 'Value and price in the Marxian system'; originally published in German in 1907 and resurrected in *International Economic Papers*, no. 2 (1952)

Bonar, J. *Philosophy and Political Economy*, London (1909)

Brody, B.A. *Identity and Essence*, Princeton, NJ (1980)

Burnet, J. *The Ethics of Aristotle*, edited with introduction and notes, London (1900)

Burnet, J. *Early Greek Philosophy*, London (1908)

Callinicos, A. *Marxism and Philosophy*, Oxford (1983)

Carr, E.H. *What is History?* Penguin, London (1964 and repr.)

Carver, T., tr. and ed. *Karl Marx: Texts on Method*, Oxford (1975)

Childe, V.G. *What Happened in History*, Pelican, London (1942 and repr.)

Clark, S.R.L. *Aristotle's Man: Speculations upon Aristotelian Anthropology*, Oxford (1975)

Cohen, G.A. *Karl Marx's Theory of History: A Defence*, Oxford (1978)

Colletti, L. *From Rousseau to Lenin: Studies in Ideology and Society*, tr. Merrington, J., and White, J., London (1972)

Colletti, L. *Marxism and Hegel*, tr. L. Garner, London (1973)

Colletti, L. 'Marxism and the dialectic', *New Left Review* 93 (1975)

Collingwood, R.G. *An Autobiography*, Oxford (1939, reissued 1970)

Collingwood, R.G. *Essays in the Philosophy of History*, New York (1966)

Copi, I.M. 'Comments on Prof. Somerville's Paper', in Somerville, J. and Parsons, H. (eds.), *Dialogues on the Philosophy of Marxism*, Westport, (1974)

Copi, I.M. 'Essence and accident', in Moravcsik, J.M.E. (ed.), *Aristotle: a collection of critical essays*, London (1968)

Davidson, D. 'Causal relations', in Sosa, E. (ed.) *Causation and Conditionals*, Oxford (1975)

Davies, J.K. *Democracy and Classical Greece*, London (1978)

Day, R.B. 'Dialectical method in the political writings of Lenin and Bukharin', *Canadian Journal of Political Science* 9 (1976)

Day, J. and Chambers, M. *Aristotle's History of Athenian Democracy*, Berkeley and Los Angeles (1962); Amsterdam (1967)

de Ste. Croix, G.E.M. *The Origins of the Peloponnesian War*, London and Ithaca, NY (1972)

de Ste. Croix, G.E.M. *The Class Struggle in the Ancient Greek World*, London and Ithaca, NY (1981)

de Ste. Croix, G.E.M. 'Aristotle on history and poetry (*Poetics* 9, 1451a36-b11) in Levick, B. (ed.) *The Ancient Historian and his Materials*, London (1975)

de Ste. Croix. G.E.M. 'Karl Marx and the history of Classical antiquity', in *Arethusa* 8 (1975)

Dobb, M. 'A reply', in *TFC = The Transition from Feudalism to Capitalism*, Hilton, R. (ed.) London (1978); originally in *Science and Society*, 1950

Dobb, M. 'A further comment', in *TFC*; originally in *Science and Society* 1953

Dobb, M. *Theories of Value and Distribution since Adam Smith*, Cambridge (1973)

Dobb, M. *Studies in the Development of Capitalism*, London (1946 and repr.)

Dobb, M. *Political Economy and Capitalism* London (1937 and repr.)

Dummett, M. *Frege: The Philosophy of Language*, London and New York (1973)

Edgley, R. 'Marx's revolutionary science', in *IMP* III = Mepham, J. and Ruben, D.H. (eds.), *Issues in Marxist Philosophy*, vol. 3, *Epistemology, Science, Ideology*, Hassocks (1979)

Edgley, R. 'Dialectic: the contradiction of Colletti', *Critique* 7 (1976)

Elson, D. 'The value theory of labour', in Elson, D. (ed.), *Value: The Representation of Labour in Capitalism*, London (1979)

Elster, J. 'One hundred years of Marxist social science', *London Review of Books*, 16 June-6 July 1983

Elster, J. *Logic and Society*, New York (1978)

Evans, C. 'A new philosophical interpretation of Marx', *Social Research* vol. 40, no. 1 (1973)

Evans, J.D.G. *Aristotle's Concept of Dialectic*, Cambridge (1977)

Fine, B. *Economic Theory and Ideology*, London (1980)

Fine, B. *Marx's Capital*, London (1975)

Fine, B. *Re-Reading Capital*, London (1979)

Finley, M.I. *The Ancient Economy*, Berkeley (1973)

Finley, M.I. 'Aristotle and economic analysis', in Finley, M.I. (ed.), *Studies in Ancient Society*, London (1974); originally published in *Past and Present* 43 (1970)

Finley, M.I. 'Technical innovation and economic progress in the Ancient World', in *Economic History Review* 18 (1965)

Finley, M.I. *The Ancient Greeks*, Pelican, London (1966, revised 1971 and 1975)

Fisk, M. *Nature and Necessity: An Essay in Physical Ontology*, Bloomington, Ind. (1973)

Fisk, M. 'Dialectic and ontology', *IMP* I = Mephem, J. and Ruben, D-H. (eds.), *Issues in Marxist Philosophy*, vol. 1, *Dialectics and Method*, Hassocks (1979)

Fisk, M. 'Materialism and dialectic', *Critique* 12 (1980)

Fisk, M. 'The state and market in Rawls', paper delivered at Second World Congress of Soviet and East European Studies, Garmisch, September 1980.

Fisk, M. 'Relatedness without relations', *Noûs* 6 (1972), and in fuller version in ch. 7 of his *Nature and Necessity*, cited above.

Fisk, M. 'Free action and historical materialism', forthcoming in *Noûs*.

Fisk, M. 'The concept of primacy in historical explanation', *Analyse und Kritik* 4 (1982)

Geach, P.T. 'Aquinas', in Anscombe, G.E.M. and Geach, P.T., *Three Philosophers*, Oxford (1963)

Geach, P.T. 'Teleological explanation', in Körner, S. (ed.), *Explanation*, Oxford (1975)

Geras, N. 'Essence and appearance: aspects of fetishism in Marx's *Capital*', *New Left Review* 65 (Jan-Feb 1971)

Geras, N. 'Marx and the critique of political economy', in Blackburn, R. (ed.), *Ideology in Social Science*, London (1972)

Godelier, M. 'Structure and contradiction in *Capital*', in ibid.

Goldman, L. 'The thought of the Enlightenment', *Annales* vol. 22, no. 4 (1967)

Gould, C. *Marx's Social Ontology*, Cambridge, Mass. and London (1978)

Gould, S.J. *Ever Since Darwin; Reflections in Natural History*, Penguin,

London (1980)

Gould, S.J. *The Panda's Thumb*, New York (1980)

Hardie, W.F.R. *Aristotle's Ethical Theory*, Oxford (1968)

Harré, R. *The Philosophies of Science*, Oxford (1972 and repr.)

Harré, R. and Madden, E.H. *Causal Powers: A Theory of Natural Necessity*, Oxford (1975)

Hartman, E. *Substance, Body and Soul*, Princeton, NJ (1977)

Hayek, F.A. von *The Road to Serfdom*, London (1944 and repr.)

Hegel, G.W.F. *Phenomenology of Spirit*, tr. A.V. Miller, Oxford (1979)

Hegel, G.W.F. *Lectures on the Philosophy of World History; Introduction: Reason in History*, tr. H.B. Nisbet, Cambridge (1975 and repr.). Another translation, though not as extensive, of the Introduction is *Reason in History*, tr. with introduction by Hartman, R.S., Library of Liberal Arts, Indianapolis (1953 and repr.). The full lectures are to be found in the edition of J. Sibree, *Lectures on the Philosophy of World History*, London (1857 and repr.)

Hegel, G.W.F. *Lectures on the History of Philosophy*, tr. E.S. Haldane and F.H. Simson, in three volumes, London (1894)

Hegel, G.W.F. *Science of Logic*, tr. A.V. Miller, intro. by J.N. Findlay, London (1969); New York (1976)

Hextor, J.H. *On Historians: A Scrutiny of some Modern Practitioners*, London (1979)

Hill, C. Review of G.E.M. de Ste. Croix's *The Class Struggle in the Ancient Greek World*, *London Review of Books*, 4-8 February 1982

Hill, C. *The World Turned Upside Down*, Penguin, London (1975)

Hill, C. *God's Englishman: Oliver Cromwell and the English Revolution*, Penguin, London (1972 and repr.)

Hilton, R.H. and Sawyer, P.H. 'Technological determinism: the stirrup and the plough', *Past and Present* (1963)

Hilton, R.H. *The English Peasantry in the Later Middle Ages*, Oxford (1975 and repr. 1979)

Hilton, R.H. Introduction to *TFC = The Transition from Capitalism to Feudalism*, London (1976 and repr.)

Hilton, R.H. 'A comment', and 'Capitalism – What's in a Name?', in *TFC*.

Hintikka, J. *Time and Necessity; Studies in Aristotle's Theory of Modality*, Oxford (1973)

Hintikka, J. 'On the ingredients of an Aristotelian Science', *Noûs* 6 (1972)

Hirsch, E. 'Essence and identity', in Munitz, M.K. (ed.), *Identity and Individuation*, New York (1971)

Hobsbawm, E.J. 'Karl Marx's contribution to historiography', in Blackburn, R. (ed.) *Ideology in Social Science*, London (1972)

Hobsbawm, E.J. Introduction to *Karl Marx: Pre-Capitalist Economic Formations*, London (1964)

Hobsbawm, E.J. 'From feudalism to capitalism', in *TFC*

Hobsbawm, E.J. and Baran, P. 'Stages of economic growth', *Kyklos*, vol. 14, no. 2 (1961)

Hull, D. *Philosophy of Biological Science*, Englewood Cliffs, NJ (1974)

Humphreys, S.C. 'History, economics and anthropology: the work of Karl Polanyi', *History and Theory* 8 (1969)

Joachim, H.H. Introduction and commentary on Aristotle's *On Coming-to-be and passing-away*, Oxford (1922)

Jordan, Z.A. *The Evolution of Dialectical Materialism*, London (1967)

Kay, G. 'Why labour is the starting point of *Capital*', *Critique* 7 (1977); reprinted in Elson, D. (ed.), *Value*, London (1979)

Kay, G. 'Political economy: Hegel versus Ricardo', *Critique* 10-11 (1979)

Kripke S. *Naming and Necessity*, Oxford (1980)

Kripke S. 'Identity and necessity', in Schwartz, S.P. (ed.), *Naming, Necessity, and Natural Kinds*, Ithaca, NY (1977). Reprinted in Honderich, T. and Burnyeat, M. (eds.), *Philosophy As It Is*, London (1979); originally published in Munitz, M.K. (ed.), *Identity and Individuation*, New York (1971)

Kuhn, T.S. 'Concepts of cause in the development of physics', in *The Essential Tension*, Chicago (1977)

Laycock, H. 'Some questions of ontology', *Philosophical Review* 81 (1972)

Lefebvre, H., *Dialectical Materialism*, tr. J. Sturrock, London (1968 and repr.)

Linsky, L. *Names and Descriptions*, Chicago (1977), esp. ch.7

Lippi, M. *Value and Naturalism in Marx*, tr. H. Steedman, London (1979)

Lloyd, G.E.R. *Magic, Reason and Experience*, Cambridge (1979)

Lubasz, H. 'The Aristotelian dimension in Marx', *Times Higher Education Supplement*, 1.4.77

Lukács, G. *The Ontology of Social Being*, tr. D. Fernbach, London, in three volumes: vol. 1, *Hegel* (1978); vol. 2, *Marx* (1978); vol. 3, *Labour* (1980).

Lukács, G. 'The ontological bases of human thought and action', *Philosophical Forum* 8 (1975)

McBride, W.L. *The Philosophy of Marx*, London (1977)

McMurtry, J. *The Structure of Marx's World View*, Princeton, NJ (1978)

McMurtry, J. 'Making sense of economic determinism', *Canadian Journal of Philosophy*, vol. 3, no. 2 (1973)

Mackie, J.L. *The Cement of the Universe*, Oxford (1974)

Mackie, J.L. *Problems from Locke*, Oxford (1976)

Mandel, E. 'Ten theses on the social and economic laws governing the society transitional between capitalism and socialism', *Critique* 3 (1974)

Mandel, E. *The Formation of the Economic Thought of Karl Marx: 1843 to Capital*, New York and London (1971)

Mandel, E. *Late Capitalism*, tr. J. de Bres, London (1975)

Mandelbaum, M. *History, Man and Reason*, Baltimore and London (1971)

Marquit, E. 'Nicolaus and Marx's method of scientific theory in the *Grundrisse*', *Science & Society*, vol. 41, no. 4 (1977-8)

Marx, K. *Capital*, vol. 1, tr. Moore and Aveling, Moscow and London (1970) and tr. Ben Fowkes, Penguin, London (1976)

Marx, K. *Capital*, vol. 2, Moscow (1967), London (1970); and tr. D. Fernbach, Penguin, London (1978)

Marx, K. *Capital*, vol. 3, Moscow (1971), London (1972); and tr. D. Fernbach, Penguin, London (1981)

Marx, K. *CHDS* = 'Critique of Hegel's doctrine of the state', in *KMEW* = Colletti, L. (ed.), *Karl Marx: Early Writings*, Penguin, London (1974 and repr.)

Marx, K. 'A contribution to the critique of Hegel's philosophy of Right' in *KMEW*

Marx, K. *EPM* = *Economic and Philosophical MSS*, in *KMEW*

Marx, K. *GI* = *The German Ideology*, in *MECW* = Marx and Engels, *Collected Works*, an English edn. in 50 vols., Moscow, London and New York (1975 +)

Marx, K. *A Contribution to the Critique of Political Economy*, introduced by Maurice Dobb, London (1971)

Marx, K. *Gr* = *Grundrisse*, tr. M. Nicolaus, Penguin, London (1973 and repr.)

Marx, K. *MEW* = Marx and Engels, *Werke*, I-XXXIX, Dietz Verlag, East Berlin (1961-8)

Marx, K. *TSV* = *Theories of Surplus Value*, (vol. 4 of *Capital*). Part I, Moscow (1963 and repr.); Part II, Moscow (1968); Part III, Moscow (1971)

Mattick, P. *Marx and Keynes: The Limits of the Mixed Economy*, Boston (1969)

Meek, R.L. *Studies in the Labour Theory of Value*, second edn., London (1973)

Meek, R.L. *Social Science and the Ignoble Savage*, Cambridge (1976)

Meikle, S. 'Dialectical contradiction and necessity', in *IMP* I = Mepham, J. and Ruben, D-H. (eds.), *Issues in Marxist Philosophy*, vol. 1, *Dialectics and Method*, Hassocks (1979)

Meikle, S. 'Aristotle and the political economy of the *polis*', *Journal of Hellenic Studies* 79 (1979)

Meikle, S. 'Dialectics and cognition', *Critique* 6 (1976)

Meikle, S. 'Marxism and the necessity of essentialism', *Critique* 16 (1984), a review article of G.E.M. de Ste. Croix's *The Class Struggle in the Ancient Greek World*

Meikle, S. 'Reasons for Action', *Philosophical Quarterly* (1974)

Meszaros, I. *Lukács' Concept of Dialectic*, London (1972)

Mepham, J. 'The *Grudrisse*: method or metaphysics?'. in *IMP* I = Mepham, J. and Ruben, D-H. (eds.), *Issues in Marxist Philosophy*, vol. I, Hassocks (1979)

Monod, J. *Chance and Necessity: An Essay in the Natural Philosophy of Modern Biology*, London (1972)

Mourelatos, A. 'Aristotle's "powers" and modern empiricism', *Ratio* 9 (1967)

Mussachia, M. 'On contradiction in dialectical materialism', *Science & Society*, vol. 41, no. 3 (1977)

Nagel, E. *The Structure of Science*, London (1961)

Nussbaum, M.C. *Aristotle's De Motu Animalium*, text with translation, commentary and interpretive essays, Princeton, NJ (1978)

Nussbaum, M.C. Review of E. Hartman's *Substance, Body and Soul: Aristotelian Investigations*, Princeton, NJ (1977), in *Journal of Philosophy* (1980)

O'Brien, G.D. *Hegel on Reason and History*, Chicago and London (1975)

Ollman, B. *Alienation: Marx's Conception of Man in Capitalist Society*, Cambridge (1971)

Ollman, B. 'Marx's vision of communism: a reconstruction', *Critique* 8 (1977)

Pannekoek, A. *Marxism and Darwinism*, Chicago (1912)

Phillips, D.C. *Holistic Thought in Social Science*, London (1977)

Pilling, G. *Marx's Capital: Philosophy and Political Economy*, London (1980)

Plantinga, A. *The Nature of Necessity*, Oxford (1974)

Pleket, H.W. 'Technology in the Graeco-Roman world: a general report', *Talanta* 5 (1973)

Popper, K. *Unended Quest: An Intellectual Autobiography*, revised edn., London (1976)

Preobrazhensky, E. *The New Economics*, Oxford (1965 and repr.)

Procacci, G. 'A survey of the debate', in *TFC*.

Putnam, H. 'Is semantics possible?', in Schwartz, S.P. (ed.), *Naming, Necessity, and Natural Kinds*, Ithaca, NY (1977)

Putnam, H. 'Philosophy of language and philosophy of science', in Cohen, R.S. *et al.* (eds.), *Boston Studies*, vol. 32 (1974)

Putnam, H. 'On properties', in Rescher, N. *et al.* (eds.), *Essays in Honor of Carl G. Hempel*, Amsterdam (1970)

Putnam, H. 'Explanation and reference', in Pearce and Maynard (eds.), *Conceptual Change*, Amsterdam (1973)

Putnam, H. 'Meaning and reference', *Journal of Philosophy* 70 (1973)

Putnam, H. 'The "corroboration" of theories', in Honderich, T. and Burnyeat, M. (eds.), London (1979)

Putnam, H. 'Reference and understanding', with comment by M. Dummett and reply by H. Putnam, in Margalit, A., *Meaning and Use*, Amsterdam (1979)

Renfrew, C. *Before Civilization: The Radiocarbon Revolution and Prehistoric Europe*, Penguin, London (1976)

Renfrew, C. 'British prehistory: changing configurations', in Renfrew, C. (ed.), *British Prehistory*, London (1974)

Rosdolsky, R. *The Making of Marx's 'Capital'*, tr. P. Burgess, London (1977)

Rosdolsky, R. 'The distribution of the agrarian product in Feudalism', *Journal of Economic History* (1951)

Ruben, D-H. *Marxism and Materialism: A Study in Marxist Theory of Knowledge*, Harvester (1977)

Ruben, D-H. 'Marxism and dialectics', in *IMP* vol. 1.

Rubin, I.I., *Essays on Marx's Theory of Value*, Detroit (1972)

Rubin, I.I., *A History of Economic Thought*, tr. and ed. D. Filtzer, London (1979)

Russell, B. *Human Knowledge: Its Scope and Limits*, London (1948)

Sayer, D. 'Method and dogma in historical materialism', *Sociological Review*, 23 (1975)

Sayer, D. *Marx's Method*, Hassocks (1983)

Selučky, R. 'Marxism and self-management', *Critique* 3 (1974)

Shaw, W.H. *Marx's Theory of History*, London (1978)

Sluga, H. *Gottlob Frege*, London (1980)

Sluga, H. 'Frege and the rise of analytical philosophy', *Inquiry* 18 (1976)

Smith, A. *The Wealth of Nations*, Books I-III, Pelican, London (1970)

Smith, G.A.E. 'The industrial problems of Soviet agriculture', *Critique* 14 (1981)

Smith, G.A.E. 'Wages, profits, and employment: some recent developments in conventional economic theory', *Critique* 16 (1984)

Sorabji, R. *Necessity, Cause, and Blame: Perspectives on Aristotle's Theory*, London and Ithaca, NY (1980)

Steedman, I. *Marx after Sraffa*, London (1977)

Suppes, P. 'Aristotle's concept of matter and its relation to modern concepts of matter', *Synthese* 28 (1974)

Sweezy, P. *The Theory of Capitalist Development*, New York and London (1942 and repr.)

Taylor, C. 'Marxism and empiricism', in Williams, B., and Montefiore, A. (eds.), *British Analytical Philosophy*, London (1966)

Taylor, C. 'The agony of economic man', in LaPierre, L. *et al.* (eds.), *Essays on the Left*, Toronto/Montreal (1971)

Thompson, E.P. *The Poverty of Theory*, London (1978)

Ticktin, H.H. 'Towards a political economy of the USSR', *Critique* 1 (1973)

Ticktin, H.H. 'The political economy of the Soviet intellectual', *Critique* 2 (1973)

Ticktin, H.H. 'Socialism, the Market, and the State', *Critique* 3 (1974)

Ticktin, H.H. 'The contradictions of Soviet society and Professor Bettelheim', *Critique* 6 (1976)

Ticktin, H.H. 'The class structure of the USSR and the Elite', *Critique* 9 (1978)

Ticktin, H.H. 'The transitional epoch, finance capital, and Britain', *Critique* 16 (1984)

Trotsky, L. *The History of the Russian Revolution*, London (1977)

Trotsky, L. *In Defense of Marxism*, New York (1973)

Trotsky, L. *Problems of Everyday Life*, New York (1973)

Trotsky, L. *My Life*, Penguin, London (1975)

Trotsky, L. 'Philosophical tendencies of bureaucratism', in *Challenge of the Left Opposition*, New York (1980)

Weber, M. *Roscher and Knies: The Logical Problems of Historical Economics*, London (1975)

Weber, M. *The Methodology of the Social Sciences*, tr. and ed. E. Shils and H. Finch, New York (1949)

Weber, M. *Critique of Stammler*, tr. and intro. G. Oakes, New York and London (1977)

White, L. 'The expansion of technology 500-1500', in *The Fontana Economic History of Europe: The Middle Ages*, London (1972 and repr.)

Wieland, W. 'The problem of teleology', in Barnes, J. *et al.* (eds.), *Articles on Aristotle*, vol. 1, London (1975)

Wiggins, D. *Sameness and Substance*, Oxford (1980)

Wood, A. *Karl Marx*, London, Boston and Henley (1981)

Wright, G.H. von 'Time, change and contradiction', Eddington Memorial Lecture, Cambridge (1968)

Index

24^{95} 9I   DuP

10^{95}